Stay Healthy Abroad

The essential guide for all travellers

Rob Ryan

General editor
Michael Corr
MCommH CTCMH CTPHC
(Fellow of the Royal Society of Tropical Medicine and Hygiene)

Note: Phone numbers and addresses for organisations mentioned in the book are listed on pages 319–322.

Published in 1995
Health Education Authority
Hamilton House
Mabledon Place
London WC1H 9TX

ISBN: 0 7521 0 170 6

A CIP catalogue record for this book is available from the British Library.

Typeset by DP Photosetting, Aylesbury, Bucks
Printed in Great Britain by Biddles, Guildford, Surrey

For Deb and Bella

Thank you to the following people for allowing us to reproduce their work in this book:

Dr Peter Barrat at MASTA
Jane Miller
Nomad
World Health Organization (WHO)

Contents

Preface

Stay Healthy Abroad grew out of articles written for *Arena* and the *Sunday Times* Travel section, where I attempted to present a variety of medical and travel health problems in an entertaining but informative way (if indeed there is entertainment to be squeezed out of mosquito life cycles and nematode infections). The aim of the book is to continue with the premise that an analysis of the health risks facing travellers can be presented in a readable, non-technical fashion.

Stay Healthy Abroad is not aimed at doctors, nurses or health professionals, but at anyone travelling abroad. For that reason, it contains very few recommended dosages and routes of immunisation, and the minimum of confusing terminology. (Where the odd 'lesion' and 'febrile' has survived intact, I apologise.) Nor is it intended as a substitute for seeking medical care – hence there is no field first aid, and no free syringe and needles taped to the front cover. It is all about analysing the risks involved in travel and health, and telling you when you should be practising your Hausa for 'Where is the doctor?'. There are also suggestions for avoiding being in that situation in the first place. If it only convinces you of the need to take the full course of anti-malarials, even when your hair is falling out and you are plagued by mouth ulcers, I will be a happy man.

Many people helped in the preparation of this book, and although I don't want this to turn into an acknowledgment list as long as that on the back of the average soul diva album ('... and I would like to thank God Almighty for the mixes on tracks 3, 7 and 9'), my thank-yous must include: Michael Corr, Project Manager – Immunisation at the Health Education Authority, who acted as general editor; Christine Walker, David Wickers and Jonathan Futrell at The Sunday Times; Dr Peter Barrett at MASTA; Drs Emma Wollfenden and Yvonne Ganley at the Liverpool School of Tropical Medicine; Dr Jon Dallimore at AMRFT; and Deborah and Bella Ryan at home. They all know why, so I won't bore you with it. I'd also like to thank all those who shared their gruesome illnesses and horror stories with me. If you didn't get in this time, maybe next.

The manuscript was read at various stages by Dr Peter Barrett, Dr Emma Woolfenden, Dr Hugh Stradling of Haddenham Health Centre Travel Clinic, Dr Jon Dallimore, Dr Eric Walker of TRAVAX, Dr Eric Le Fevre of Thomas Cook Travel Clinic, Amanda Byrett of Mérieux UK and Paul and Larry Goodyer of Nomad. Dozens of other eminent people too numerous to mention gave up their time to speak to me over the telephone. Any glitches that remain, of course, are property of Rob Ryan. Every effort has been made to ensure the information is accurate and correct at the time of going to press. However, neither the author nor publishers can accept any liability for unforeseen errors, omissions or changes in a country's regulations.

Part I
Travel Health and Medical Problems Abroad

1 Assessing the risks

There is an occasional dining and drinking club called the Oates Club, which convenes in London perhaps once or twice a year. It is named after Captain Lawrence Oates (1880–1912), the man who courageously left the Scott tent, saying 'I am just going outside . . . I may be some time.' The criterion for membership is to be a travel writer, to know one or more of the founding members and, most tricky of all given the profession, to be in the UK at the right time.

A typical evening will consist of dinner at a venue with an agreeably late licence, followed by a lengthy session of digestifs. Sometime during this latter phase, talk inevitably turns to the hazards of modern travel. The dialogue usually begins to resemble the scene in *Jaws* where Robert Shaw and Richard Dreyfuss compare their shark bites ('I got that beat. I got that beat. Look . . . moray eel . . . bit right through my wetsuit.').

Over the years the Oates club has furnished tallish tales of African revolution, air misses and too-close-for-comfort encounters (the most terrifying being, thanks to a little on-the-job-training for an inexperienced ranger, with a female leopard protecting her cubs).

This session usually encompasses a 'diseases-I-have-known-and-lived-through' section, and, given the total number of miles and the assortment of countries the members have visited, it has to be said that this can be a disappointing part of the proceedings. Where for instance, are the snake bites? I can recall a few '. . . and then it slithered away' anecdotes, where the snake has obviously been more terrorised by a bleary-eyed travel hack than vice versa, but in terms of toxic avengers, the best we have managed in 5 years is a couple of scorpion stings, none fatal.

And what about the legendary candiru fish of the Amazon? Famed for following a stream of water to enable it to lodge in another fish's gills, the myth (and I was always a big fan of it, true or not) is that if you wade into a South American river to urinate and create a stream of water, you can find yourself with a very confused candiru lodged up your urethra.

Unfortunately for the myth, the Oates Club members have never met anyone stupid enough to wade into a South American river to urinate (not surprisingly the legend of the piranha is even more powerful than that of the candiru).

So what have these globetrotters actually suffered from? Well, some sort of intestinal problem clocks in at close to 100 per cent, but then who can claim never to have had such a bout at home? A couple of malarias, a dengue fever, a suspected leishmaniasis (a scarring caused by sand-flies) which turned out to be a fungal infection, leeches, those scorpion stings, a couple of bad cases of altitude sickness, sunstroke, ear infections from swimming in suspect water, and a concussion after falling down some stairs while under the influence of alcohol, this latter being disqualified as self-inflicted.

The point is, these people spend their lives travelling on all the continents, indulging in every kind of travel barring those 'hopping-to-the-Pole' expeditions favoured by the likes of Ranulph Fiennes, and not only have they all lived to tell the tale (though one of the malarial cases could have been serious had the patient not diagnosed it faster than the doctor), but their collective experiences have failed to put them off their chosen career.

Yet the list of things these people could, theoretically, have caught is terrifying: flies that lay their eggs on clothes, so that maggots burrow under the skin surface; disfiguring facial scars from sandflies; heart damage from bugs that live in hut walls. There were even some cases in New Mexico in 1993 of contact with chipmunks being fatal. And then of course there are the candiru fish.

But as the ad hoc survey of the Oates Club shows, the chances of the traveller catching anything wonderfully exotic is quite low (the risks are, of course, different for those working long-term in some areas of the world), though the possibility of having your plans disrupted by some intestinal invader is quite high.

Travellers' health, in fact the whole business of travelling, is really all about risk assessment. After all, there is the remote possibility that the plane you are on may have a compressing engagement to keep with a mountainside, and the gruesome accounts of foreign afflictions in some travel literature would make even the most hardened Oates Club member re-book for Bournemouth this year. The intention of this book is neither to frighten you into staying at home, always a danger when you start discussing the gamut of potential problems, nor to suggest you travel as a paranoid 'don't-point-that-unpeeled-vegetable-at-me-my-man' Howard Hughes figure.

Its aim is to try and make travellers, be they package tourists, backpackers or long-stay workers, aware of the risks, both high and low, and enable them to make informed judgements as to what precautions they should take. It covers not only basic health, but also some of the other hazards that may await you, from shallow swimming pools to messing with water buffalo, preparations before departure, including what equipment to pack, and continuing vigilance upon your return.

The conclusion from the Oates Club is that, with proper immunisation and reasonable care, ill health does not have to spoil your trip. And should something go wrong (and if it doesn't, where are you going to get your stories to tell over brandy?), perhaps you will adopt the attitude of the Oates Club member who has clocked up the most hours in small, unhygienic rooms and behind bushes: 'I treat the odd stomach upset or viral infection like a hangover that tells you that last night was a great night out. A small price to pay for the experience.'

The risks

Even my knowledge of statistics is adequate enough to appreciate that the Oates Club is hardly a representative study of the travelling public. There are other more reliable indices of troubles abroad. General Accident keep a track of the most common causes of claiming against their insurance policies. Fifty per cent of all claims are for medical expenses (including those as the result of accidents). The top six, *excluding* trauma from road accidents, etc. are:

- **travellers' diarrhoea and other gut problems**
- **urinary infections**

- **heart attacks**
- **unstable angina**
- **respiratory problems, including asthma**
- **skin problems due to bites or rashes.**

The head of this list stays remarkable constant, regardless of where the travellers are headed. For instance Dr Hugh Stradling conducted an audit of problems encountered abroad by clients who had attended his clinic at Haddenham, Buckinghamshire. He found the majority of respondents had no problems at all, with a strong showing by diarrheoa as the most common complaint, followed by minor illnesses (chest infections, toothache, vertigo, tooth problems), with accidents accounting for the bulk of the rest.

Even in areas we might consider more life-threatening, where the shock to our industrialized systems is greater, minor health hiccups dominate. Figures given in *Mason's Tropical Diseases* of the likelihood of coming down with something nasty suggest that, for every 100,000 travellers to the tropics, just over 30% will succumb to travellers' diarrheoa, another 25% will have a bout of a non-specific 'felt ill', 0.04% will be hospitalised, 0.06% will be evacuated by air ambulance and one of the 100,000 to make a small corner of that foreign field forever his or her own.

Up until relatively recently such statistics would be of little interest to most travellers, but the last decade has seen a significant increase in long-haul travel, with such destinations as The Gambia, about as tropical as you can get, opening up to package charters. In a 1994 travel survey by Meriuex, 50% of the people surveyed at London's airports had visited a tropical country in the last five years, an increase of 14% over their 1989 survey.

Of course, not everybody who visits the tropics is likely to need instigate every precaution mentioned in this book – some spend their entire tenure whisked from air-conditioned hotel to car to conference centre and back again. In many ways people on shoddy package holidays to the Med are at as much, or more, risk of health problems ruining their trip.

The best travel health advice is carefully tailored to your itinerary – the requirements and precautions for Hong Kong are very different to those for China, a week in Bangkok far less likely to expose you to potential pathogens than trekking in Chiang Mai. The risks also vary with the seasons. What you don't want is someone reading off a list of recommended immunisations for your destination, and leaving it at that. But whether you are going for two weeks in the sun, a few days' business in Asia, are working for 2 years in Africa or are clutching that much coveted, open-ended, round-the-world ticket, there are things in this book you should know before you board that plane.

Different strokes for different folks

The package holiday

It must be the word 'package' that does it. In my experience of dealing with readers' complaints on the *Sunday Times*, normally resourceful, independent people suddenly become great sacks of potatoes when they give themselves up to a travel company. As Eric Le Fevre, manager of the Thomas Cook Travel Clinic, says: 'People generally do not want to take responsibility for their own health, and this is particularly true when they take a package holiday. "But nobody told me I needed jabs for Kenya" is something we hear quite a lot of.'

Just as importantly, the same abrogation of responsibility extends to their safety while abroad. Some people taking part in relatively hazardous activities, such as whitewater rafting, somehow feel that if it wasn't safe, the company wouldn't suggest it. It isn't necessarily, and, yes, they would.

Similarly, package holidaymakers are not necessarily more immune from illness than backpackers. On the contrary, hotels may present a whole new set of health hazards, such as the microbiological nirvana that is the lunchtime buffet, complete with ice-cream which melted yesterday, but has now been re-frozen, salmonella-strewn mayonnaise and shellfish carefully nurtured near the sewage outlets down the beach.

Under EC laws, travel agents are required to give out certain health advice to holidaymakers when they book their package, but that only refers to health *formalities* rather than risks. And anyway, we don't ask our doctors for travel advice, so why should we ask our travel agents for health information?

A *World in Action* programme on malaria (*Dying for a Holiday*, 18 July 1994) quizzed 40 travel agents on what precautions holidaymakers should take in Kenya, one of the most malarious countries in the world. Over half made no mention of malaria at all. Only seven recommended seeing a doctor.

While on a tour of the drug company Merieux, which runs an advice line for doctors and nurses dealing with travel vaccinations, I heard one call from a woman who had been told categorically by her travel agent that smallpox is required for Egypt, and so would not leave without the jab. Smallpox, of course, has been totally eradicated from the world for more than a decade.

Smallpox may have gone, but look in the back of the brochure of, say, Thomson Worldwide or Thomas Cook, and examine some of the farther flung places and the recommended immunisations these countries carry. You will find some pretty impressive pathogens lurking out there even in what have become mass-market destinations (Kenya, the Gambia, Goa, parts of Thailand etc.). It may be a package holiday, but even the slickest travel company cannot protect you from exposure to endemic diseases. That part is up to you.

Yet it seems the holidaying public is loathe to take responsiblity for its own well-being: in one survey of holiday and business travellers to the tropics and subtropics, only 65 per cent had had the recommended vaccinations; and a SmithKline Beecham survey found that 37 per cent of the people interviewed had not sought any kind of medical advice at all.

Dr Jonathan Cosser of The Communicable Diseases (Scotland) Unit at Ruchill Hospital in Glasgow, has done much work on following up holidaymakers' patterns of illness. His findings confirm that alimentary problems are to the fore, and that they are more likely the further you travel south and east, culminating in a massive 77 per cent of people afflicted during their summer package holiday in North Africa.

The independent traveller

These days the line between the package and the *Lonely Planet/Rough Guide* traveller is increasingly blurred. Dozens of companies exist which offer the illusion of independent travel, while hovering around like some faithful retainer to ensure everything runs smoothly. However, whether discreetly chaperoned or not, we can consider the independent traveller to be anyone who has created their own itinerary (which may include getting a short-term job en-route), which will often involve moving away from established tourist centres. And there is the first problem. If anything goes wrong in Bali, Bangkok or Rio, slick hospital treatment is only minutes away. If it happens on the Laos border or the Bolivian *antiplano*, then the cry of 'Is there a doctor in the *casa*?' may sound very hollow indeed.

Anyone who is likely to find themselves more than a few hours from a hospital should consider very carefully what they need to take with them, including a set of disposable syringes and needles and a first aid kit. The more adventurous will need to think about such items as water purification tablets or a water filter.

They are also more likely to be moving and staying among locals in rural areas, so a different profile of immunisations will be needed, including ones not required for most standard tourist routes, such as Japanese B or tick-borne encephalitis. They are also four times more likely than conventional tourists to get hepatitis A.

It may be a generalisation, but independent travellers (and volunteer aid workers) tend to be below 30 years of age. The research findings of Dr Jonathan Cosser and others (including figures from Travellers Medical Service) show that this age group (16–30) is particularly prone to health problems while abroad. This may be because the squeaky-cleanness of our shrink-wrapped society means they have not been exposed to the kind of pathogens that would enable them to build up immunities, or because their budgets mean they live and eat in less salubrious places than their older counterparts, and just possibly, particularly with regard to accidents, the commonest problem with young travellers, because they think they are invulnerable and immortal.

The international aid worker

This includes people working for the likes of Voluntary Service Overseas (VSO), Overseas Development Agency (ODA) and Save the Children Fund (SCF), who may be posted well away from western-style medical centres and will, by definition, have intimate contact with the locals.

Yet another immunisation programme will be needed, including ensuring full protection against such prolonged-contact infective agents as diphtheria, meningococcal meningitis and tuberculosis. Some drugs that are quite safe for short-term use may have cumulative side effects when taken over months or years, so, a different anti-malarial regime may be needed. Long-term hygiene practices, the purification of water, off-road driving skills and self-treatment of conditions such as malaria should be a consideration.

What this book does not offer is a comprehensive survival guide to being stranded in the bush or desert. For that try *Stay Alive, A Handbook on Survival* by Maurice Dunlevy (Australian Government); *Stay Alive in the Desert*, Dr K.E.M. Melville, (Roger Lascelles); *Survive*, by Xavier Maniguet (Facts on File) or, for those real pessimists among you, *The SAS Survival Handbook* by John Wiseman (Collins).

In a survey of Peace Corps Volunteers, suicide came in as the fourth most likely cause of death (after car and motorcycle accidents and drowning). There is no doubt that long-stay workers may suffer culture shock, stress, over-work, loneliness and a feeling of helplessness. The best agencies are prepared for this, and will offer the option of counselling (something they should be at pains to ensure you are not afraid or ashamed to ask for). There is also the possibility of reverse culture shock upon return, of course. Much of the information covered throughout this book will be of relevance to the long-stay worker, and Chapter 16 is dedicated to volunteer's special needs.

2 Preparing for your trip

Hilary Bradt is a tour leader and author who has taken many groups to South America, Africa and Madagascar. In all that time she has only refused to take one customer. 'She was terribly overweight, and obviously distressed when we met her at La Paz, where she was waiting for us before we started the trek, and where she had been robbed on arrival. I was very concerned. She was a lay preacher from a small town in midwest-America, and had obviously saved up for a long time for this trip. So I asked her if she had done any preparation at all. "Oh yes," she replied, "the whole congregation is praying for me."'

Now I don't want to denigrate the power of prayer, but I would suggest a little additional forward planning. However, Hilary has also come across the opposite extreme. 'I have had people turn up with suitcases full of medicine, everything short of blood plasma, and no room left for clothing.'

Good preparation is essential, but so is pitching the level correctly. There is a sensible middle ground.

The list

'All journeys begin in the same way,' said V.S. Naipul, with something completely different in mind to what I find: all travel begins with lists. There follows a check-list of things you should consider, including where you are going, how long you are staying in each place, and what you are taking with you. Most subjects touched on here are covered in more detail in Chapter 3.

- **Check all travel documents.** Make sure your passport has adequate time to run – I was once almost turned away from the USA because mine only had 2 months left on it. The fact I was only going to be in the country for 5 days cut little ice with the immigration at JFK airport. If appropriate, ensure that your children are on your passport.

- **Have somewhere secure to keep travel documents,** money, photocopies of travellers' cheques and your passport.
- **Check visa requirements with the appropriate embassy.** And remember, they often take longer to process than they tell you over the telephone.
- **Check required and recommended immunisations for all the countries you will visit.** You may need a yellow fever immunisation certificate, even if you just transit through an 'endemic zone'. For long-stay workers, some countries insist on an 'all-clear for AIDS' certificate. If consulting a travel clinic be sure to be specific about type of holiday – whether it is rural, urban or high altitude, and the season, will make a lot of difference.
- **Get your teeth checked.** Toothache or a broken crown can ruin a holiday; HIV or hepatitis B caught from irresponsible dentists can ruin your life.
- **Get a spare pair of glasses/contact lenses.** I once broke my spectacles while away, and spent 3 weeks looking at the world through prescription sunglasses (and looking like a prize idiot in the bars at night).
- **Medical checks.** A full medical is unnecessary unless you are planning to be away on an extended trip, have recently had a medical condition or are over 50. However, most aid agencies insist on a full check-up, including a chest X-ray, before your spell in the wilderness. Also if you are going high altitude walking or doing any other strenuous activity, it may be worth having the once-over. Note that some conditions, however, are contra-indications to some immunisations (e.g. being pregnant, certain serious allergies), and those on beta-blockers should not take mefloquine anti-malarials.
- **If you are away on an extended trip, make sure you will not be deregistered by your GP** (most charities/government agencies make sure this doesn't happen).
- **If there is any doubt, check you *aren't* pregnant.**
- **Insurance.** About 800,000 claims are made each year by UK travellers. Of these, around 200,000 are for medical expenses, about the same as for loss or theft of luggage. Check you have enough cover for your particular type of trip.
- **Clothing.** There is nothing worse than lugging inappropriate clothing around the world, as if it needed its own holiday, or finding what you have got just isn't up to the job.

- **Insects.** You may need to take malaria tablets, which have to be started a week before leaving. You should also look at insect repellents and mosquito nets – the plan is to not get bitten at all (see Chapter 12).
- **Medical supplies.** For some it may be no more than a Band-Aid and some aspirin, others may want enough stainless steel and sutures to perform major surgery, and certain nationalities seem to insist on travelling with most of the known antibiotics. You don't need to go that far, but you should take appropriate medicines and equipment with you, including sunscreens.
- **Sunglasses.** Take a *good* pair, able to screen out UV light (there is a British Standard, BS 2724, for sunglasses. Also look for the UV400 sign for effective filtering of UVA and UVB).
- **Consider a first aid course.** St John Ambulance or St Andrew's Ambulance in Scotland can advise you of local courses. If, however, you are going to really remote places with no medical facilities, Dr Jon Dallimore and Barry Roberts run a course called Advanced Medicine for Remote Foreign Travel, which picks up where first aid courses leave off. It covers diagnosis and emergency therapeutic manoeuvres, including stitching wounds and inserting a drip. Very comprehensive, possibly life-saving, it is most suitable for expedition members, mariners and the like who have no recourse to professionals. It costs £275 for 5 days and places are limited.
- **Other equipment.** There may come that moment when you look at the only available bed in town, and swear it moves. Consider taking a sleeping bag or a cotton liner (useful for those unexpected overnight stops). A torch is always a good idea, a compass may be useful, and somewhere to stash your money about your person is without doubt essential.
- **Are you in the right shape for your holiday?** This may, of course, be your normal one ifyou intend to lie on the beach. If, on the other hand, you are going walking at altitude, or even skiing, you may need a few more resources, and getting yourself fit will help prevent injury (most skiing accidents happen when people are cold and tired). Note that, in the top six of travel claims for General Accident, heart problems hogged the number two and three positions.

- **Make a will.** Yes it might happen, and though you may be beyond worrying, it will make things easier back home. And if only one of a couple dies, being intestate can cause the survivor no end of problems.
- **Every year the British Red Cross receives hundreds of requests to trace missing friends or relatives** who may – or may not – have been swallowed by war, famine or plague. The vast majority are, of course, fine, having found a beach shack and a shack partner somewhere and decided to sever all links, but it costs the organisation thousands of pounds to trace these people. They recommend leaving your passport details and a detailed itinerary with family/friends, sending postcards and, if in an area for some time, registering with the local consulate. If there is a local disaster, tell the consulate you are OK so that relatives will have their minds set at rest.
- **Try *not* to take your worries with you.** Holidays are one of the major causes of stress. *Travelwise '94*, a newsletter published by a guide-book company, reckoned that some 15 million Britons will suffer some degree of anxiety or stress prior to (consultations with GPs increase in the week before a holiday) or during their vacation. It is not uncommon for someone to fret about how the office is going to cope without them during the run up to and first week of a holiday, and then to switch to worrying that they are coping, and they may be dispensable after all.

What you don't need to add to such concerns is worry about whether you have taken enough medical precautions. There was a time when travellers would, if they were very pessimistic, get a tetanus jab before they went. These days, given the amount of literature, clinics and travel nags, it is all too easy to let concerns about health dominate everything else. Don't let them. Worry about whether somebody is doing your job better instead.

3 Immunisations

These are going to take some forward planning, perhaps as much as three months.

When

As a travelling nation, we leave medical matters to the last minute. In a survey for SmithKline Beecham of 4000 holidaymakers travelling to hepatitis A risk areas, 37 per cent sought no medical advice, and a quarter of those who did left it too late to have the full course of recommended injections. In the 1994 Merieux survey, 54 per cent of travellers had booked their holidays a month or less before departure, which is cutting it fine for jabs.

'The backpackers are the worst,' says Dr Emma Woolfenden of the Liverpool School of Tropical Medicine. 'They come in the day before they are due to leave for India and Asia, and ask what immunisations they need. I can give them some, but they often go away under-protected.'

The message Dr Woolfenden gives is that you should start planning three months ahead if your trip is likely to take you anywhere remote. This may be erring on the side of extreme caution, but at least a month is advisable.

In an ideal world you should start your schedule of immunisations 12–14 weeks before departure, by checking that tetanus, diphtheria, and, if required, tuberculosis are all up to date, and arranging boosters if not. (Note that if you have a polio booster you should allow 3 weeks before having hepatitis A immunoglobulin, if using, because the polio immunisation interferes with the antibody response.) Then arrange a schedule to take in those immunisations which need multiple jabs:

- **Japanese B encephalitis and rabies:** days 0, 7, 28–30 (many clinics are happy to truncate this to two jabs with a booster at one year).

- **Hepatitis B:** weeks 0, 4 and 8, with an antibody level check to ensure there has been a response.
- **Tyhpoid: weeks 0 and 4.** There is also the new Typhim Vi, one shot which offers the same protection, with less debilitating reactions.
- **Hepatitis A:** the one-shot Havrix Hep A now available replaces the previous two-dose immunisation. One shot of Monodose 2–4 weeks before travelling protects for 1 year. This can be boosted to a decade.

Then there are others, such as meningococcal meningitis, cholera (if travelling to certain African and South American countries), and yellow fever – the certificate for which does not become valid until 10 days after the jab.

The schedule may have to be varied as there are certain problems if your basic immunisations aren't up to scratch. Live viruses (yellow fever, BCG, oral tyhpoid, yellow fever, oral polio) have to be given all on the same day or three weeks apart. Confusing isn't it? The sooner you get to that clinic, the better.

Where

Getting accurate advice on travel immunisations is tricky. Many of the problems hinge on the words 'required' and 'recommended'. The only immunisation that is internationally recognised as being a requirement of entry to certain countries is yellow fever. Cholera (see below) is not. So never phone up a tourist board and ask what is required for their country. They may say yellow fever, they may say nothing is required, but they are unlikely to volunteer the information that drug-resistant malaria is sweeping rural areas, or that hepatitis A is endemic. After all, they are in the business of getting you there on holiday.

Traditionally the cheapest way to get advice and a set of injections is to use the NHS. Although not all immunisations are free (e.g. rabies unless you are at 'occupational risk'), it still works out cheaper than a dedicated travel clinic. Your GP can, in fact, give everything except yellow fever (only WHO-approved centres can do that), and in a 1994 survey of 1032 travellers, 87 per cent had gone to their doctor for advice.

However, with the changes in the NHS, many GPs have noticed that travel immunisation is a steady earner for BA, Thomas Cook etc., and have set up their own travel clinics. Here it is normally the practice nurses who deal with immunisations.

Traditionally the objection to using GPs/practice nurses is that they are less likely than the clinics to be up-to-date with current requirements (although it is the clinics who often point this out). In fact, GPs do have access to accurate information, they can go on-line free to the NHS TRAVAX Service (though whether they choose to use it is another matter – in a 1990 survey, only 34 per cent of Glasgow GPs knew about TRAVAX, and it is based in the city). Many magazines (*MIMS*, *Practice Nursing*, *Pulse*) also produce immunisation charts for the world, but, as we shall see, this rather sketchy information should really be just the core material, not the sum total of advice.

One of the drug companies also runs an advice line for medical professionals, and it takes over 70,000 calls a year. Cynics, of course, would say it is in a drug company's interest to promote immunisations, and that they would tend to suggest immunisation more often than not. It is, however, really all down to how well-versed in the subtleties of travel immunisation the person using the service is. When my wife and I went on separate occasions to the same GP's clinic, we were given conflicting advice about whether we should have meningococcal meningitis (we didn't really need it).

Not that the big travel clinics are immune to this. A survey published in the Sunday Times (conducted by Edward Welsh with the help of Dr Richard Dawood) in September 1993, found that clinics varied in the standard of their advice, some tending to over prescribe jabs and pills (malaria and Japanese encephalitis for high altitude trekking in Nepal, for instance), and others failing to mention the full range of appropriate jabs. Basic immunisation costs ranged from £49–£68; a more exotic battery, for an adventurous African safari, came in at £103–£121. So it may be more than your left arm hurting. The information the clinics provided about such essential matters as altitude sickness and food and water hygiene was often sketchy.

If you want to be pre-briefed about what they should be telling you, Medical Service for Travellers Abroad (MASTA) has a telephone advice line (with postal back-up). Calls cost 39p/49p per minute, but may save you more in unecessary jabs. The MASTA database (also used by BA clinics) is sophisticated enough to take into account seasonal variations and different standards of travel, from backpacker to five-star. As someone who doesn't particularly like syringes, and also does not approve of taking a sledgehammer to my immune system, I tend to try and make sure the recommendation isn't a 'well-let's-give-it-just-in-case' scenario, when 'just in case' is on a par with the risk of being hit by frozen lavatory waste from a passing jet plane. Remember also, that very few of the immunisations give 100 per cent protection.

You should also expect any advice centre to give you information about other risks in the country you are visiting (e.g. whether there is a possibility, usually remote, of scarring leishmaniasis from sandfly bites, or dengue fever from mosquitoes) and an update on how to avoid the all-too-common travellers' diarrhoea.

The Merieux survey of travellers asked the subject what feeling they got from having been immunised. Sixty-two per cent said peace of mind, 37 per cent said a sense of security. But it can be a false sense of security; the immunisations are just a small part of the defence against disease.

Eric Le Fevre, manager of the Thomas Cook Travel Clinic, comments, 'It is estimated that 95 per cent of the illnesses it is possible to catch abroad are not immunisation-preventable. People have the whole balance of travel health wrong, and often leave thinking the jabs give them carte blanche to eat, drink and do what they like. They don't.'

So consider the following to be *part* of your overall protection plan. Immunisation centres are listed on page 322.

What

You are unlikely to need the entire range, but these are the immunisations in the clinics' armoury:

Cholera

It is over two decades since the WHO declared that cholera immunisation certificates were no longer needed as a condition of entry to any country. It was always a nasty jab, with adverse reaction (fever and generally feeling like death) common, and when it was recognised that it is less than 50 per cent effective, there seemed no reason at all to have it. However, some countries, such as Tanzania and Liberia, cling to it, and stories persist of over-zealous border guards elsewhere demanding proof of cholera shots. These stories are very difficult to verify, but they are always at fairly remote crossings, and usually in Africa and South America.

An AIDS worker I met swears she came across a case where the only possible route of infection was an enforced injection with a re-used needle at a border post. It may be advisable for travellers to South America and Africa, or at least those off the standard tourist routes, to get one cholera jab and an official-looking certificate from their doctor just in case. MASTA and the London School of Tropical Medicine and Hygiene actually produce a phoney certificate with a large CHOLERA stamp on it, with the words 'unnec' (i.e. unecessary) tucked away, but some doctors do not like to indulge in such deception, though the cause seems just. At the Liverpool School of Tropical Medicine, they inject a tiny amount of the immunisation, arguably more as a conscious-salving exercise, and then issue the certificate; Thomas Cook has a similar policy. You may have a doctor who will just issue the certificate without a jab. Just remember, if you are caught in an 'epidemic' area without a piece of paper, officials will immunise anyone, so your own supply of syringes and sterile needles is also essential.

Whether you have the jab or not, cholera remains a risk if you are dallying with untreated water in primitive, slum conditions in Africa, Asia and Central and South America. It is not a disease of tourism, but takes hold in conditions such as those seen in the Rwandan refugee camps. The South American version is an epidemic which was triggered by a strain that crossed from Asia. A new, more lethal strain is currently brewing up in Pakistan and Nepal and spreading east. The immunisation is even more useless against this robust variation (even though there are reports of some border officials on the subcontinent asking for certificates), so prevention by good hygiene is essential in endemic areas. The symptoms of cholera include vomiting, explosive watery diarrhoea, muscle cramps and weakness. If untreated, it can cause death through dehydration in as little as 6 hours (see Chapter 10).

Diphtheria

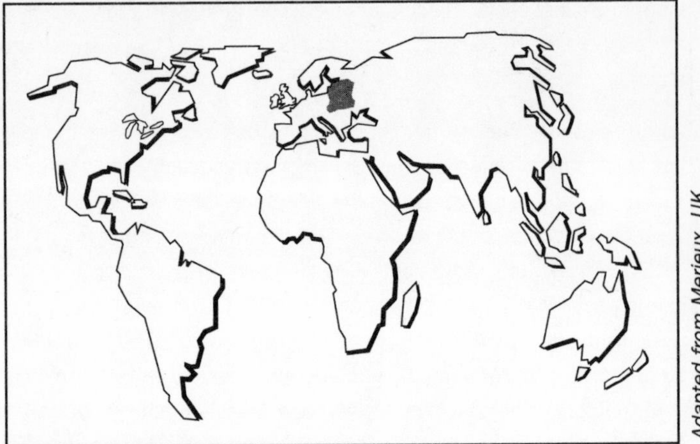

Adapted from Merieux, UK.

Most people in the UK will have been routinely immunised in childhood (if not, it is three injections, one month apart), and anyway it is a disease of prolonged close contact with locals. But if you are spending time living among the population in Eastern Europe, Africa, Asia, Central/South America or Vietnam, and given the evidence that immunity does wane over time, consider having a booster, which lasts for 10 years. (Note that in the UK a booster is now routinely being given to all school leavers, along with tetanus and polio boosters.)

A new low-dose, low-side-effect adult immunisation is now available, called Diftavax. It is, however, combined with tetanus, so if you have had a tetanus booster recently, expect a sore arm.

Hepatitis A

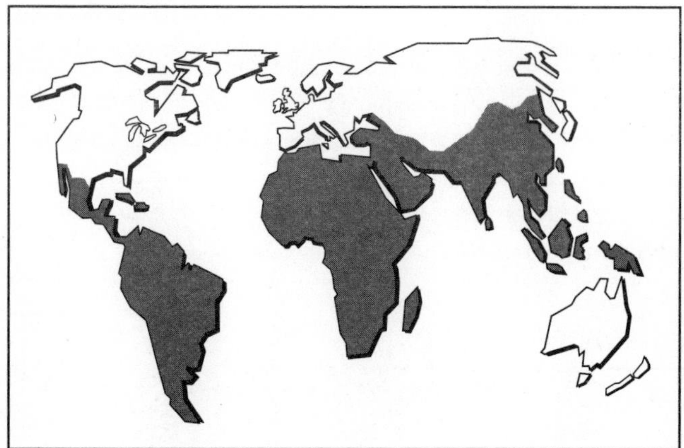

Adapted from Merieux, UK

One of the great miseries for the frequent traveller to the less hygiene conscious regions of the world was the gammaglobulin injection: a hefty packet of purified blood products pumped into the buttocks. The misery came from knowing that within a few months you would need another one.

In 1990 the Havrix Hep A immunisation changed all that: two injections one month apart gave protection for 12 months, and a booster at 6–12 months added a buttock-relieving 10 years. The two-shot has now been replaced by Monodose, one jab 2–4 weeks before leaving, again extendable to a decade. Note the 2 weeks minimum: the tardy back-packer who turns up the day before leaving will still get it in the rear.

Hepatitis A is endemic across Asia, the Middle East, and the central and southern Americas. However, it is a disease of poor sanitation/hygiene, and not every traveller will need protection (though, as Dr Emma Woolfenden points out, one rogue ice-cube is all it takes, and the Liverpool clinic suggest hepatitis A for all travel outside Europe, USA, Canada and Australasia).

Hepatitis A is a virus which invades the liver, reproducing there and infecting faeces. So it is caught from contaminated water, but also, notoriously, from eating seafood, especially shellfish, which can accumulate the virus. It causes flu-like symptoms, possibly jaundice and liver damage and it can kill.

Good hygiene practices will help protect the unimmunised traveller. The older person may well have immunity (which can be checked), but someone in their twenties (the classic backpacking age) may well have not been exposed. (Although it can be very serious in adults, hep A is quite mild in children, and will confer immunity. However, a 'junior' immunisation for those over 12 months is now available.)

Hepatitis B

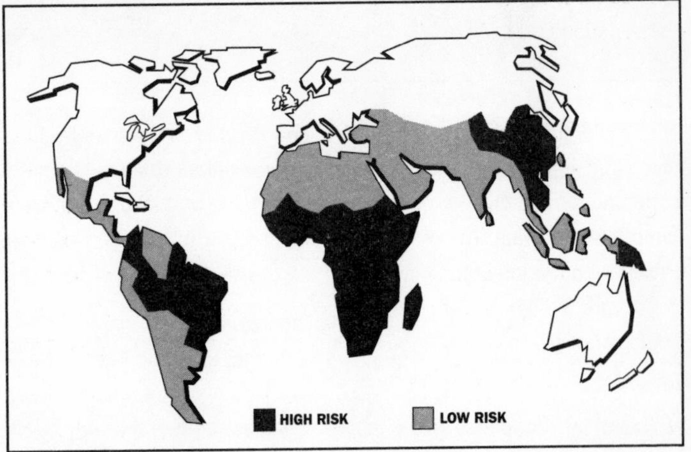

Adapted from Merieux, UK

Whereas the average traveller may well have a close-ish encounter with hep A, its even less attractive sibling is no real threat except in certain circumstances (which include unprotected sex). It has the same symptoms as hep A, but is more insidious, slower-acting and may cause permanent liver damage or even death, and it is implicated in liver cancer. It is caught through sexual contact, blood transfusions or from contaminated needles. There is also an unknown infection mechanism at work, whereby African children pick up the virus by an, as yet, undiscovered route (they may even have been born with it).

Anyone working in an endemic country (particularly if it involves contact with children who may have open wounds, grazes, sores, burns, etc.) is recommended to have the immunisation. So should any children, especially if attending local schools. Five-year protection is conferred by three injections over a 6-month period, though there is also an accelerated three jabs over 2-months, followed by a booster at 12 months. (Note it doesn't always 'take' – antibody levels have to be checked.)

The hepatitis family has a few more ugly relations. Hep E is a water- and food-borne version that has a record of high mortality in pregnant women; C is like B, with a similar transmission pattern through infected blood. You are very unlikely to come across D, F and G, but they are out there (and some authorities reckon we will one day exhaust the alphabet with the variations that will be discovered).

Japanese B encephalitis

This is caused by yet another pathogen that hitches a lift in the mosquito, though this time it is a *Culex* species (malaria is transmitted by the *Anopheles* species). The culprit is a virus, though it is thought that most people who are infected show no signs. However, ifthey do appear, the death rate is high, at 30 per cent. Of those who survive, some 80 per cent are left with a 'neurological deficit', nerve damage ranging from pins and needles to paralysis. Nasty stuff.

Travellers are at risk in rural areas of Asia, particularly where there are paddy fields, and especially if they are travelling for several weeks in such an area. The monsoon season is Jap B time in Thailand, India and Nepal, though trekkers at high altitudes are not at risk, due to the absence of the mosquitoes. The immunisation is three shots, on days 0, 7 and 28, and protects for 2 years. There is also a two-shot version of the immunisation, followed by boosters at 1 and 3 years, which some clinics favour. As with malaria, the best defence is not being bitten.

Meningococcal meningitis A and C

Africa has a meningitis belt. This girdles the country from below the Sahara, skirting across the top of Gabon, Zaire and down into Kenya, and

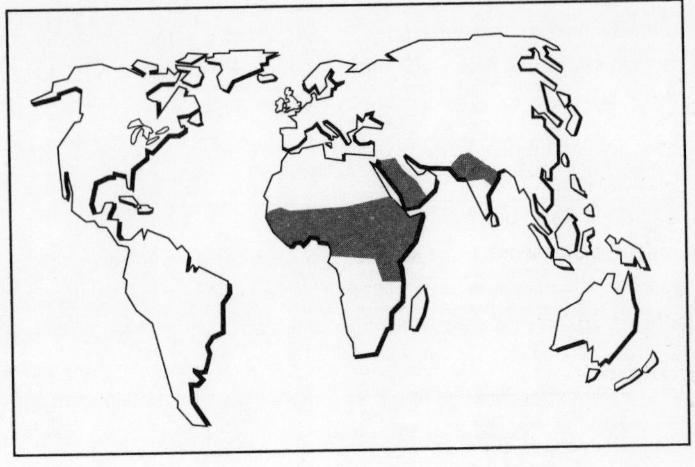

Adapted from Merieux, UK

there is strong evidence that the belt is slipping further south, with cases reported as far down as Namibia and Malawi. There have also been outbreaks in Brazil, Delhi and Nepal. It is caused by a bacterium, and spread by moisture in the form of airborne droplets, so it is a disease of close contact, and once you have it, the onset is lightening fast: fever, chills, rash and seizures are closely followed by death.

It is advised that all health workers, children (over 2 years old) attending local schools and teachers are immunised. One injection protects for 3 years. Up-to-date information about outbreaks is essential for anyone travelling independently in risk areas. Around 80 per cent of all cases of meningitis occur in the under-25 age group, so children should be protected (though, ironically, the immunisation is not as effective in children as adults). There is no immunisation against the B strain – one of the commonest.

Note that Hib meningitis (*Haemophilus influenzae* type B) is the most common cause of meningitis in very young children on the Indian sub-continent. Have your children immunised against Hib if not already done as part of the childhood schedule.

Information on recognising the signs of meningitis is given on p.160.

Polio

Polio is another disease we tend to ignore, thinking the entire population has beaten it, but surveys suggest that there are gaping holes in our protection, and a reinforcing booster dose, which lasts 10 years, might be a good idea. Check its current status: for instance it is widespread in South East Asia, but the incidence is very low in Malaysia and non-existent in Singapore. But just in case we get too complacent, in 1993 there was a hefty outbreak in Holland.

Rabies

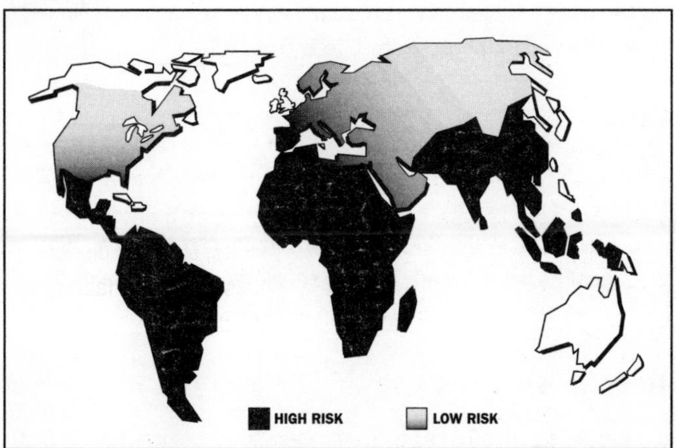

Adapted from Merieux, UK

I have a slight fear of rabies because a mangy, restless cur, with all the classic symptoms of incipient rabies, once bit me in North Africa. Fortunately, fashion at the time dictated I had rather high lace-up boots on despite the heat, and though I had some pinch marks on my skin, it wasn't penetrated. I should, of course, have sought treatment, but the thought of all those injections in the stomach put me off. Had I developed any symptoms at all, death would have been inevitable.

The old-fashioned regime of multiple jabs in the stomach has, in most parts of the world, been replaced by less terrifying methods. There is now a pre-exposure immunisation of three jabs (at 0, 7 and 28 days) and also a two-jab, 4 weeks apart, booster at 1 year version. Even if you have had these jabs, you must seek more treatment after a suspected bite, with jabs on days 0 and 37. With no pre-bite immunisation, you will need human rabies immunoglobulin plus immunisation on days 0, 3, 7, 14 and 90.

The pre-exposure immunisation is particularly recommended for anyone who will be more than a few hours from a medical centre equipped to deal with a bite (or, though it may seem like a joke, a nasty lick, especially to the face). Some authorities would like to see more people travelling to Thailand and, especially, Bangkok, being immunised. (Incidentally ignore the old advice to catch the animal and observe to see if rabid: you just end up with two bites.) Rabies can also be carried by other animals, some of them cute and cuddly, so treat any bite as suspect.

Tetanus

The bacterial spores that cause tetanus live in soil and dirt, and can easily be caught through a graze or burn. The symptoms include muscle spasms, which give it the name lockjaw, and it can be fatal. Have a booster (usually every 10 years), though check your current status first if you can – overimmunisation can lead to a very sore arm.

Tuberculosis

In most people's minds TB remains a disease of the depression. In fact, it has made a re-appearance in many areas, including the USA, where mass immunisation of the population was halted in the 1980s out of a very false sense of security. The disease is on the rise in New York among the homeless: there were 4000 reported cases in 1993 (though it clocked up 15,000 per annum in the early part of the century). It is also one of the growing number of AIDS-related illnesses. The WHO estimate it now kills 3 million people a year, and describes the situation as 'a global emergency'.

Most people in the UK, however, receive the BCG immunisation at secondary school (though if taking younger children abroad, get them immunised earlier). If you had it, you won't have forgotten, as it will have left that little moon crater on your left arm. If you haven't, and you are travelling off the beaten track in Africa, Asia or Latin America, and will be in prolonged contact with locals, you will need a skin test to establish your immunity. If you need a BCG, it should be given 2 months before departure, so the status of your TB protection should be one of the first things a long-term traveller checks.

Note, there is no doubt that children should be vaccinated if at risk, but there is evidence that the BCG is less effective in adults. Whether to vaccinate or not in adults is a controversial area: you may hear conflicting opinions.

Typhoid

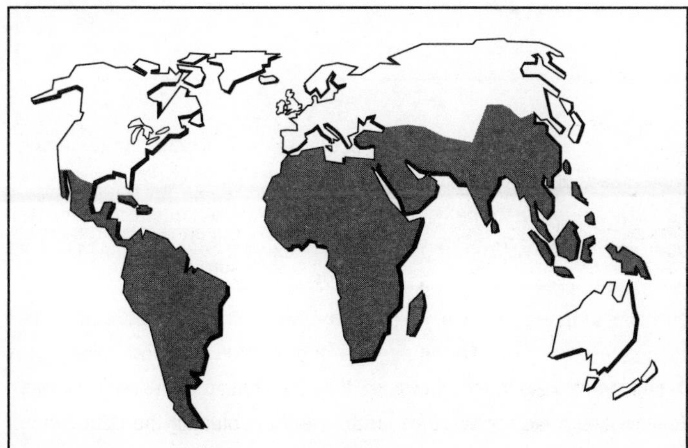

Adapted from Merieux, UK

More danger from dirty water, this time from the Salmonella family. It causes the usual battery of effects: fever, vomiting, dehydration. Anyone who had the old style injections (two jabs, a month apart) will have had a short taster of this. An oral version is now available (one capsule a day for 3 days; protects for 1 year; no side effects, but can't be taken with antibiotics, oral polio or the anti-malarial mefloquine), and a one-off Typhim Vi jab, effective for 3 years. Typhoid is not used quite as widely as it once was: backpackers etc. should have it, but a couple off for two weeks in an all-inclusive resort in Jamaica should probably not bother.

Yellow fever

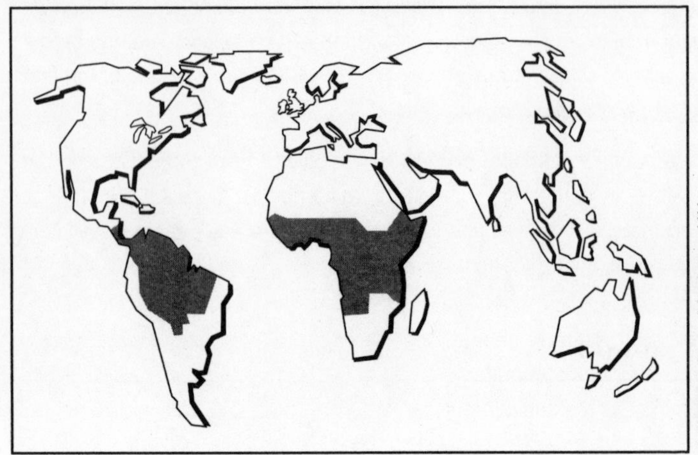

Adapted from Merieux, UK

Yellow fever is endemic in parts of South America, Central America and Africa (see map). Only a WHO centre can give this injection and provide you with an internationally recognised certificate, required by some countries for entry. (It is important to check your routing; you may not need a certificate to go into a country from the UK direct, but you may if you have stopped off in a yellow fever zone.) It is a virus carried by mosquitoes, this time *Aedes aegypti*, and is often fatal, as there is no specific treatment for it. However, the one-shot immunisation is very effective and lasts for 10 years. Both the immunisation and the certificate only become active 10 days after the jab.

Yellow fever infected countries, according to the WHO at the time of writing, are: Angola, Bolivia, Brazil, Cameroon, Colombia, Ecuador, The Gambia, Ghana, Guinea, Kenya, Mali, Nigeria, Peru, Sudan and Zaire.

However, some countries insist on certificates when travelling from certain countries, even if yellow fever is no longer active there. Bangladesh, for instance, has a long list of countries it considers to be a yellow fever risk, a list that grows all the time. Some countries want *all* travellers to have one.

The Liverpool School of Tropical Medicine recommend yellow fever for: Angola, Benin, Bolivia, Brazil, Burkino Faso, Burundi, Cameroon, Central African Republic, Chad, Colombia, Congo, Cote d'Ivoire, Ecuador, Equatorial Guinea, Ethiopia, French Guiana, Gabon, The Gambia, Ghana, Guatemala Guinea, GuineaBissau, Guyana, Kenya, Liberia, Mali, Mauritania, Niger, Nigeria, Panama, Peru, Rwanda, Sao Tome & Principe, Senegal, Sierra Leone, Somalia, Sudan, Suriname, Togo, Tanzania, Uganda, Venezuela and Zambia.

But check carefully, some countries put Zaire and Trinidad & Tobago on to their list of countries in the yellow fever zone, and will require a certificate if you have been through there recently. Note that even though some countries' requirements stipulate 'all travellers' or 'all travellers over 6 months', children under 9 months (preferably 12) should not be immunised: get an exemption certificate.

Others

For completists only, who have to have the full set of everything, there are a couple of other shots. You can have a jab against plague. Although linked with the Middle Ages, plague has never gone away from the rest of the world. Every so often, however, a journalist notices it in the WHO listing and does a global epidemic story.

There *is* an increase in plague: in 1992 there were 1768 cases worldwide, with some 198 deaths. Countries affected that year included Vietnam (437 cases, 13 deaths), Madagascar (198 cases, 26 deaths) and even the USA (13 cases, two deaths), but it is not a disease of tourism. The immunisation is expensive, not particularly effective, can cause hefty reactions, and is hard to obtain in the UK. Those at risk should consider taking an antibiotic (e.g. tetracycline) as prophylaxis or treatment instead.

At the time of writing, India is just recovering from a prime example of plague panic. French, Germans and Japanese have pulled out of tours in their thousands, yet the number of deaths remains small, and no tourists have (to date) been affected, even though pneumonic plague, the variation in question, can be spread by human-to-human contact. As the newspaper reports stressed, it is a nasty old business, tightness in the chest, cough and fever, leading to death within as little as 48 hours. However, it is still true that this is a disease of poverty and overcrowding and the risk to the average visitor, even at the height of the outbreak, was, to quote MASTA, 'very, very small', and treatment is fast and effective. The advice remains to avoid prolonged contact with locals in crowded conditions, something not that easy in India, and to seek advice if chest symptoms, such as coughing up blood, or a fever appears.

Similarly the immunisation for tickborne encephalitis (see Chapter 12) is limited to those at extreme risk, working in the forests where the ticks are found. However, MASTA and the London School of Hygiene and Tropical Medicine recommend that hikers, campers, etc. in Austria seriously consider it. Note it must be ordered specially: you can't turn up the day before you are due to go and expect to be immunised.

Travel clinics and hospitals

There are a number of organisations that can arrange or advise on immunisations, and these are listed in the section beginning on p.00. Incidentally, do not expect a consensus here different clinics, even doctors within clinics, have slightly differing ideas.

Summary

Type	Course	Lower Age Limit	Effective After	Effective For	Notes
Yellow Fever	One injection	9 months	10 days	10 yrs	Compulsory for some countries
Typhoid	1 inj (Typhim V_1)	18 months	10 days	3 yrs	Oral version available effective for 1 yr

Type	Course	Lower Age Limit	Effective After	Effective For	Notes
Tetanus	1 inj if received DPT in childhood	6 weeks	Immediate	10 yrs	If no childhood immun, 3 inj one month intervals
Hepatitis A (HAVRIX) Immunoglobin	One inj monodose One	16 yrs (junior version of 2 inj available) None	2–4 weeks Immediate	1 yr 10 yrs if booster at 6–12 months 2–4 months	Relatively mild in children. May be worth checking if you have immunity
Hepatitis B	3 inj, 0, 1, 6 months or 0, 1, 2 months + booster at 1 year	None	3rd dose or booster	5 yrs	Need to check antibodies to ensure protection in place
Cholera	1	1 year	6 days	3–6 months	Poor efficacy – consider *only* if cert needed
Meningococcal memingitis	1	18 months	15 days	3–5 yrs	A + C only
Rabies	3 inj at 0, 7, 28 days *or* 0, 28 and booster at 1 year	12 months	3rd dose	12 months if 2 dose; 2–3 yrs otherwise	Still need post-exposure if bitten
Japanese B encephalitis	3 inj 0, 7, 28 days (there is a 2 jab version)	1 year	10–14 days (one month if two jabs)	2 yrs	Consult travel clinic/GP for risks areas
Polio	Primary course in childhood (if not 3 doses 1 month apart)	6 weeks for inj; none for oral	Immediate after final dose or booster	Oral booster every 10 yrs	Check your status with GP

Type	Course	Lower Age Limit	Effective After	Effective For	Notes
BCG (TB)	1 inj, but test should be given first to check immunity	None	2 months	? but no booster advised	Believed to be less effective in adults
Diphtheria	Most have DPT as child; 3 inj	6 weeks	3rd dose	Every 10 yrs	At risk groups only – new combined DIP/TET boost available

Adapted from *International Travel and Health: Vaccination Requirements and Health Advice. Situation as on 1 January 1994.* Geneva, World Health Organization, 1994. Thanks to Yvonne Ganley, Liverpool School of Tropical Medicine

You can also check current requirements at your local library by consulting *MIMS* magazine, which carries a monthly update on countries and the advised immunisation/malaria prophylaxis, or the GP's *Pulse* magazine.

N.B. HIV-positive individuals should not be given live vaccines. Check carefully with your doctor.

4 What to take

As if the immunisations didn't cost enough, there is a whole host of other equipment you should also consider. Note, consider. One thing that emerges from conversations with regular travellers is that their list of essentials diminishes over the years as they learn to do without, to buy when they get there and discard on leaving, or to improvise using local materials.

Insurance

This is one thing you are not going to be able to get on the ground, and you shouldn't leave home without it. Europ Assistance, one of the repatriation organisations that subcontracts to the insurance companies, has seen a five-fold increase in moving uninsured people over the past few years. Being coverless means you may have to pay for an air ambulance with a doctor and nurse, a nurse to escort you home, or an extra seat on the plane to prop up your broken leg. It can cost an absolute fortune (£7–8000 from Spain, over £30,000 from the USA), enough to make the heftiest of premiums look like a bargain.

Choose your insurance with care. Insurance companies are, by nature, some of the most slippery beasts you will come across on your travels – if they can wriggle out of your claim, they will.

Read the policy carefully. Yes, it is very boring and full of confusing terminology. It is designed like that. And note that on many policies your passport is not covered unless it is on your person or in a safe, the amount of cash is limited to £250, personal accident is invalid if due to 'solvent abuse or alcohol' (and the latter is a distinct possibility; see Chapter 13). It may also have an excess on it. Travellers' Insurance Association (part of Commercial Union) for instance, will not pay out the first £35 on any claim, nor will they pay out more than £250 on any one article (get anything you really value – such as your camera, laptop, favourite jacket, etc., on your all-risks home policy). Columbus drops its upper limit from £100 down to £75 if the theft occurs on a beach, which may seem stingy until you realise that many companies regard such theft as carelessness and void the claim altogether.

Ask also under what conditions you can cancel or curtail your trip. Jury service usually counts, death of the cat doesn't. The amount of cover provided must be enough to reimburse the cost of your trip. It is usually £3000, but exotic holidays often cost more than that (American Express offers £7600 and £12,500 options on its Centurion policies).

Arguably, the most essential thing is medical cover. Losing your luggage, camera and so on and finding out you missed the clause explaining they will deduct wear and tear from replacement value is annoying in the extreme, but it isn't life-threatening. Finding yourself facing an operation in a foreign hospital with no cover could be. Always check the medical section very carefully.

To those of us used to the NHS, having £2m medical cover might seem ridiculous; and annual policies often have a dream-figure of £5m. I asked Alan Cousins, a manager of Europ Assistance, how many people had run up bills of £2m recently. None, he said, though several had bounced through the £250,000 barrier. 'But sooner or later, someone will end up on a life-support machine in America with a court case pending. That is why you need it.'

Several companies have said that over the last 4 years the actual value of each individual medical claim has risen by 40–50 per cent. The number of claims has also increased by 35 per cent in that time, and some insurance companies have noted that people over 65 are eight times more likely to claim medical expenses and cancellations than others, and have hiked the premiums accordingly (usually doubling them). Note that BCWA has no age loading, Club Direct do not penalise until the age of 70, and Age Concern arranges its own policies.

If you have a pre-existing medical condition, and this may mean just being on a waiting list for a minor op, do declare it, otherwise it may invalidate your claim. Douglas Cox-Tyrie has a policy where diabetes is not considered a pre-existing medical condition. Leisure care Insurance has a Special Care policy aimed at 'the medically disadvantaged' who may have a problem getting cover elsewhere.

Also check what is excluded in terms of activities. Many companies use the term 'hazardous activity' very vaguely: anything that involves standing up seems to be disqualified. You may be allowed to undertake activities if they were not the sole purpose of your holiday, for example General Accident claim you may be covered if the activity was spur-of-the-moment. However, if you are going on a dedicated white-water rafting trip, they would expect you to contact them for a quote the normal policy would not apply.

TSB has an option which, for £12 over normal policy price, adds abseiling, scuba diving, orienteering and several other mildly threatening activities, while £15 gives you the full testosterone-fuelled options of bob-sleighing, hang-gliding, parachuting, pot-holing and white-water rafting.

Your policy must have a 24-hour contact number (phone, fax, telex) for the emergency medical service, and you need to know the dialling code for the UK from the country you are in (currently being standardised to 00 44). Note that insurance companies want letters and receipts for absolutely everything – I am afraid that your word is no longer your bond.

If you travel more than a couple of times a year, consider an annual policy, or a family policy. Again, check carefully what the restrictions on travel are. General Accident in its £78 world-wide, year-round policy specifies that no single trip must last longer than 31 days; it will also cover one winter sports holiday. BCWA allows 90 days per trip, again with 17-day winter-sports cover. With WEXAS (joining fee £39.58), you can travel for ten weeks, plus a three-week winter-sports holiday. Leisurecare has a medical-only annual policy for £49. Europ Assistance has a policy for mammoth trips up to 18 months, but the level of cover is lower than its standard policies and cost is calculated on a sliding scale depending on trip duration, with a whopping £724 worldwide cover for the full 18 months. But that is *continuous* cover. Family policies are offered by many of the companies (though the age when children attain adulthood and cost full price varies from 15 to 21 years), but check whether the policy is in force if the individual family members holiday separately.

Try also Travel Direct, Frizzell and Crispin Speers. Note that some companies have medical-only cover, others offer a cheaper rate if baggage is excluded (Columbus says 53 per cent of all claims are for baggage, as opposed to 18 per cent for medical).

Note there is no regulation on air ambulance and repatriation/assistance companies. There is a British Aeromedical Practitioners' Association, which has a code of practice, but there is no compulsion for members to comply. The situation was highlighted in a report in the *Daily Telegraph* (20 August 1994) describing the plight of a holidaymaker who slipped a disc in Minorca and was air ambulanced home. The ambulance stopped off en route to pick up other cases, stretching the flight time to a very painful 14 hours (7 hours after her family got back). There is little you can do about not finding yourself in the same situation, because most of us buy our insurance from an insurance company, and the names of the assistance companies are meaningless apart from a couple of the larger ones.

Mosquito nets

You are not likely to need a net if your itinerary features the hotel groups Mandarin, Taj, Amandari and so on; they usually have nets or screens and air-conditioning. If you intend to venture away from such comfortable cocoons in Africa, Asia or South and Central America, you will need one. There is much debate over nets. The very small mesh nets will stop through-biting by insects, but tend to be very stuffy. Lighter nets with a larger mesh size will allow the odd sneaky proboscis to be probed through.

'If you treat your net with permethrin,' says Jane Miller, a net expert at the London School of Hygiene and Tropical Medicine, 'then mesh size is less critical because contact will kill them. People argue against the single-point bell-shaped ones, because you are more likely to touch the sides, but again, if treated adequately you don't have to worry.' However, permethrin breaks down after a time, so the best approach is one of belts and braces: a net with a small enough mesh to stop mosquitoes and the even tinier sandfly, *and* treated with permethrin.

Some of the rectangular tents require more than one ceiling attachment point, which can be a nuisance. Weight must also be a consideration. I have in my office a free-standing, double-bed net, absolutely wonderful, but very bulky and very time consuming to set up. Many companies produce neater alternatives. Oasis sells cotton/synthetic mix nets that weigh in at $8\frac{1}{2}$ ozs. They cost £31.40 and come pre-treated with the insecticide permethrin, which remains effective for 6 months in use

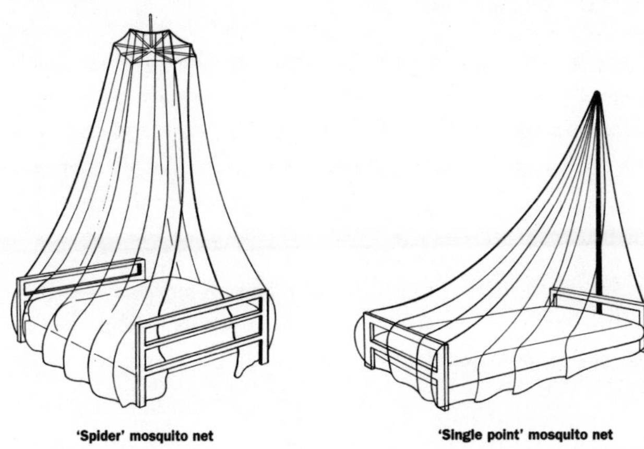

'Spider' mosquito net **'Single point' mosquito net**

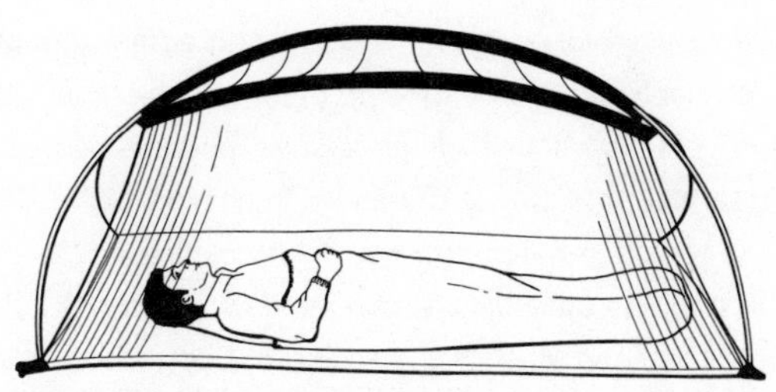

'Bubble' mosquito net

(handling and light diminish the concentration). After this time Oasis will retreat it or will supply a home chemistry kit for £5. SafariQuip has introduced a hexagonal-holed net, which it claims resists stretching. It is designed to hang from a wall or the side of a truck, and both its weight (300 g/10½ oz) and its price (£15.99, £24.99 treated) make it an interesting proposition. Nomad has a treated box net which converts to a wedge for £15.99. (See Useful Addresses for other suppliers.)

Hilary Bradt swears by a self-contained 'bubble' type net made by US company Long Road. These are available through Travel Medicine Inc or direct from Long Road. A one-person net costs $79, a two-person $99, plus 24 per cent to cover foreign delivery.

I was sceptical about them: they are not light the double is 2.8 lb and you do feel a little like the boy in the bubble in one, minus the oxygen supply, but once I had handled one, I had to admit they beat the opposition hollow. The sewn-in ground sheet, and the shape mean that the chances of a bite through are very slim, which in turn eradicates the need for insecticide treatment.

For those who really hate insects, Travel Medicine Inc also features Ben's Bug Armor Suit, which means you basically walk around all day in a tailored mosquito net. Very chic.

Repellents

See also Chapter 12.

You should equip yourself with plenty of mosquito/insect repellent. Remember it isn't only the tropics that are plagued – the mosquitoes in Alaska seem to hold a particularly fierce grudge, perhaps because they missed out on carrying malaria. DEET (diethyl toluamide) is the standard formulation, and comes as roll-on, sprays, low concentration creams and impregnated in arm and anklebands, and as slow-release formulations (e.g. Ultrathon). It is good stuff, but has its drawbacks. Do not use on children under six, and discontinue if you have a skin reaction.

MASTA's MosiGuard Natural is a non-DEET alternative with a similar repellent effectiveness (including leeches and the like). Also DEET-free are X-Gnat and Gurkha (which, I am reliably informed, is a variation on Avon's Skin-So-Soft: conditions and softens as it repels). Permethrin-treated clothing is also a good idea, as are permethrin knock-down sprays.

Sleeping bags

I finally disposed of my old bag: I decided my sleeping bag days had come to an end, and it was starting to leak down. These days I stick to taking a simple cotton sheet liner, which is cool, and also lets you sleep easier on suspect sheets. Exodus sells a nifty combination of sleep mat (a slab of foam which helps keep you warm), inflatable pillow and sleep sack for £17.35. SafariQuip also sells good cotton bags, both square-cut and tapered. Nomad has army-issue bags with built-in pillows.

I bought my down bag before the good synthetics came on the scene. The latter (such as Quallofil, Hollofil and Polarguard) have the advantage that they continue to work when wet – down just collapses. So if you do choose down (and it still offers the best insulation rating), make sure you keep it dry.

There is no hard and fast advice on buying a bag, it has to be tailored to your itinerary. How warm do you actually need it? The crude way is to look at the season rating, one season means summer use only, and they go through to five seasons (the 'who-do-you-think-you-are-ChrisBonnington?' bag). Will it be an advantage to be able to zip two together? Is it going to be very cold (in which case look for a hood and draft collar and an insulation mat to stop 'compression spots')? What shape do you want? The tapered mummy shapes offer the best insulation, but limited leg room for those of us who like a good bit of tossing and turning before dropping off.

Choose a shop where the staff will go through the relative merits of each type of bag for your trip, and try out everything, especially the zip, making sure it doesn't snag and that it is baffled to prevent heat loss. Some zips have velcro fasteners to help prevent them 'creeping' open during the night. Some dispense with zips altogether, which saves weight, but means no ventilation. There are various construction methods. The simple stitched-through method of quilting gives flat (read cold) spots, and is only suitable for one season bags. Some bags get over the problem by double or triple layering, off-setting with each layer where the stitching falls. More sophisticated bags use a method of 'box walling', where the insulation materials is stuffed into its own walled compartment. There are any number of variations on these themes.

You also need to see how easily they pack into the stuff bag (which must be waterproof and well stitched). Finally, do not be afraid to get into it in the shop, particularly if you are tall – sleeping bags which come up to your armpits are no use at all. Remember that when in use a lot of your heat will go through the ground, particularly as your body weight will compress the filling. Again, an insulating sleep-mat will enhance the performance of any bag you choose.

Clothing

Hats

Hat sales continue to decline. Which is a shame, because they are wonderful things. The original reason for wearing hats in the tropics was to prevent sun (now heat-) stroke. However, as you tend to lose heat through your head, the effect is to really make you sweat more: a fedora functioned more as a sun-shield. A wide-brimmed hat will shade the eyes and cover the neck. Real Panamas (woven in Ecuador), which shade without trapping too much heat, are widely available in this country now (try Genuine Panama Hat Co), as are various cotton hats, usually punched through with mesh-covered holes, which ventilate the head while keeping insects out (e.g. Norfolk Headwear). If it's warmth you are after, try something a little less flattering (see below).

Footwear

There are all sorts of things that get in through your feet, both on land

and in the sea. A pair of flip-flops will protect against stones, but are not really adequate against many soil-borne parasites, and I, for one, hate walking in them. You may want to consider more robust footwear. Deck shoes are light, comfortable and will deter jigger fleas and the like. Desert boots give good grip plus ankle support. Plastic sandals may look less chic, but are better for wading in water and keeping the sea urchins at bay. Some of the mail order shops mentioned stock 'travel sandals'. (See Useful Addresses.)

What you wear the rest of the time is purely a matter of taste. There are those who swear by travelling in trainers, personally I dislike them, and not just on aesthetic grounds – most of them make perfect hothouses for athlete's foot. However, should hiking be on the agenda, a good pair of boots is invaluable. Paul Goodyer of Nomad suggests you look for tough Vibram soles, with leather uppers, rather than any fancy fabrics, for durability (the fewer seams the better). At the lower end of the range he suggests the Neuwald Axim (£50), though serious walkers/trekkers should consider splashing out on the Karrimor KSB (£110). Don't buy them too tight, because your feet may swell. Good long, loop-stitched socks are essential if you are in leech/tick country.

Footwear featuring a water-repellent outer or inner material, such as Gore-Tex, is a good idea. US company, Rockport, produces something called Dressports, a sort of Q-boot which looks like a heavy-soled brogue, but is completely waterproof and tough enough for hiking. They cost around $139. SafariQuip sells a Gore-Tex trekking boot that doesn't look quite as stylish, but is probably a little more practical, for £61.99.

Other clothing

You will need to be aware of local mores when packing. In certain countries (e.g. Malawi) a skirt is essential for women, and even for men shorts can be an inappropriate garment in many cultures. Good cotton trousers as opposed to jeans are a good bet. They look smarter, allow air to circulate (which can prevent all sorts of fungal problems and heat rashes) and do not rub as much as denim. The US company, Haggar, produces 'no-iron' trousers that really do look good after washing. They cost £40 a pair, from most department stores. Jackets and shirts are promised. Cotton rip-stop trousers are useful if you are going to 'layer' they are baggy enough to wear long johns/track suit bottoms underneath.

Always pack a sweater. Every summer San Francisco is full of freezing, half-naked tourists who think that California doesn't get cold. And you never know when you will encounter over-zealous air-conditioning or that unexpected trip into the mountains or desert (see also Chapter 8).

A waterproof garment is also a good idea. Whether you can bring yourself to buy a cagoule is up to you – they do the job, but generally look awful. A space-saving, poncho-type number made from synthetic material often does the trick, and can double as a ground-sheet or sun canopy.

Generally speaking, whatever the climate, the concept of layering – being able to take off and add a thin garment as appropriate – is the best option. Adapting local dress is often recommended – the cooling jebalas in North Africa, sarongs in Asia, etc. If you can carry it off and keep a straight face, then fine.

If you are trekking to very cold climates – and something like the Kilimanjaro 'walk', often rather disingenuously sold as 'soft' mountaineering, will take you to bitterly cold conditions – choose your clothing very carefully. I first came across Gore-Tex when I used to windsurf a lot. I bought a remarkable thing called a dry suit, which could slip over my clothes. Despite covering me from neck to toe, it was never uncomfortable, because Gore-Tex 'breathes', i.e. lets moisture out. Unfortunately, due to strain on the seams, the suit eventually started to let moisture in, lots of it.

The leaks weren't the Gore-Tex's fault, and I remain impressed by the material as an insulating outer garment. As for what you wear underneath it, make sure it is layers, which help trap and warm the air. Many experts now favour some sort of fleece (bunting) intermediate layer (fleece jackets double as soft pillows), with a thin sweater, woollen shirt and woollen (or silk or synthetic) vest underneath. Do not wear cotton next to the skin – it loses its insulation properties when wet. The legs should be similarly layered. A woollen hat that can be rolled down into a balaclava is also a good idea, even if you do end up looking like a mass murderer.

The first aid kit

The idea of travelling with a first aid kit seemed unthinkable a few years back. Some Band-Aids, paracetamol (more for hangovers than anything else) and sting relief cream used to be about it. These days people depart for holiday with a small branch of Boots in their case. The chances are they will come back with about three of the various packets and bottles open, and two of those only because they split in transit.

Think carefully about whether you need to take lots of medication, especially if you expect to meet others you can cadge from: some seem to pack as if the Masque of the Red Death is on the itinerary. Many countries have better equipped pharmacies than ours, with quite powerful drugs available without prescription. And US drug stores are a hypochondriac's paradise: a whole two aisles of painkillers, two dozen different fungal creams, 16 ways of curing motion sickness, a score of anti-diarrhoeal preparations . . .

However, if you are travelling to remote areas, or are worried about bootlegged proprietary medicines (as is increasingly common – look for colour variations or misprints on labels), then you should pack more than the Band-Aid. You can buy ready-packaged kits, but is just as easy to tailor-make your own: only you know whether it is worth taking a pack of Kwells for motion sickness. Consider some of the following, however:

- **Most importantly for many countries, sterile needles, sutures, canulae etc.** (see Chapter 13). If you feel your intentions might be misconstrued (increasingly unlikely as more travellers pack kits), get a letter explaining these are not for your on-going drug habit. All clinics sell packs, as do the mail-order companies mentioned above. Try also: WellCare, InterHealth, Travel Medicine Centre and SAFA.
- **Aspirin and/or paracetamol or, better yet, panadiene paracetamol with codeine** for sunburn, mild altitude sickness etc – as well as hangovers.

- **Insect repellents,** both personal (DEET) and knock-down sprays (permethrin) plus coils for burning.
- **Calamine lotion** for bites or sunburn or skin irritations.
- **Factor 15 or higher suntan cream.**
- **Insect bite/sting relief cream** (with hydrocortisone; can also be use for mild sunburn). I use Benadryl anti-histamine ointment bought in the USA.
- **Anti-diarrhoea treatment** (brand names such as Arret or Imodium). **Be careful.** These should never be given to children under 12 (although some syrups aimed at kids are available) because loperamide, the active ingredient in many preparations, and other drugs can halt all intestinal activity. Even for adults, they are at best a temporary relief.
- **Oral rehydrating salts** (ORS), such as Dioralyte, which make up for the effects of diarrhoea (and hangovers), and are better than loading yourself up with loperamide. Also useful for dehydration treatment. Some of the mail order companies above produce a salt/sugar measuring spoon for making your own.
- **Crepe bandage** (John Hatt, author of The Tropical Traveller, recommends these doubled as somewhere to keep valuables and money, strapped closely to your leg).
- **Sterile gauze; various sizes of plaster.**
- **Scissors and tweezers** (or Swiss army knife with built in scissors and tweezers, though the latter are a bit feeble).
- **Zinc, or baby, talcum powder.**
- **Sterile gauze, different sized fabric plasters** (more adheshive), melolin non-adherent dressings plus micropore or zinc oxide tape for holding down. A triangular bandage (for slings), safety pins, pressure bandages.
- **Parenthood brings with it an appreciation of 'wet ones'** wipes of various sorts ideal for wiping the face (or cutlery) of grime.
- **Water purification tablets** (iodine the most effective against organisms such as Giardia) and/or filter/purifier. Iodine tincture can also be used as antiseptic for cuts. Water containers are also essential for storing/ carrying your treated supplies.
- **Anti-malarial regime** (including permethrin soaked net); plus possibly selftreatment (see below).
- **Spare glasses or contact lenses** or, at the very least, your prescription.
- **Also ensure you have adequate supplies of any personal medication** for

conditions such as asthma. Medicines may be difficult to get, and may even be widely pirated.

- **A torch** to scare away those snakes and water buffaloes at night.

You may also want to consider:

- **A clinic thermometer.**
- **Antiseptics, e.g. Savlon.**
- **Antifungal creams** such as Daktarin (miconazole) or Canesten (clotrimazole) and athlete's foot powder (fungal infections are very common in the tropics).
- **Dental repair kits** (if you have crowns and bridges), though in my experience they are a very temporary measure. Oil of cloves might be more might be more useful to help numb things until help can be found.
- **If you expect to be away from reliable medical care, consider taking a supply of broad spectrum antibiotics** such as Trimethoprim, ciprofloxacin (Ciproxin) or doxycycline; Flagyl (metronidazole) for amoebic dysentery or giardiasis; perhaps even mebendazole for treating a variety of worm conditions. It is essential you talk over what you might need, doses and possible side effects with a doctor. Doxycycline, for instance, is not suitable for children under 12 or pregnant women, and co-trimoxazole has had a bad press recently about its safety.

  Many authorities suggest not taking antibiotics in case you use them incorrectly, but all the travelling doctors I know admit to a fondness for the likes of ciprofloxacin, including Dr Jon Dallimore who runs the Remote Medicine course and leads treks in Nepal: 'Well, it is handy, because, like Domestos, it kills 99 per cent of all known germs.' If it's good enough for them, you might think it good enough for you.
- **Again, you may need to take a course of malarial treatment** (as opposed to prophylaxis) such as quinine or Fansidar. If you are very ill in a remote area you may not be able to even get out to get them, and the few tablets you need to start you off won't weigh very much. Discuss with your clinic/doctor before you leave to ensure that the course does not react unfavourably with your anti-malarial regime.
- **You should also consider whether you feel the need for eye ointments (against, for instance, conjunctivitis) or treatments for vaginal infections such as yeast.**

- **A good first aid book.** *Where There Is No Doctor* by David Werner (see further reading) would be suitable for the isolated aid worker, though it is too large and far too specialised for the average traveller. The *British Red Cross Practical First Aid* is a handy-sized alternative.

  At the time of writing MASTA were preparing a simple diagnostic guide to travel illnesses, though no publication date had been fixed.
- **If you have diabetes, a rare allergy or blood group, a history of epilepsy, etc., consider getting a Medic Alert bracelet,** which will contain details and a 24-hour emergency number.
- **Condoms, contraceptive pills, tampons** are often hard to get
- **A short wave radio** that will pick up BBC World Service (Sony and Aiwa both do excellent ones), in case the only sickness you get is home sickness.

Travel checklist (general)

BAGGAGE
Rucksack
Day pack
Document wallet

SLEEPING
Sleeping bag/liner
Inflatable pillow
Inflatable neck cushion
Mosquito net
Tent/groundsheet/foam mat

EATING
Mess tins/bowl
Cup
Knife/fork/spoon
Cooker/fuel bottle
Rations

SECURITY
Money belt
Padlock
Chain

ESSENTIAL TRAVELLING COMPANIONS
Swiss army knife
Cord/strong string
Gaffa tape
Universal plug
Sewing kit/strong thread
Safety pins
Prit Stick
Electric adaptor
Ear plugs
Maps
Books
Guide books
Pocket dictionary
Note book/pens/pencils
Compass
Playing cards/games
Alarm clock
Plastic bags

LIGHT
Torch/spare batteries
Lighter/matches
Stub candle

WATER
Water bottle (1 or 2 litres)
Water purification chemicals

CLOTHING
Long-sleeved shirt (x 2 - 1 smart)
T-shirts (x 2)
Sweat shirt/jumper
Thermals
Trousers/skirt (x 2 – 1 smart)
Shorts
Swim wear
Underwear (x 3)
Socks (x 3)
Hat
Scarf
Walking boots
Sandals/flip flops
Waterproofs

HYGIENE
Soap/soap box
Toothpaste
Talcum powder
Travel wash
Folding toothbrush
Razor/cream
Towel
Wipes
Loo roll
Shampoo
Sanitory protection
Condoms

HEALTH
Insect repellent (DEET)
Insect killer
Medical first aid kit
Vitamins
Malarial tablets
Sun screen
Moisturising cream/lip salve
Sun glasses
Prescription drugs/antibiotics/ course of malarial treatment

DOCUMENTS
Passport/visas
Air/travel tickets
Driver's licence
Passport photos
Immunisation certificates
Addresses of British Consulates *en route*
Money (currency/dollars)
Traveller's cheques
Credit card

OTHERS
Camera/film
Personal stereo/radio (recording)
Tapes
Binoculars
Fan

Travel checklist (medical)

The Nomad pharmacy recommend you consider the following medical list for short holidays (under six weeks) which are mainly hotel based.

- ❑ **Aspirin soluble 300 mg**
- ❑ **Loperamide 2 mg**
- ❑ **Dioralyte**
- ❑ **Panadiene**
- ❑ **anti-histamine tablets**
- ❑ **steripod**
- ❑ **Savlon dry spray**
- ❑ **fabric plasters (7.5 x 2cm/3.8 x 3.8cm)**
- ❑ **Band aid waterproof plasters**
- ❑ **Micropore tape 2.5cm**
- ❑ **wound dressing BPC14**
- ❑ **cotton buds**
- ❑ **anchor bandage**
- ❑ **crepe bandage 7.5 cm**
- ❑ **gauze swabs**
- ❑ **lancets**
- ❑ **mediswabs**
- ❑ **melolin 10 cm**
- ❑ **scissors**
- ❑ **tweezers**
- ❑ **antimalarials**
- ❑ **sting relief**
- ❑ **insect repellent**
- ❑ **repellent coils**
- ❑ **sunscreens**

Ch.3 Immunisations

Prescription items: e.g. malarial treatment or antibiotics for amoebic dysentery: SEEK SPECIALIST MEDICAL ADVICE.

For the tropics, under 2 months, mainly backpacking, Nomad suggest adding to the above:

- ❑ **hydrocortisone cream**
- ❑ **Dioralyte tablets and sachets**
- ❑ **miconazole cream**
- ❑ **melolin 10 cm and 5 cm**
- ❑ **foot blister plasters**
- ❑ **HIV/hepatitis B sterile kit**
- ❑ **water purification tablets**
- ❑ **mosquito net (treated)**

Plus: ointment/drops for conjunctivitis (especially for wearers of contact lenses), antifungal powder/talc. Plus your prescription items.

For trips longer than 2 months you need to discuss your itinery carefully with a pharmacist, otherwise you can find yourself leaving the UK looking as if you are going to open your own chemist somewhere - remember you may be able to stock up *en route* with many items.

5 Malaria: the Big One

This disease gets a chapter all on its own, even before we figuratively up and leave these shores. Throughout this book you will find mention of various equally nasty conditions that you often have as much chance of catching in Trafalgar Square, however, as abroad. Malaria is a different matter. Aid agencies report this as the commonest serious disease among returning workers, and increasingly, holidaymakers to Africa and, to a much lesser extent, Asia are being infected.

On average some 2000 people a year bring this liver/blood parasite home to the UK as unwanted baggage, over 90 per cent of it from Africa. Usually around 10–12 of these will actually die (though figures for 1993 were down to five), mainly because they do not seek treatment quickly enough or because it is misdiagnosed. The figure could be higher: over half of those with the disease are harbouring *Plasmodium falciparum*, the most lethal variant (capable of causing cerebral malaria and death within 48 hours). Malaria demands respect from even the most jaded traveller.

Although malaria is not a reason to avoid a country, it is very serious for pregnant women: if you are pregnant, as the old slogan used to say, is your journey really necessary?

What is it?

It isn't really the mosquitoes' fault. Any jury would acquit them as innocent dupes in this matter, just out for a blood snack, a minor misdemeanour on the scale of things. 'How was I to know my saliva contained a parasitic protozoan, M'Lud?'

The protozoan (or single-celled) organism in question comes in four forms, the highly dangerous *P. falciparum* (which causes over 80 per cent of all cases in sub-Saharan Africa, plus a hefty contribution in South America) or malignant malaria, and three comparatively benign forms *P.*

vivax, *P. malariae* and the rare *P. ovale*. That doesn't mean the latter trio are a bundle of laughs, you still get the chills, the fevers, the shakes, the sweats, the diarrhoea . . . it just isn't going to kill you. ('You do the shake and bake,' as one doctor described the symptoms.)

How you get it

The mosquito that will infect you with malaria is inevitably a female *Anopheles*, because only they suck blood. Great play is often made of being able to decide whether a mosquito is a male or female, but 'Sexing the mosquito' comes some way behind Scrabble as a holiday treat for me. Anyway, how often do you see the one that got you? Often the first evidence of assault is that itchy lump.

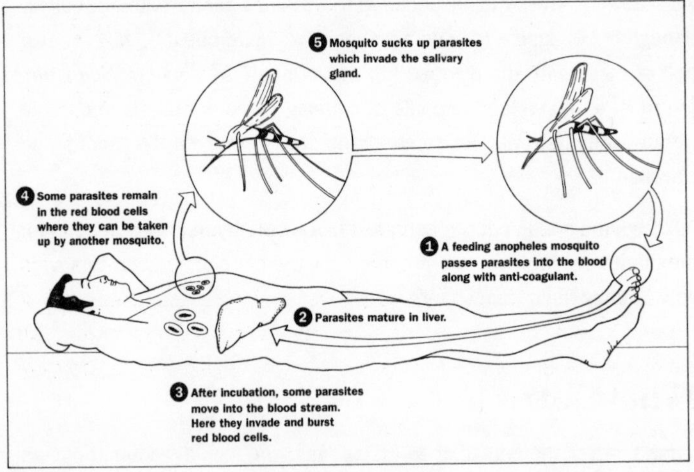

SIMPLE MALARIA LIFE-CYCLE

Once in your bloodstream, the parasite moves to the liver, multiplies, and then some decamp back into your blood, reproducing and bursting red blood cells. It is this that causes most of the symptoms – the cells aren't meant to blow apart while in circulation; the malignant form may destroy up to 80 per cent of the red blood cells, littering the place with debris. The parasite then settles down at a stage where it needs to be picked up by a mosquito to complete its life cycle.

Where to catch it

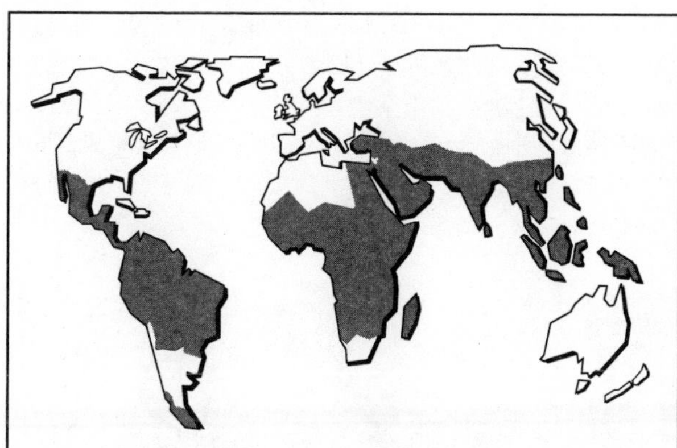

Adapted from Merieux, UK

As the map shows, malaria is widespread (at least 101 countries), although its occurrence within a country can be very patchy (places such as Hong Kong and Bangkok are not normally risk areas). Note that even if malaria is present, the number of carrier mosquitoes varies, from an estimated 20 per cent of *Anopheles* species in parts of Africa carrying the parasite, to just 1 per cent in Asia.

How not to get it

Malaria prophylaxis

There is no drug regime that is 100 per cent effective against malaria. Furthermore, the drugs are getting less and less useful.

In the golden age of malaria, only one drug needed to be prescribed,

WORLD MAP SHOWING DISTRIBUTION OF CHLOROQUINE-RESISTANT MALARIA

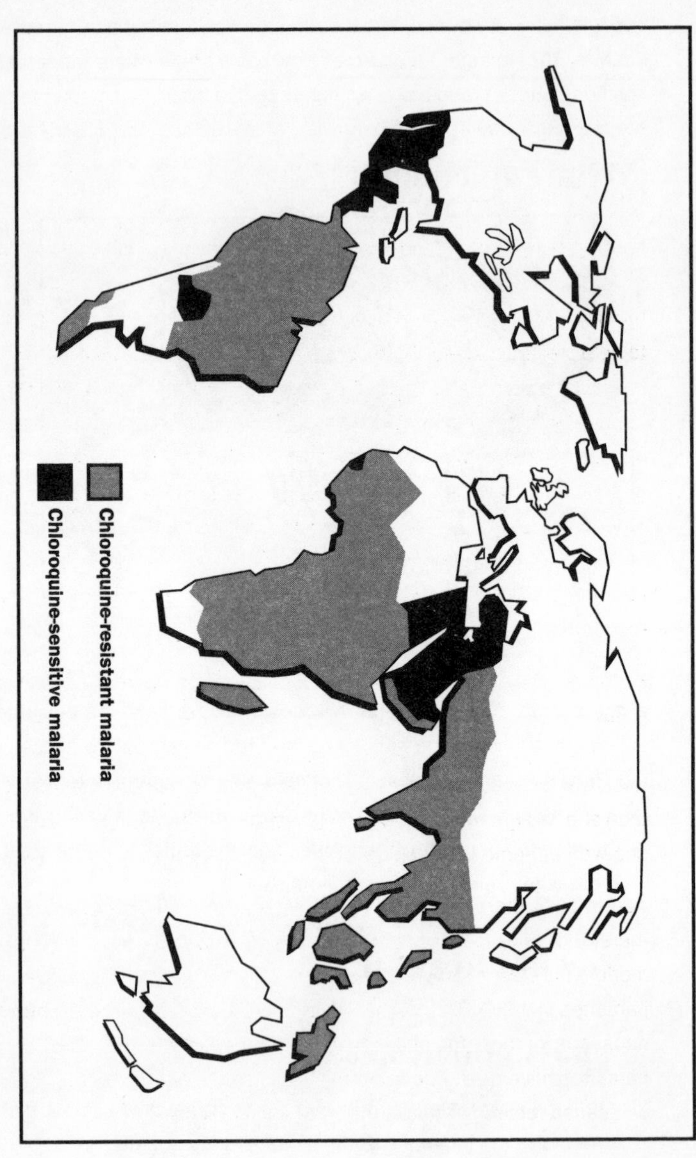

Based upon information from the World Health Organization.

usually a synthetic variation of quinine called chloroquine. Although there are still some areas where chloroquine alone will work, around 25 years ago it became obvious that chloroquine-resistant strains of *Plasmodium* (not the mosquito) were appearing, and in those countries the regime was tweaked so that a weekly dose of two chloroquine tablets (trade names: Avloclor or Nivaquine) was reinforced with a daily dose of two proguanil (Paludrine).

For the UK (the USA never took to proguanil/Paludrine) the relatively low toxicity and proven effectiveness meant C&P became the classic formulation. It is important to take these tablets after food, and with water, to help prevent nausea. For those who are forgetful, a dispensing 'wheel' is available from MASTA (£2.95). Like all anti-malarials there is a chance of side effects with these drugs. Chloroquine can cause stomach upsets, nausea may be associated with hair loss and high doses (*much* higher than you would normally take) can damage the retina. Proguanil/Paludrine can also cause stomach upset and mouth ulcers. The incidence of side effects seems to be much higher when the two are taken in combination (some estimate that up to 30 per cent will get a reaction).

For those who get them, these side effects can be depressing, and after a few weeks of feeling permanently sick, it is tempting to think about skipping the tablets. A friend of mine suffered hair loss on a trans-African truck trip and, fed up with waking up and leaving more hair on the pillow than she had left on her head, stopped taking the tablets. Within a month she was at home in hospital with malaria. Try and carry on.

Just in case there are side-effects and to give protection when you get there, the course should be started a week before leaving (2 weeks with mefloquine). Most importantly, because the drugs tend to trap the parasites in the liver rather than kill them, the course must be continued, nauseous or not, for at least 4 weeks upon returning, until all the parasites have died. *P. ovale* tends to be sneakier than the others, and can cause recurring attacks for up to a year or more.

Over the past few years, however, these magic bullets have lost their shine. Multidrug resistant strains – once it was resistant to chloroquine, proguanil seemed just like a short hop for *Plasmodium* – have muscled in to Africa and Asia (see map) and another drug was needed. Mefloquine (trade name Lariam) was wheeled in to combat malaria in countries such as Kenya, Tanzania and Thailand.

And this is where the real confusion starts. Clinics vary in their advice. Mefloquine is a once-a-week drug, so it may be more convenient than the C&P regime (though some argue that it is far easier to forget a once-a-week drug than a daily dose). However, it has some potential side-effects (pilots, for instance cannot take it due to its effect on concentration), which include dizziness, drowsiness and much more rarely, psychotic episodes and seizures.

Save the Children Fund and other UK agencies will not recommend it for more than 3 months (at the time of writing it was about to be licenced for 12 months' continuous use, and some clinics were already doing so), though Peace Corps workers have taken it for up to 2 years with, it is claimed, few problems. US troops took it in Somalia, with, again, few incidences of severe reactions. However, it is contra-indicated for small children (less than 2 years old or 15 kg in weight), those with heart, liver and kidney complaints and during the first trimester of pregnancy. Even becoming pregnant is not recommended until 3 months after completing a course of mefloquine. It is worth taking mefloquine for two weeks before leaving, just to check there are no unforeseen manifestations.

Different clinics, doctors and countries have varying attitudes to mefloquine. Some, for instance, recommend it for Zimbabwe as the first choice, others insist C&P is perfectly adequate. The variation comes from the UK method of drawing up guidelines. As Professor David Bradley of the Public Health Laboratory Service Malaria Reference Laboratory explains: 'To review the guidelines I convene a meeting of those who have special expertise and responsibility in the area, attempting to get at least one person from the main groups, centres and other interested organisations. I chair the meeting but seek the sense of the meeting rather than my own views.' The results of this meeting are turned into a consultation document, which then become the current UK guidelines, published in the *British Medical Journal*. This judgement-by-consensus is why the UK recommendations sometimes seems at odds with, say, the WHO guidelines, which have favoured mefloquine much more than the UK (it is possible the US's lack of proguanil has helped bring this about).

One school of thought in the UK thinks that mefloquine should be restricted, and brought in only when absolutely necessary, because over-subscribing will hasten the day when the disease becomes totally resistant to mefloquine as well. This is why the latest guidelines have moved from favouring C&P/mefloquine regimes equally for West and Central Africa, to a slight preference for mefloquine, rather than jumping in feet first and recommending mefloquine only.

The caution is justifiable: mefloquine resistance is already showing up in Kenya and on the Thai/Cambodia and Thai/Myanmar (Burma) borders. Here doxycycline, a drug which numbers photosensitivity among its side-effects, is being used, though it is again not recommended for children or during pregnancy.

In various islands of the South Pacific a drug called Maloprim is sometimes combined with chloroquine, mainly because it is a popular regime with the Australasians. Maloprim is another once-a-week regime, though there have been cases of death by bone-marrow failure in people who doubled the dose: that narrow margin of error is a little too close for comfort for many in the UK. But Maloprim may well move centre-stage as mefloquine loses its efficacy.

Professor David Bradley: 'How long has mefloquine got? After use in some parts of Thailand for around 8 years there is about 40 per cent resistance. I would guess that in Africa we also have about 8 years, but it depends on what other alternatives are around, on cost, on whether vaccines are developed, and in any case the relative protection will only decrease slowly.'

It is no surprise that, given this ducking and diving, many feel it is only a matter of time before malaria becomes resistant to *all* drugs.

Because of the shifting pattern of resistance (for instance at the time of writing chloroquine-resistant malaria was moving from Guatemala to Mexico, and similarly robust strains were making their presence felt in Rajasthan, India) you must consult a clinic or your GP for the latest information on the spread of resistance and the most suitable regime. Note though, that any drug prophylaxis is better than none. Even where people taking the full course of C&P have got malaria (and, sorry to repeat this, no regime is 100 per cent effective), they have been less ill than if they had not taken any drugs.

Pregnancy

Malaria in pregnancy carries a grave prognosis for mother and unborn child. Pregnant women may wish to consider postponing visits to malarious areas. Eric Le Fevre of Thomas Cook Travel Clinic is quite clear on his attitude to malaria and pregnancy: 'Malaria is a very serious for a pregnant woman, and may cause a miscarriage. Yet I get people who insist this visit to Africa or wherever will be their last fling before settling down to family life. I tell them to go to Florida.' If travel is undertaken, it is imperative that bites are avoided and anti-malarial prophylactic drugs are taken. Chloroquine is safe in pregnancy. Proguanil and Maloprim are safe in pregnancy, but a folate supplement should be taken. Mefloquine is safe to use after the first trimester.

Children

Children must be protected, with cot nets and repellents etc. (MosiGuard Natural is safe to use on children). Anti-malarial tablets or syrups should be used. Again Eric Le Fevre of Thomas Cook Travel Clinic advises thinking again: 'Malaria is very serious in children. I would not recommend taking children on holiday to malarious areas if it could be avoided.'

Children's doses

Age	Weight	Chloroquine/ Proguanil	Mefloquine	Maloprim
0–5 weeks		$\frac{1}{8}$ adult dose	Not rec	Not rec
6 weeks – 11 months	Up to 10 kg	$\frac{1}{4}$ adult dose	Not rec	$\frac{1}{8}$ adult dose
1–5 years	11–19 kg	$\frac{1}{2}$ adult dose	Not under 2 years, then $\frac{1}{4}$ adult dose for 2–5 years	$\frac{1}{4}$ adult dose
6–11 years	20–39 kg	$\frac{3}{4}$ adult dose	6–8 years $\frac{1}{2}$ adult dose 9–11 years $\frac{3}{4}$ adult dose	$\frac{1}{2}$ adult dose
12 years up	45 kg up	Adult doses		

Children's doses table with kind permission of WHO.

Key to antimalarial chart overleaf:

CHL	Chloroquine 300 mg base weekly (Avloclor 2 tabs weekly or Nivaquine 2 tabs weekly)
PRO	Proguanil 200 mg daily (Paludrine 2 tabs daily)
CHL + PRO	Chloroquine 300 mg base weekly + proguanil 200 mg daily
MEF	Mefloquine 250 mg weekly
MAL	Maloprim 1 tablet weekly
MAL + CHL	Maloprim 1 tablet weekly + chloroquine 300 mg base weekly
DOX	Doxycycline 100 mg daily
LOW RISK	Very remote possibility of malaria. No anti-malarial prophylaxis drugs advised, but be aware of risk and avoid bites.

When two alternatives are given, either can be used. We, generally, advise the first alternative unless there are contraindications to its use. If the advised prophylactic drug is contraindicated and no alternative is given, then specialist advice should be sought.

A guide to antimalarials

North Africa, West and Central Asia

Country	Regimen	Alternative	Comment
Afghanistan	CHL + PRO		Below 2000 m May–Nov
Algeria	Low risk		
Azerbaijan	CHL	PRO	Risk only in some southern border areas
Egypt	CHL	PRO	Most tourist areas free. Risk only in El Faiyum area, June–Oct
Iran	CHL + PRO		Parts of Iran. Mar–Nov
Iraq	CHL	PRO	Risk in rural north, May–Nov
Libya	Low risk		
Morocco	Low risk		
Oman	CHL + PRO		
Saudi Arabia	CHL + PRO		Low risk in north, Asir Plateau and western border cities
Syria	CHL	PRO	Northern border areas May–Oct
Tajikistan	CHL	PRO	Risk only in southern border areas
Turkey	CHL	PRO	Most tourist areas free. Risk on plain around Adona, Side, South-east Anatolia. Mar–Oct
Yemen	CHL + PRO		
United Arab Emirates	CHL + PRO		Northern rural only

Sub-Saharan Africa

Country	Regimen	Alternative	Comment
Angola	MEF	CHL + PRO	
Benin	MEF	CHL + PRO	
Botswana	CHL + PRO	MEF	Only in northern half of country, Nov–June
Burkina Faso	MEF	CHL + PRO	
Burundi	MEF	CHL + PRO	
Cameroon	MEF	CHL + PRO	
Cape Verde	Low risk		
Central African Rep	MEF	CHL + PRO	
Chad	MEF	CHL + PRO	
Comores	MEF	CHL + PRO	
Congo	MEF	CHL + PRO	
Djibouti	MEF	CHL + PRO	
Equatorial Guinea	MEF	CHL + PRO	
Eritrea	MEF	CHL + PRO	Below 2000 m
Ethiopia	MEF	CHL + PRO	
Gabon	MEF	CHL + PRO	
Gambia	MEF	CHL + PRO	
Ghana	MEF	CHL + PRO	
Guinea	MEF	CHL + PRO	
Guinea-Bissau	MEF	CHL + PRO	
Ivory Coast	MEF	CHL + PRO	
Kenya	MEF	CHL + PRO	
Liberia	MEF	CHL + PRO	
Madagascar	MEF	CHL + PRO	
Malawi	MEF	CHL + PRO	

Country	Regimen	Alternative	Comment
Mali	MEF	CHL + PRO	
Mauritania	CHL + PRO	MEF	Southern half of country all year Northern half Jul–Oct
Mauritius	CHL		Risk only in rural areas
Mozambique	MEF	CHL + PRO	
Namibia	CHL + PRO	MEF	Only in northern one third of country Nov–June
Niger	MEF	CHL + PRO	
Nigeria	MEF	CHL + PRO	
Rwanda	MEF	CHL + PRO	
Sao Tome et Principe	MEF	CHL + PRO	
Senegal	MEF	CHL + PRO	
Sierra Leone	MEF	CHL + PRO	
Somalia	MEF	CHL + PRO	
South Africa	CHL + PRO	MEF	Parts of Natal and Transvaal only
Sudan	MEF	CHL + PRO	
Swaziland	MEF	CHL + PRO	
Tanzania	MEF	CHL + PRO	
Togo	MEF	CHL + PRO	
Uganda	MEF	CHL + PRO	
Zaire	MEF	CHL + PRO	
Zambia	MEF	CHL + PRO	
Zimbabwe	CHL + PRO	MEF	Areas below 1200 m Nov–June All year in Zambezi Valley

South Asia

Country	Regimen	Alternative	Comment
Bangladesh (1)	CHL + PRO		All areas except east (no risk in Dhaka city)
Bangladesh (2)	MEF	CHL + PRO	East in Chittagong hill tracts
Bhutan	CHL + PRO		Southern districts only
India	CHL + PRO		Most of India. No risk in mountain states of north
Nepal	CHL + PRO		Below 1300 m (no risk in Kathmandu)
Pakistan	CHL + PRO		Below 2000 m
Sri Lanka	CHL + PRO		Most of Sri Lanka (No risk in and just south of Colombo)

South-East Asia

Country	Regimen	Alternative	Comment
Bali	LOW RISK		
Borneo	CHL + PRO		
Cambodia (1)	MEF		No risk in Phnom Penh
Cambodia (2)	DOX		In Western provinces. Very resistant malaria
China (1)	LOW RISK		Main tourist areas
China (2)	MEF		Rural parts of Hainan and Yunnan provinces
Indonesia	CHL + PRO		No risk in Jakarta and big cities
Irian Jaya	MEF		

Country	Regimen	Alternative	Comment
Java	CHL+PRO		No risk in main resort areas
Laos	MEF		No risk in Vientiane
Malaysia (1)	LOW RISK		Except Sabah and deep forests
Malaysia (2)	CHL+PRO		Deep forests
Mayotte	MEF		
Myanmar (Burma)	MEF		
Philippines	CHL+PRO		Throughout year in some rural areas below 600 m
Sabah	MEF		
Sarawak	LOW RISK		
Sulawesi	CHL+PRO		
Sumatra	CHL+PRO		
Thailand (1)	LOW RISK		Main tourist areas (Bangkok, Chieng-Mai and islands are free of malaria)
Thailand (2)	MEF		Backpacking in rural areas
Thailand (3)	DOX		Borders with Cambodia and Myanmar. Very resistent malaria
Timor	CHL+PRO		
Vietnam	MEF		No risk in urban centres and deltas

Latin America

Country	Regimen	Alternative	Comment
Argentina	CHL	PRO	Small area in north west only
Belize	CHL	PRO	
Brazil	MEF	CHL + PRO	Amazon basin only
Bolivia (1)	CHL + PRO	MEF	Rural areas below 2500 m
Bolivia (2)	MEF	CHL + PRO	Amazon basin area
Colombia	MEF	CHL + PRO	Most areas below 800 m
Costa Rica	CHL	PRO	Rural below 500 m
Dominican Republic	CHL	PRO	
Ecuador	CHL + PRO	MEF	Areas below 1500 m
El Salvador	CHL	PRO	
French Guiana	MEF	CHL + PRO	
Guatemala	CHL	PRO	Below 1500 m
Guyana	MEF	CHL + PRO	All interior regions
Haiti	CHL	PRO	
Honduras	CHL	PRO	
Mexico	CHL	PRO	Some rural areas not often visited by tourists
Nicaragua	CHL	PRO	
Panama	CHL + PRO		Parts of Panama
Paraguay	CHL	PRO	Some rural parts of Paraguay
Peru	CHL + PRO	MEF	Rural areas below 1500 m
Surinam	MEF	CHL + PRO	Except Paramibo and coast

Country	Regimen	Alternative	Comment
Venezuela (1)	CHL + PRO	MEF	Rural areas other than on coast
Venezuela (2)	MEF	CHL + PRO	Amazon basin area

Oceania

Country	Regimen	Alternative	Comment
Papua New Guinea	MEF	MAL + CHL	Below 1800 m
Solomon Islands	MEF	MAL + CHL	
Vanuatu	MEF	MAL + CHL	

Note: this chart is only suitable for advice if travelling to a single country; more complex itineraries will need expert advice. Table courtesy of Dr Peter Barrett at MASTA.

Bit players

There is no doubt that the situation with anti-malarial drugs is something of a mess, and smacks of rearguard action as the chemical arsenal, certainly in Africa and parts of Asia, becomes increasingly depleted. It comes as something of a relief to realise that there is something else you can do: stop the mosquitoes biting you in the first place.

This does not necessarily mean immersing your skin in chemicals 24 hours a day. Like many other bloodsuckers, *Anopheles* mosquitoes come out to play at night, with something of a feeding frenzy at dawn and dusk, so this is the time to cover up, with long sleeves and trousers. Cocktails on the terrace at sundown in shorts is not a good idea – legs and ankles are particularly vulnerable.

A compound called DEET (diethyl toluamide) is extremely unpleasant to mosquitoes (and other insects), and can be bought as sprays and roll-on sticks (e.g. Autan, Jungle Formula) or impregnated in arm- and ankle-bands. It can also be applied to clothes by soaking them in a diluted solution of DEET (1:8). How long your application lasts depends on many factors, such as absorption and 'sweat-off'. Dr Ron Behrens of the

Hospital for Tropical Diseases has been conducting research into various repellent formulations for the last 5 years, and his findings suggest that 'slow release' formulations remain effective the longest. 3M's Ultrathon is one common version of these extended time treatments. Unfortunately DEET can cause skin problems, and it has a tendency to attack plastics.

However, there are now DEET-free formulations such as X-Gnat and Mosi-Guard Natural being marketed as effective low-toxicity alternatives to DEET (see Chapter 12).

Rooms can also be mossie-proofed, by spraying with a 'knock-down' compound, the use of screens, or by burning mosquito coils or plug-in hot plates that release vapour. The coils and hotplates are both liable to problems: draughts, which may include a ceiling fan, can cause the coils to burn out quickly, and power failures can play havoc with hotplates. It is best to use mosquito nets treated with permethrin, which actually kills the mosquitoes, just to be certain.

One thing the mosquito does after feeding is settle on the wall for a quick breather, which enables you to swat the bloated culprit. If you enter a strange hotel room and it has walls like Al Capone's garage, there is obviously a problem.

Anyone staying in a malarious area for some time should examine the surroundings for stagnant water, no matter how shallow, where larvae may hatch out. Insecticide paint is also available, but redecorating a room every night is probably a bit of an overreaction for the average tourist.

You've got it

Despite all the drugs, nets and sprays, some people still get malaria. The important thing is to recognise it when it happens, and not think 'Can't be malaria, I've got most of Hoffman La Roche sloshing around my veins. Must be flu.'

And it might seem like flu, because malaria is not user-friendly enough to follow the classic cycle of dry and wet fevers so beloved of most prison camp dramas (this is mainly *P. ovale*). The important thing is to treat any flu-like or feverish symptoms, either while in a malarious country or upon your return (and it may be up to a year later, though around 28 days for *P. falciparum*), as the real thing.

Incidentally, there is evidence that malarial mosquitoes have made it to Europe in luggage and sleeping bags, and may have one last bite in them. In August 1994 it was reported that one man died and two people became seriously ill with malaria in the area around Charles de Gaulle airport in Paris: it is likely that a mosquito or two survived fumigation and got out into the streets. Similar outbreaks have happened around Schiphol.

Diagnosis for the disease is usually a simple blood test. The parasites can be stained to show up skulking within the red blood cells. Treatment is normally fast and effective.

But what if you aren't coming home and are well away from any medical care? Well, you can self-treat malaria, though you have to be careful with doses, and consider it to be a temporary action. In particular do not try and self-treat with high doses of mefloquine, unless you *want* to turn into Jack Nicholson in *The Shining*.

For long-term residents or travellers to relatively isolated areas, the WHO recommend you pack three treatment courses for each 6 months of travel. Self-treatment consists of one dose of three tablets of Fansidar. It cannot be taken by anyone with an allergy to sulphonamide drugs, and there are parts of the world where Fansidar resistance has taken hold. Alternatively a course of quinine sulphate three times a day for 7 days, followed by a course of tetracycline preferably under medical supervision (and preferably not if you have been taking mefloquine). Quinine tastes horrible and has some side effects, such as nausea and ringing in the ears. Still, it's better than malaria.

There are other possibilities. Halofantrine (Halfan, three doses of two tablets, taken 6-hours apart, and repeated after 7 days) has had serious cardiac side effects in a small number of cases, though it is still highly regarded by some (WHO recommend an ECG test before administering Halfan, just to be sure sudden death isn't likely). As already mentioned, mefloquine, which was originally marketed as a treatmentonly drug, is sometimes recommended (only if not using it as a prophylactic), but the high doses – two tablets, 250 mg, followed by two more after 12 hours – mean the side-effects are more likely (1 in 750 cases, according to Prof Bradley).

Every doctor and pharmacist I consulted concurred that this is not a good area to start your DIY medical degree, as there is a risk of over-doing the self-healing: SEE A DOCTOR WITHIN 24 HOURS IF YOU EVEN SUSPECT MALARIA.

The future

In the fight against malaria, humans may be down, but they are not out. Dragon Pharmaceuticals is a Welsh/Belgian company which is marketing a compound called Artenam, an extract of *Artemisia annua*, or sweet wormwood. At the moment it is used for treatment, and is available on prescription from pharmacies in Uganda, Kenya and Vietnam. The company is optimistic it may be developed as a prophylactic. This is a controversial area, though, because there are those, notably the WHO, who would like to keep Artenam in reserve until the current crop of drugs are sidelined. In a recent *World in Action* programme (*Dying for a Holiday*, 18 July 1994) one of the researchers managed to buy Artenam over the counter from a pharmacy in Kenya without a prescription. This is not the way to control the use of a new drug.

A Colmbian, Manuel Patarroyo, has developed an immunisation that is currently undergoing WHO trials in Tanzania, The Gambia and Thailand. However, it seems it will fall well short of 100 per cent protection in adults, though we will probably have to wait 3 years to find out.

Summary

- **Malaria is one of the most likely diseases, after stomach complaints, you will pick up in the tropics and sub-tropics. It kills.**

- **Prevention is by means of an appropriate drug regime** (seek up-to-date advice) and not being bitten, by using DEET or other effective repellents and insecticide-soaked mosquito nets, covering up at dawn and dusk and mosquito-proofing rooms. (Carry repellant in your hand luggage the walk from plane to terminal leaves you exposed.)
- **Start drugs one week before departure (two for mefloquine).** Continue for at least 4 weeks upon return. Don't stop until the course is completed.
- **If you vomit after taking tablets, do not re-dose yourself.** Diarrhoea should not affect your levels too much.
- **Treat any flu-like symptoms, fever or general ill-health within 3 months as malaria.** Seek medical help immediately. Some forms can hit you up to a year after exposure.
- **If you cannot get to a doctor within 24 hours, self-treat using Fansidar or quinine (care!).** Then see a doctor.
- **Any of the clinics listed on p.322 will be able to provide advice on malaria.** The Malaria Reference Laboratory at the London School of Hygiene and Tropical Medicine has a recorded information line. The Liverpool School of Tropical Medicine is also a centre of expertise (Sir Ronald Ross, who first discovered malarial parasites in the gut of *Anopheles* mosquitoes, trained there).

6 Coping with the journey

I was reared on the pre-Judge Dredd generation of comic heroes that inhabited the frames of *Lion, Tiger* and *Victor*. The Steel Claw, Archie the Robot, Tough of The Track and, above all, Paddy Payne, Battle of Britain Ace (though he seemed to have flown in every other theatre of World War II as well). Paddy, along with my impressive collection of Airfix models convinced me that I would make a natural pilot. But the eyes didn't have it. By the age of 11 even the largest letter on the optician's chart was just a blur. Still, even if I wasn't destined to have a Mig in my sights, I thought I would make a good flier.

It came as something of a surprise to discover, on my first flight, that, not to put too fine a point on it, I was scared shitless. The flight was out of Tangiers. As I walked out onto the tarmac I realised the plane was a Comet 4B. Now I had built a model of the Comet 4B. I knew it was a direct descendant of the Comet 1, the first commercial passenger jet, whose wings had a tendency to form large cracks and fall off. Whether it was this knowledge, the shock of how flimsy the whole thing was (the overhead lockers burst open on take off, and I was nearly concussed by a goatskin drum), the feeling of lack of control or the appalling quality of the inflight catering I shall never know, but something snapped and I found myself enrolled as a lifetime member of the White Knuckle/Sweaty Palm Club.

I took several more flights and monitored my progress. Yup, still scared shitless. I thought philosophically that I could take my holidays on trains with just the very occasional flight. God then dealt me a particularly vicious hand, and decreed I should start to earn my living as a travel writer.

That first flight was some time ago, and my condition has improved, though the odd jolt can bring it bubbling back to the surface. I was flying on a very rocky flight to Salzburg a few years ago when the air hostess came over and asked gently, 'Is this your first flight?' My companions guffawed, and it was the funniest joke ever until Salzburg proved to be fog bound and we had to endure two aborted landing attempts. I got little satisfaction from seeing that flash of fear in their eyes when the tops of tower blocks poked their aerials thorough the foggy blanket. Well, perhaps just a tiny amount.

I am not, of course, anything like alone here. In the USA, fear of flying is reckoned to be the fourth most common phobia, tying with a visit to the dentist. Many who suffer from FoF are multiphobic, as in 'What are you afraid of?' 'Well, what have you got?' According to figures from Britannia Airways, in the UK something like 80 per cent of people experience some anxiety at some point before flying, 20–25 per cent are frightened, and 10 per cent simply will not fly at all.

Over the years various remedies have been suggested to me. Most calm fliers try to soothe with statistics: more likely to die on the M4/in the bath/on the job, that sort of thing. One had even read that more people are kicked to death by donkeys than die in plane crashes. However, I have yet to be shown a donkey who can take out 450 people at one sitting. And such statistics can be wonderfully manipulated: exactly how meaningful is accidents per thousands of passenger miles, when most accidents happen on take-off or landing?

The (few) other travel writers who admit to the odd bout of anxiety nearly all favour the comatose approach to flying, usually a mixture of vodka and valium. I eschew this on the grounds that impaired sense might thwart my avowed intention of being first one down that inflatable ramp if anything goes wrong.

Calm, calm, calm

Courses

One obvious cure for my problem (it is called pterophobia, by the way) is to enrol on an anti-fear of flying course, as run by Britannia Airways and British Airways. But then they would say it was safe, wouldn't they? I once spent a Saturday on a course run by Britannia at East Midlands

Airport. It consisted of an introduction by Captain Your Favourite Uncle, a man with such a reassuring smile you would buy a personal pension plan from him, trust him with your life. Which is what the 80-odd people on the course were doing, of course. Captain YFU explained the theory of flying and why the Boeing 757 we were to take to the air in that afternoon would not, repeat not, fall out of the sky. *I* knew it wouldn't because wiping out a plane load of nervous fliers would do Britannia's reputation no good at all: this would be the safest flight over the UK that day.

Then we were told of various techniques to help assuage our irrational fears. Desensitisation consists of going to watch planes land, convincing yourself that they, on the whole, complete their journey successfully, or going on a Fear of Flying course. Then there are relaxation techniques (which turned out to be alarmingly similar to antenatal classes: I kept thinking someone was about to go into labour). A last resort is medication: not alcohol (too dehydrating), but beta blockers or anxiolytics, drugs which simply give you a sense of security.

The day ended with a flight, carefully conducted by Captain YFU, who soothingly explained what every clank and bump is as the plane took off, circled over Scotland, and landed again to great applause and congratulations all round.

Does it work? Well, there was one refusal to board, one fainting and one throwing-up-the-entire-flight. Of the rest, most were reassured to some extent (though after all the cosseting of this palliative flight, the real cattle-shifting experience of, say, a flight to Corfu, might come as a bit of a shock); a few claustrophobics were not convinced by the whole experience. And me? Turns out I am not afraid of flying after all, not like my teeth-grindingly terrified companions.

Read on

There is a classic tome on this whole subject by the late Maurice Yaffe, *Taking the Fear Out of Flying*, which seeks to convince you that you would have to fly every day for 93 years before crashing and that you have nothing to fear from your 747 narrowly missing the Penta Hotel while trying to land on the A4, or the pilot forgetting to lower the landing gear (as nearly happened at Heathrow).

Yaffe's book relies on what he calls 'cognitive behaviour therapy', which he regarded as thinking yourself calm with 'coping skills' such as relaxation techniques and replacing bad thoughts ('Why has that engine gone quiet? It's cut out') with good ones (in my case 'should my final meal in this world be the chicken or beef?').

Shortening the odds

The fact is that even I accept that flying is generally, with a few obvious global hotspots, safe. At the time of writing internal flights in the former Soviet Union generate tales of over-loaded planes and patchy maintenance, though the tourist Moscow-St Petersburg route is said to be fine.

Similarly the situation over China is a bit more risky than elsewhere, mainly thanks to antiquated air traffic control. Colombia, too, is something of an aviation black spot. Elsewhere, you have to trust in those statistics.

Cabin fever

On the Fear of Flying course mentioned above, we paid a visit to the mock up cabins where the staff are trained. Looking inside, one nervous flyer burst into tears and had to be led away. I know how she feels, but not for the same reason: my heart often sinks when I realise how little leg room I am about to suffer for the next 12 or 14 hours.

However, you can suffer from more serious things than cramp: aircraft cabins can be dangerous places. Most divers know not to fly within 24 hours of a dive (the reduced pressure may bring on the bends, not funny at 40,000 feet), but there are some other conditions that should make you consider your fitness to fly:

- **Severe infection of the middle ear or sinusitis.** I have flown with ear problems. Trust, me, it hurts, and can damage ear drums. Decongestants will help if you have a cold/flu, but they cause very dry nasal passages.

- **Recent stroke, heart attack or surgery** (abdominal within the last 10 days, chest within the last 14 days.) For minor procedures, such as laparoscopy, check with your doctor if a flight is imminent.
- **Severe anaemia:** being in a plane is like being up a mountain at 6–7000 feet. This can cause problems for those with impaired oxygen carrying capacity.
- **If more than 36 weeks pregnant** (34 on long haul, though exact restrictions vary with airline. You should carry evidence if less than 34 weeks but, given your size, birth looks imminent). Those worried about cosmic radiation suggest avoiding long flights during the first 3 months (see Chapter 14).
- **If you have an infectious disease** (tuberculosis, plague, measles – not a cold).

This latter has been the cause of much concern in the last few years, with various bodies claiming that disease can be transmitted through the cabin. Up until the mid-eighties, all the air on planes was drawn from outside, with the stale air replaced every 3–4 minutes. On many modern jets, fresh air, which is expensive to warm to cabin temperature, is often mixed with filtered, recycled air. This dilution of the fresh air saves airlines a lot of money, but it increases the level of CO_2, a prime suspect in lethargy and headaches.

Although the filtering process takes out cigarette smoke, various foul body emissions and odours, and bacteria, it is theoretically possible for viruses to move around the cabin, spreading colds and 'flu. There is no hard evidence for this. An air hostess on Continental did infect her fellow crew with TB a few years back, but this was due to close contact rather than the recirculation of air. In early 1993 a businessman threatened to sue a US airline, claiming he had picked up a virulent form of pneumonia on board. Since then the Centers for Disease Control in Atlanta, Boeing and Airbus have announced investigations into cabin air quality, but the chances are the air is unpleasant rather than dangerous.

Flying fit

There isn't much you can do about the air quality in the cabin, but there are other syndromes associated with flying, mainly feeling wrung out and desiccated. Those people that the American magazine *Conde Nast Traveler* insists on calling 'savvy travelers', opt for the following guidelines:

- **The air that is sucked into the plane contains little or no moisture, so you will tend to dehydrate.** Skin moisturisers will alleviate the worst external affects. Contact lenses can give problems as eyes dry out (and prizing off dried out lenses can damage tissue), so remove them before the flight.
- **Move around a lot,** particularly in economy. This is not so simple if you are in a window seat, but it is important: cramped inactivity can put anyone at risk from blood clots (ten deaths at Heathrow in a 3-year period turned out to be from clots in the lungs), and cause swelling of the ankles. Moving about will also help your back, if you suffer from problems.
- **If you suffer from lung problems you may need extra oxygen on the flight.** Dr Owen Johnson, a respiratory specialist, tested patients with cryptogenic fibrosing alveolitis and found one in three would need supplemental oxygen at aircraft cabin pressures if they were to avoid angina, dizziness and shortness of breath. One in ten people in the UK have lung or respiratory problems: there is a simple test that can be performed at any respiratory clinic to check if you are at risk while flying.
- **Some countries insist on spraying planes to kill any stowaway pests when they have landed,** even if they are only stopping over, which means passengers may get a dose of insecticide during this 'disinsecting' procedure. The WHO claim this is safe, but admit it may cause allergic reactions.
- **Anyone who has ever gone through the free drinks binge will know what alcohol does to you on planes.** You arrive feeling parched with an industrial strength hangover brewing. This is because the alcohol exacerbates the dehydration. Drink lots of soft drinks instead. Well, maybe just that one little bottle of wine with the meal. And OK, maybe the champagne if its free.

- **Just to show you what is likely, in one year BA dealt with 2000 sick passengers in the air.** Four hundred fainted (this may be anxiety at flying), 260 had diarrhoea (usually something they had picked up before leaving), 96 asthma attacks (dry air makes it worse), 40 diabetic attacks, 40 angina attacks, 25 heart attacks and four women went into labour. Unfortunately, no airline I have spoken to will confirm the urban myth that if a baby is born on a plane it gets free flights for the rest of its life.
- **Airlines calculate the risk of being ill on an aircraft at between one in 10–12,000.** Have a good flight.

Motion sickness

I would suggest that the sick bag on planes is more often used in cases of hyperventilation, when a nervous passenger panics (breathing in and out of a bag helps restore the carbon dioxide levels in the blood which the panting has depleted). Still, I have sat and watched my companion fill up bag after bag on a roller-coaster transatlantic crossing, but thankfully such occasions are rare. Motion sickness, however, remains a problem on other forms of transport, particularly boats: some 30 per cent of people are reckoned to feel queasy even in a mild swell.

Motion sickness is due to the brain receiving confusing messages from the eyes and the ears. Co-ordinating the signals does help: that is why in cars, drivers rarely feel sick, and at sea standing on deck and watching the horizon (not the waves) may help.

A survey among yacht crews in *Conde Nast Traveler* put some motion sickness remedies to the test. Top of the queasy cures were scopolamine patches, worn behind the ear. Scopolamine is the drug featured as the German's truth serum in *The Guns of Navarone*. But while it won't have you blurting out true confessions of a secret affair, it may cause dry mouth and drowsiness. It can also induce a mild state of euphoria, though this is probably not the reason why in trials it was voted the best preservative. In the UK it is known as hyoscine and is available in both patches and as Kwells. It does have side-effects – follow instructions carefully.

Next came the various other over-the-counter motion sickness drugs including Dramamine, which had fewer side effects (though it, too, can cause drowsiness) but was somewhat less effective, and needed to be taken 30 minutes before you get that sinking feeling (some need to be administered 2–4 hours before). I used to find that Avomine (contains promethazine) worked best for me, with few discernible side-effects, but these days I try to avoid taking anything other than fresh air. Remember you cannot take alcohol with any of the above remedies. But if you need them, you won't feel much like drinking anyway.

I know someone who swears by Sea Bands, the acupressure cuffs which are designed to press on your nei-kuan point and prevent nausea. Most authorities agree their main contribution comes under the heading of Wishful Thinking. 'Maybe they are a placebo,' my sailing chum says, 'but they work for me.' Sea Bands came out badly in the Conde Nast survey, but the real secret of sea sickness is finding your own remedy, and sticking to it. My wife, for instance, is a great believer in root ginger. If you are going on a long voyage, the one consolation is the sickness usually wears off.

If you feel sick:

- **light food is better than heavy meals or no food;**
- **try to stay in the most stable part of the vehicle (in the middle of plane or boat, front of a car – you could even ask to drive);**
- **don't drink alcohol;**
- **try drugs, but follow instructions carefully and don't drive;**
- **fresh air helps, as does lying down;**
- **remember, nobody ever died from motion sickness, it just feels like it.**

Jet-lag

The problem

New Year in Los Angeles certainly sounded like a good idea at the time. I flew in on 31 December and at 4pm on the nose, midnight back home, made the obligatory hint-of-a-gloat 'How is New Year in Belsize Park-? –

Beverly Hills-is-wonderful' call. Then I went out to kill the 8 hours before it was my turn to mark the passing of the year, well aware of the seasoned traveller's maxim: always slot into local time as quickly as possible.

The first hint of jet-lag hit about 8.30 in a bar owned by the actor who played Archie Bunker on TV. First someone injected styrofoam through my left ear, gradually swamping my poor neurons, leaving all the synaptic signals stuck on red. The barman obviously thought limeys were spectacularly bad at holding their liquor – what, slurring after two drinks? – and retreated to the other end of the bar. Next came the stage where I seemed to be viewing the world on a very old 425-line TV set, all grain and fuzz. Finally, meat tenderizer was diffused throughout my limbs, giving me the opportunity to display my Rubber Band Man walk to the bartender as I made for the door.

I had every symptom of full blown, head-swimming jet lag, but I wasn't going to succumb. In order to reach the magic midnight marker my wife and I were reduced to re-enacting the Jack Lemmon/Shirley Maclaine overdose scene from *The Apartment*, except in this case both Jack and Shirl wanted to doze off. Midnight came: with relief I opened the champagne. We had made it.

The cures

The experts on jet-lag tell me that I shouldn't have got it quite so bad, that the lag is at its worst when flying west to east, because the body can adapt more readily to a day that has been artificially stretched (by staying awake until local bedtime) than one which has been concertina-ed. The theory is it takes one day per time zone for your clocks to adjust fully to your new environment – 5 days for New York, 8 for LA.

Trying to find out exactly what causes the worst feeling this side of a tequila hangover propels you straight into New Age territory. The problem is you are messing with your biorhythms. More precisely, crossing time zones causes trouble with your circadian rhythm, which refers to the way bodies run to a 24-hour clock. Without external triggers the body would settle down to a 25-hour cycle of events, but exposure to alternating

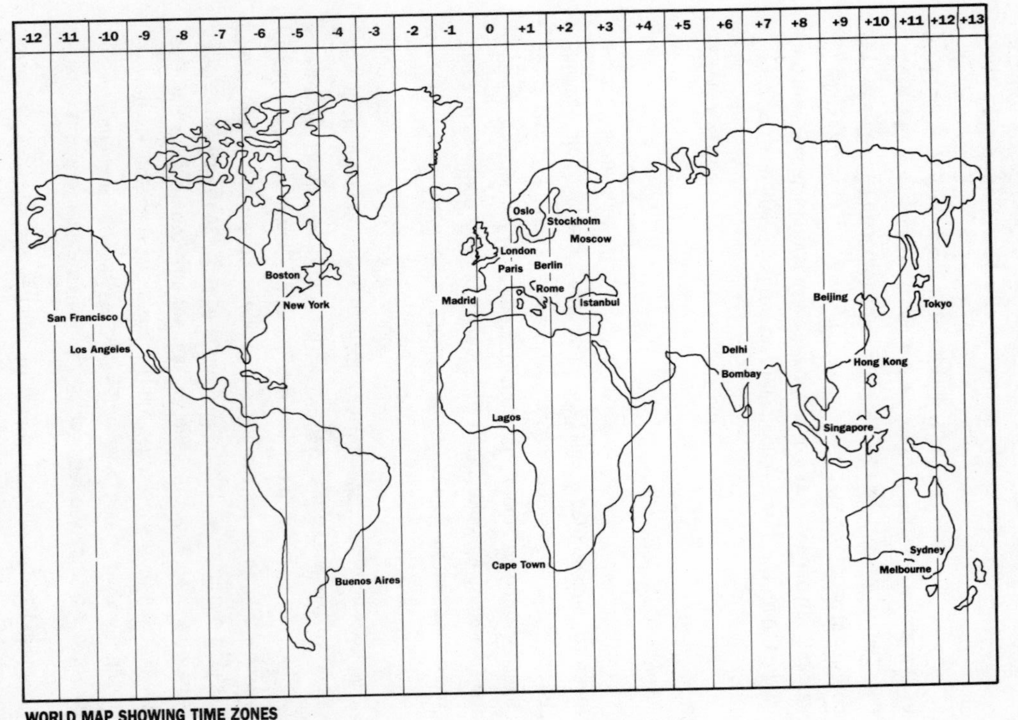

WORLD MAP SHOWING TIME ZONES

Time Zones

The county-by-country guide in Part II of the book gives the time difference from Greenwich Mean Time for each country.

The figures below indicate the number of hours each country is ahead of or behind Greenwich Mean Time.

Afghanistan	+4.5 hours
Algeria	+1 hours
Argentina	-3 hours
Australia	+8 to +10 hours
Austria	+1 hours (+2 in summer)
Bahamas	-5 hours (-4 in summer)
Bahrain	+3 hours
Bangladesh	+6 hours
Belgium	+1 hour (+2 in summer)
Brazil	-3 hours (-2 in summer)
Canada	-3.5 to -8 hours
Chile	-4 hours (-3 Oct to March)
China	+8 hours (+9 in summer)
Colombia	-5 hours
Costa Rica	-7 hours (-6 Jan to March)
Cuba	-4 hours (-5 Oct to March)
Cyprus	+2 hours (+3 in summer)
Czech Republic	+1 hour (+2 in summer)
Denmark	+1 hour (+2 in summer)
Ecuador	-5 hours
Egypt	+2 hours (+3 in summer)
Estonia	+2 hours (+3 in summer)
Ethiopia	+3 hours
Falkland islands	-3 hours (-4 in summer)
France	+1 hour (+2 in summer)
Germany	+1 hour (+2 in summer)
Ghana	+0 hours
Greece	+2 hours (+1 end of Sept to end of Oct)
Hong Kong	+8 hours
Hungary	+1 hour (+2 in summer)
India	+5.5 hours
Iran	+3.5 hours
Iraq	+3 hours (+4 in summer)
Ireland, Republic of	+0 hours
Israel	+2 hours
Italy	+1 hours (+2 in summer)
Jamaica	-5 hours
Japan	+9 hours
Jordan	+2 hours
Kenya	+3 hours
Kuwait	+3 hours
Lebanon	+2 hours (+3 in summer)
Malaysia	+8 hours
Mauritius	+4 hours
Mexico	-6to -8 hours
Morocco	+0 hours
Myanmar (Burma)	+6.5 hours
Nepal	+5.75 hours
Netherlands	+1 hour (+2 in summer)
New Zealand	+12 hours
Nigeria	+1 hour
Norway	+1 hour (+2 in summer)
Oman	+4 hours
Pakistan	+5 hours
Panama	-5 hours
Peru	-5 hours
Philippines	+8 hours
Poland	+1 hour (+2 in summer)
Portugal	+0 hours (+1 in summer)
Qatar	+3 hours
Romania	+2 hours (+3 in summer)
Russia	+3 to +13 hours
Saudi Arabia	+3 hours
Sierra Leone	+0 hours
Singapore	+8 hours
Slovak Republic	+1 hour (+2 in summer)
South Africa	+2 hours
Spain	+1 hour (+2 hours in summer)
Sri Lanka	+5.5 hours
Sweden	+1 hour (+2 in summer)
Switzerland	+1 hour (+2 in summer)
Syria	+2 hours (+3 in summer)
Tanzania	+3 hours
Thailand	+7 hours
Trinidad and Tobago	-4 hours
Tunisia	+1 hour
Turkey	+2 hours (+3 in summer)
Ukraine	+2 hours (+3 in summer)
United Arab Emirates	+4 hours
Uruguay	-3 hours
USA	-5 to -8 hours (Alaska -9, Hawaii -10)
Venezuela	-4 hours
Vietnam	+7 hours
Yemen	+3 hours
Zaire	+1 to +2 hours
Zambia	+2 hours
Zimbabwe	+2 hours

periods of light and dark, regular meal times, working hours (collectively known as environmental synchronisers, or zeitgebers) fine tune the process. But throw a spanner into your zeitgebers and you end up with the horror of a 3 am craving for lunch. The cause of this confusion appears to be a little clump at the top of the brain called the pineal gland.

The pineal gland secretes melatonin, a chemical released in darkness and suppressed by light. This hormone seems to dictate the timings of our day-to-day routine. It is also associated with longer cycles. It plays some part in seasonal depression syndrome (also called seasonal affected disorder or SAD, one of the more apposite acronyms).

However, knowing what is twiddling your dials is little comfort when, having finally made it to that lunch you fancied 8 hours earlier, you find yourself face down in the soup.

Prevention

The most effective preventative step is to go by boat. The transatlantic crossing to New York, for instance, chivvies away an hour a day, so your body hardly notices the 5 hour time difference. However, it makes a weekend in the Big Apple a little impractical when you have to add 10 days travelling time.

Assuming you must fly long haul, there are a variety of practices that are supposed to moderate the lag. Virgin and Air New Zealand offer aromatherapy packs to their (business class) passengers, with 'asleep' and 'awake' oils designed to induce the appropriate behaviour. I found little effect from my Virgin pack on the LA run, other than to make me the sweetest smelling zombie in town. However, if you fancy having a go, Harrods sells anti-lag aromatherapy kits (£35), as does the company that designed the airline kits, Danielle Ryman, for £12–£30.

That gadget repository, The Leading Edge, used to stock something called the Bioclok, an expensive (£80) calculator which computed how much light/darkness the long-hauler would need to re-set the biorhythms: that is, when to stay indoors and when to get out in the sun. I suspect it takes a strong sense of determination when your friend meets you at Sydney airport to whisk you off for a barbie on the beach to say: 'I am sorry, but my Bioclok suggests I spend the next 5 hours lying down in a darkened room.'

A few years ago scientists at Harvard claimed that exposure to very bright sunlight can stop the body clock altogether, enabling it to quickly be reset. So instead of heading for the hotel, a spell on the beach (awake` not sleeping) might help you adjust (but rememember your sun protection). Still, if sunbathing isn't your thing, there does seem to be some evidence that even just spending as much daylight time as possible out of doors upon arrival does speed up the adjustment process. Just don't go in the rainy season.

The Argonne National Laboratory in Illinois has produced an anti-jet-lag diet, which involves changing how and what you eat for 3 days before a long flight, thus tinkering with a different zeitgeber. A Qantas pilot, Carl Dransfield, also believes that adjusting to different time zones is more than a matter of light and dark. He markets a nutritional supplement called Jetzyme, which costs £20 for 30 tablets; the longer the flight, the more tablets you take.

There are other devices, such as a plastic visor with light bulbs in to shine in your eyes and suppress the chemical melatonin, extending your wakefulness, and the 'dawn simulator' an alarm clock with a big light on the top to artificially lengthen your day. However, I will suffer jet-lag any day rather than walk about looking like some B-movie card sharp, or carrying a small searchlight around the world with me. And anyway, nothing is guaranteed with any of these methods.

There are, of course, those irritating people who hardly seem to be affected, whose body clocks seem to have some sort of adjustment knob, an internal watch winder they can pull out and turn. One thing you can be certain of: if you suffer from jet-lag now it isn't going to get any better. It appears things deteriorate as you pass 30 (hey, what doesn't?) and the debilitation moves up a notch with every passing year.

The greatest hope for suffers is melatonin, the chemical released by the pineal gland which comes out to play after dark and tells you its time for bed. It has long been available in the USA as a food supplement. Professor Vincent Marks at the University of Surrey first published work on melatonin and jet-lag in the early eighties. 'There is no doubt it works. Everybody here who has tried it has reported marked improvements. However, timing is crucial. You must take it at midnight in the country you are travelling to, or at least as late as you can. If it is midnight in my destination while I am on the plane, I set my watch to that and take the tablet then. If you get it wrong and, say, take it at midday, it exacerbates the effects. It is quite a sophisticated concept I have heard of people taking the tablets three times a day, which will do them no good at all.' (Melatonin is available from health food shops in the USA.)

Professor Marks maintains that all the toxicological work on melatonin has been done, and he is hopeful it will soon be available in the UK. Remember, though, that many of the symptoms of jet-lag may be due to simple dehydration, which is why you can still feel bad after a long north-south flight, where you cross no time zones, so take plenty of fluids. Melatonin's effect is also subtle: it shortens the period of readjustment, but does not eradicate it altogether. Do not expect miracles. In the absence of the wonder drug, many frequent travellers have formulated their own regimes. These can be summarised as follows.

- **Travelling west,** you lose time, so you will usually arrive the same day. Do not sleep during the flight, avoid stimulants, go to bed reasonably early (not too soon, otherwise there will be the 3am hunger for lunch).
- **Travelling east,** which is often more debilitating, you will usually leave early evening and arrive at your destination in the early morning. Eat lightly, no stimulants, try and sleep on the plane (getting up early the day of travelling is a good idea).
- **Sleeping tablets are often recommended,** though I loathe the feeling of fuzziness they give. If you do use them, keep to mild sedatives, and stick with the advice of your GP.
- **John Hatt, author of *The Tropical Traveller*, was the first person I heard recommending oral-rehydration salts** (as used for the treatment of diarrhoea) as a way of perking up your dried-out body. It works.

- **Don't drink excessive alcohol,** which exacerbates dehydration. However, the odd glass with a meal will not transform you into a desiccated husk.

  Incidentally, many people find that jet-lag hits harder after their return hourney, because they have to try and slot back into a far more rigid work/home routine (particularly if children are involved). Again, there are those who swear by sleeping tablets; I swear by leaving a couple of days free at the end of a trip before I have to go to the office.

7 When you first arrive

It is a moment to savour, as you step out of the plane and the local flavours and smells hit you (admittedly usually leavened by a mixture of kerosene and bad drains, though often only the former disappears from the bouquet when you leave the airport). It is also a moment of extreme vulnerability.

After a long, disorientating flight we have all succumbed to little tricks of the trade: the man who grabs your bag and runs off towards (if you are lucky) a waiting rogue cab, the taxi driver who takes you to a hotel other than your choice, the meter being 'broken'. I once lost $100 between baggage reclaim and the cab rank without, to this day, knowing how. According to a report in the *Independent*, Murtala Muhammed, Lagos, Nigeria's main airport, is one of the more hazardous places to arrive. The local wheeze is for muggers to get hold of passenger lists, and hold up the names in the arrival hall, drive the poor victim off to some remote place and rob them. The USA has banned direct flights to Murtala Muhammed.

If you are in a country where the usual 'don't wear flashy jewellery, keep money in money belt, dress according to local customs' apply, then do it from the moment you step foot on their soil. And, especially if you arrive at night, apply insect repellent on the plane. It is also worth having at least the first night accommodation pre-booked.

Being suspicious when nothing happens makes you feel a little churlish, but better than that naive feeling when a fool and his luggage/money/passport are parted. I haven't actually met anyone who has been slipped a Mickey Finn, but reliable reports have come out of the Philippines, Thailand, Mexico and Czechoslovakia of the friendly Coca Cola having a little more kick than anticipated, and a groggy gringo or *farang* waking up many pounds/dollars lighter. Of course, the downside to this is that paranoia will stop you meeting the locals at all, which would be crazy. Just pour your own drinks, that's all.

If you are fly/driving, the usual procedure is to pick the car up at the airport and drive into an unfamiliar city, often in the dark or at rush hour. This can be madness, particularly in places such as Miami, where great swathes of downtown seem to be populated by opportunists waiting for a couple of lost, tired out-of-towners to come cruising slowly by. Spend a night in the city or at the airport, and pick up a car when you are feeling sharper; car charges are often cheaper away from airports anyway.

When driving to and from airports watch out for the helpful men who flag you down to point out a flapping exhaust or wobbly tyre. This popular Neapolitan pastime, now spread to other countries, is a device to distract you while an accomplice rifles through the car, stealing bags, etc.

Checking in

So you get to your hotel. Try and see the room before you hand over money/credit cards etc. I have been put in the basement with the waterfall-effect walls before now. It took me a while to realise this wasn't an intended design feature, but a ruptured pipe up above. The receptionist shrugged and moved me, hoping that sooner or later someone would appear who was too tired to notice.

Remember that foreign hotels operate to different standards: check and see if there are fire exits, and if they are open. It is ridiculous to expect UK standards of fire doors and sprinkler systems in many developing countries, so the best you can do is make sure you can get out. The favoured option is often to be on a low floor (ground floors tend to be more vulnerable to burglary) where you can either jump (not recommended) or fire equipment can reach.

The advice if trapped in a fire is to get down on the floor; smoke tends to rise, and crawling is safer than running or walking. However, there is a risk of being trampled. This may seem excessively paranoid, but one company does market an in-hotel safety device. It hangs on the back of your door, and consists of a portable smoke alarm, and an intruder alert. If someone opens the door it triggers a sensor and makes an almighty row. There is also a smoke hood. The ALERT is expensive at £48.50, but

I know of one lone woman traveller who sleeps a lot easier with it in place.

It isn't only hotels that are risky. If you are in an apartment with any sort of gas or water heater, check how it is vented to the outside. There have been several deaths on the Algarve and in the Canaries from carbon monoxide poisoning due to faulty heaters. Carbon monoxide detectors are available, but the best are expensive, bulky monitors and not the sort of thing the casual holiday maker will want to pack. If in doubt, turn the heater off.

There are other dangers in hotels. The most lethal part of the building, as already mentioned, may well be the hotel buffet, with its variable refrigeration and open invitation to any fly with an Access All Areas pass, which is all of them. And then there is legionnaires' disease, a type of pneumonia caused by a bacterium which thrives in hot water systems and Jacuzzi pipes. Although outbreaks tend to generate a lot of publicity, to be honest you are more at risk from the prawn vol-au-vents (see Chapter 10).

And finally ... Take it easy. Although your chances of getting anything more than a stomach bug are slim, remember that 15- to 45-year-olds are twice as likely as other age groups to die in accidents abroad, whether it is on the road or in the swimming pool (see Chapter 13 for more details). You are also most at risk from the sun in the first few days.

The climate

If you are about to enter a completely different climatic zone from your own, the best advice is to give your body time to adjust. It is very easy to expose yourself to a potent mix of jet-lag, unaccustomed temperatures and hectic schedules, and for that not-quite-with-it feeling to last the whole trip. It can be difficult, but try and avoid anything that says '8am arrive hotel; 8.30 meet in lobby; 9.00 start walking tour of the Great Valley of The Burning Sun ...'

If you have no idea of what the climate will be like, ask the tourist board, or consult the World Weather Guide (Hutchinson £12.95).

Hot, hot, hot

Switching from a temperate to a tropical climate can cause all kinds of problems, the most likely of which is commonly known as feeling shagged out. The heat seems to sap your energy, particularly if you are overweight. The effects vary according to humidity: a very damp atmosphere prevents the sweat evaporating properly, stoking the furnaces of your metabolism, and making overheating more likely. When you sweat, salt is excreted from the body, and losing too much screws up certain metabolic processes, such as muscle action. This salt loss does decrease over time, as the body realises things are not as they were.

The main thing to do is go gently to begin with, wear suitable clothing (see Chapter 4), including a hat (apart from anything else a sunburned scalp is very painful and it makes combing your hair difficult, too). It is essential to drink plenty of fluids you need far more than your thirst response will indicate, possibly 10 litres or more under extreme conditions. Things to watch for are:

Heat exhaustion: Thumping headache, vomiting, possibly weak pulse but not a raging thirst. You should lie down in a cool place and drink a **lot** of slightly salty water or soups (see below). Rest for a day or so.

Sun or, more accurately, **heatstroke**: The temperature of a person with heat exhaustion does not rise, but with sunstroke the temperature shoots up and sweating stops. Nausea followed by unconsciousness is the norm (though giddiness and headache coupled with pains in the limbs are early warning signs), so get the victim into the shade, loosen or remove clothes completely and cool them down immediately, using cool, or room temperature, water (not cold or iced), and a fan if possible (if there is air conditioning, even better).

Take the victim's temperature if you can – it may be 41°C or more; keep cooling until it drops to 39°C. If you suspect heatstroke rather than straightforward exhaustion, call a doctor. Once the cooling has worked, cover the victim up and keep warm, you don't want to kill them with hypothermia. Rehydrate (see below) when they are conscious.

Cramps: Your body's way of telling you that you are losing far too much salt. You can get cramp from exercising (which may just be kicking a ball around) in the heat. It can be insidious, so drink plenty of fluids before, during and after exercise, preferably with a small amount of added salt. Coconut milk will do nicely, otherwise add a quarter of a tea spoon of salt to a pint (550 ml) of water, or make a point of putting extra salt on your food each time. (**Don't give salt to babies**.) The colour of your urine is a good guide to your fluid balance: it should be quite pale, if it darkens, your kidneys are scavenging it back to try and keep water loss to a minimum, so you need to drink more.

Prickly heat: A nasty rash caused by blockage of sweat glands, which usually occurs in areas subject to friction from clothes (jeans, as I once discovered, are not ideal tropical clothing). Wear loose, well aerated items, preferably cotton or linen or a mix. Leave the nylon Y-fronts behind.

Prickly heat can be alleviated by washing, talc and calamine lotion, but avoid too much soap – it probably helped clog up the pores in the first place.

The heat and moisture can make other skin complaints, particularly fungal ones such as athlete's foot and ringworm, extra rabid. If you suffer from any of these, pack some medication. If you don't and don't want to, keep clean, dry and go heavy with the talc. Not walking barefoot in the shower is a good idea, as is taking an anti-fungal cream such as Daktarin or Canesten, just in case.

The bacterial bonanza of the tropics also means that small scratches, bites, etc. can become infected in record time: clean and use antiseptics on even innocuous seeming damage.

Burn, baby, burn

It is over a decade since, theoretically, the Golden Age of Tanning ended. The news from Australia probably signalled its demise, when the whole populace down under began to chant 'Slip, Slop, Slap', meaning slip on a shirt, slop on the sun tan cream and slap on a hat. With the increasing incidence of skin cancer, Oz became a land of the pale and interesting rather than bronzed Ockers. The news that the skin version is the second most common cancer in the UK, most of which is related directly to exposure to sun, helped spread the word here.

Well, kind of. They still have suntans on *Home and Away*, and the Med remains the prime holiday destination for Britons, and we cannot pretend they are going there to sample the indigenous culture. The fact is that, despite the risk of long-term damage to our skin, our eyes and our DNA, and despite dire warnings to women that their handbags will have better skin than they will by the time they are 50 (it's called photoaging), most of us look and feel better with tan than without. What is out of fashion is the deep George Hamilton permatan, and blistering.

The human body can adapt to most things, it can even adapt to strong sunshine given the right skin type (redheads may have a little more of a problem here) and time. What you have to do is build up enough pigment in the skin to help screen out the worst excesses of ultraviolet light, particularly the lethal UVB, the type linked to melanomas (its chum UVA seems to be content with just leathering and wrinkling up your dermis, though recent evidence suggests it may not be as benign as once thought).

The following advice is fairly standard, but all of us get taken by surprise once in a while, caught out by altitude, water, snow, a cooling breeze or a hazy sky, all of which can magnify or mask the effect of sun. So, just to remind you:

- **Take it easy.** Limit yourself to 20 minutes' exposure on the first day. Avoid the high intensity time, between 10am and 2pm.
- **Use a sun screen that will filter out UVA and UVB.** Use a high SPF (sun protection factor) cream. The SPF is based on how long the lotion will protect you over and above the standard 20 minutes it takes someone (an average someone) to start to burn. So if you usa a factor 10, it will protect you for 10 × 20 = 3 hours 20 minutes. It's all very approximate, however, and what is true in Malaga may not hold in Marrakesh. So start with high factor numbers, 15 or 20 (25 for the very pale), dropping down to 6 or 8 once you have built up a tan (you can still burn once that base is established). Note that SPF is based on UVB only, which is why your lotion must filter out UVA as well.

- **Re-apply lotion frequently,** particularly after swimming (waterproof ones are meant to last 90 minutes in water, but friction from towels can often reduce that).
- ***Good* sunglasses that screen out UV are essential.** Sunshine also causes cataracts and bad sunglasses dilate the pupils without filtering out the harmful rays.
- **Lips, extra pale bits that never see the sun and *children* need extra protection:** there is evidence that even one bad childhood sunburn can increase the risk of melanoma in later life.
- **Wear a hat or scarf** (and a t-shirt if snorkelling).
- **You can buy little patches called Sun-Spots,** which absorb radiation and change colour, warning you of over-exposure and the need to reapply sun screen. They also leave little white circles on your skin, which seems something of a design fault (although they can be placed on your clothes, I suppose). The Lancaster cosmetic company produces a small card which can be placed next to you and will change colour when you are 'done' on that side. MASTA have a somewhat Heath Robinson device designed by Dr Brian Diffey, called MASTABLOC, a ruler with a little vertical arm, which throws a shadow onto a scale to tell you whether and how long you can stay in the sun without protection.
- **Watch the moles.** If they bleed, change size, join up, take on an irregular shape and/or pigmentation or generally start acting suspiciously, go and see a doctor.
- **Consider fake suntan preparations.** Sometimes, it's just easier.

If you do get burned, painkillers and calamine or other soothing lotions help, as do cold compresses. If it is a mild burn, hydrocortisone 1% will help. If you are blistered, seek medical attention: human skin shouldn't be treated like pork crackling.

8 Mountain hazards

Cold comforts

I have been cold lots of times, but only once have I begun to think I just might be in for the Big Chill. It wasn't anywhere terribly remote, just enthusiastic skiing in the Trois Vallées area with someone much better than me. It certainly stretched me, to the point where we were a long way from home and realised lifts would start to shut down soon.

As we started to head back, a wind came up, one of those winds that drives needles of ice into every pore. Visibility started to go, and I was having trouble seeing the marker poles. I fell a couple of times, and realised just how tired I was. My partner helped me to my feet, but by this time I was also getting cold, the wind making my jacket all but transparent, and I was aware of cold sweat coating my skin. I recall racking my brain on how to build a snow cave.

The spat lifted as quickly as it had arrived, and with the wind down we got back, transmuting incipient panic into the usual mindless apres-ski story. But I can still conjure up a little panic when I want, because I was inadequately prepared, with not a Mars bar to my name.

People die in far more mundane circumstances than skiing in the Trois Vallees. Every year walkers die in the hills of the Lake District and Scotland (there were 54 deaths on the Scottish mountains and hills in 1993, and the annual total is rising). In 1994 much was made of the case of 51-year-old Jaqueline Greaves, a woman who went missing for several days in the Scottish mountains, only to be found alive and well. It was no fluke. Not only had she attended survival courses and knew how to construct a snow cave, but she had on several layers of winter clothing, including a hi-tech jacket, three vests and waterproof boots, around £500-worth in total, and was carrying such aids as a whistle (six blasts mean you are in trouble) and rations. However, even as well equipped as she was, she had started hallucinating, and probably could not have lasted much longer, death would have been from hypothermia.

Hypothermia is when the core body temperature (not the skin) drops to below 35°C from its norm of 37. The chances of getting hypothermia are not only dependent on external temperature. There is the wind chill factor, whereby the wind makes it feel very much colder than it actually is, and damp. Trapped moisture, be it sweat, rain or melted snow or ice, rapidly negate the insulation effect of clothing (which is why so much emphasis is laid on 'breathable' fabrics such as Gore-Tex). Other factors may include when you last had food (carrying high-energy snacks on mountains and hills is highly recommended), general fitness, and current level of exhaustion. Women are also better at surviving cold, due to their even distribution of fat (men's is laid down over the abdominal area), helping keep the core warm longer. A beer gut is a serious survival risk. All this means that people who are cold, wet, thin and tired (and usually lost) are at greatest risk.

According to David Snadden, Medical Officer of the Cairngorm Mountain Rescue Team (1985–92), hypothermia is best divided into mild and severe. Mild is when the body is at 33–35°C, which gives strong involuntary shivering, lack of co-ordination, tachycardia (increased heart rate) and peripheral vasoconstriction the skin loses its blood supply. Urine production may increase, leading to dehydration. Severe hypothermia starts below 33°C, and involves rigidity, more loss of co-ordination, confusion, hallucination and coma (oddly, the shivering reflex often disappears).

If the hypothermia is severe, the victim must be treated as a stretcher case, insulated from further heat loss and got the hell out of there. One complication is that the victim may go into a kind of suspended animation, with low heart rate. David Snadden claims that the potential victim must be 'both warm and dead' before you can be sure the hypothermia has killed them. Severe hypothermia does occur on mountains, but is more likely from immersion in cold water.

There is a problem with treating severe hypothermia. If you warm someone by, say, putting them in a bath of hot water, the blood vessels in the skin re-dilate, and cold blood from the skin hits the core, pushing the temperature further down (the so-called after-drop) which can shock the heart into failing. Some experts now recommend, if possible, rewarming by dialysis in an intensive care unit. (Incidentally, don't drink alcohol in excessive cold, it also vasodilates the peripheral blood vessels leading to increased heat loss. A 'warming' brandy can be lethal.)

In cases of mild hypothermia, there is no need for such drastic measures, just getting the victim away from the cold, into shelter and if possible into dry clothing, coupled with warm drinks and high-energy foods, will lead to rewarming.

Many of the deaths on the Scottish mountains are not from hypothermia: the fashion for sophisticated fabrics and expensive jackets means that many people are suitably equipped. Well over half the annual toll is due to heart attacks and other medical conditions: people take up walking and launch themselves into it with a gusto that takes their previously sedentary body by surprise. The danger is exacerbated by lack of navigational experience and by the refusal to abandon walks when the weather turns nasty. Being an enthusiastic amateur can also kill you if you are not careful.

Frostbite is another risk of extreme cold. It occurs when the extremities, toes, fingers, ears, tips of noses, start to freeze, killing the tissue. As you might imagine, it hurts. But not for long. The pain eventually goes, leaving the area literally frozen – numb and white. The best way to prevent frostbite is to use adequate clothing; balaclavas, face masks, gloves, socks and boots must all be up to the job. Any area that becomes painful must be re-warmed, by chemical packs that generate heat, covering up, using a cosy crotch or armpit, anything that does the job. Do not walk on frostbitten feet, if possible. Don't rub the affected part – you may damage the skin.

In extreme conditions members of a group usually keep an eye on each other for the tell-tale patches of white. If frostbite is suspected never adapt a 'carry on regardless' attitude. Stop, find some shelter and treat it, and make sure the area doesn't refreeze: it is pointless treating it if it is likely to be damaged again.

For further information consult the Medical Handbook for Mountaineers by Peter Steele (Collins, £8.95).

Bad altitude

'It was like a combination of the worst motion sickness with the most savage hangover you can imagine.' This is how *Travelog* presenter Robert Elms describes his brush with altitude sickness. 'I had been up high before in Chile and Mexico, and felt a little breathless, but nothing prepared me for this.'

Elms had flown into Bhutan, the Himalayan mountain kingdom, with a film crew for 2 weeks. Within 20 minutes he had had to stop the bus from the airport to be sick. 'By the time I reached Thimphu, the capital, I couldn't even stand up. I had to lie down in a darkened room for 24 hours before I started to feel better. I honestly thought I would have to go down again. Luckily, it improved.'

Elms **was** lucky. He was in a particularly dangerous situation: he had flown straight to high altitude without time for his body to adjust, and a feeling of responsibility to himself and others (abandoning a film shoot, particularly half way around the world and up a mountain, is not a good career move) prevented him from insisting they leave.

Fortunately the acute mountain sickness (AMS) he was suffering abated, but there are other insidious complications, such as fluid in the lungs (pulmonary oedema) or brain (cerebral oedema) that could have struck. The nausea, breathing difficulties and sleep disorders are normally characterised as benign AMS, which may progress to the lethal malignant AMS and can quickly lead to a coma. The oedemas cause bad coughs, chest tightness and mental confusion. Trek leader Hilary Bradt: 'It gets to the point where you don't know if someone with some mountain sickness is just being stroppy, or is in the first stages of oedema and so are very confused. If in doubt, you must go down.'

About two-thirds of all people will experience some symptoms of AMS over 10,000 ft (3120 m); women are more prone to the related swelling of extremities (particularly nasty when it is the eyelids). It is reckoned 2 per cent of people will get the full blown version, usually at over 14,000 ft (4300 m). In the case of malignant AMS, pride often comes before death. People feel like wimps, even though there are cases of fit, strong soldiers suddenly succumbing. It is a physiological roulette wheel – you never know if or when your number will come up. It usually wears off in 2–3 days, but if in doubt, there is one straightforward course of action that will save your or someone else's life, descending to a low enough elevation (1500 ft, around 500 m should do it) for the symptoms to disappear.

All altitude sickness is caused by a simple physical fact: the higher you go, the less air pressure there is and the less oxygen is available to you. People who live at high altitude have larger lung capacities and masses of haemoglobin to compensate. Given time, your lowly self will also up its red blood cell count, giving you blood like tomato puree: problems start when you rush things, usually by flying straight into a high region.

Some elevations

Place	*Feet*	*Metres*
		Above sea level
Death Valley	–178	–54
Vlissingen, Neth	3	1
London	16	5
Rome	56	17
Rio de Janiero	201	61
Paris	246	75
Atlanta, USA	1054	321
Sofia, Bulgaria	1805	550
Las Vegas	2006	612
Madrid	2165	660
Katmandu	4388	1338
Cameroon Highlands, Malaysia	4750	1448
Santa Fe	7000	2134
Mexico City	7575	2309
Bogota, Colombia	8678	2645
Quito, Ecuador	9446	2879
Cuzco, Peru	10581	3225
La Paz, Bolivia	12000	3658
Lhasa, Tibet	12080	3685

To prevent mountain sickness you must ascend slowly, preferably with some time spent at around 7000 ft (2250 m – symptoms rarely start below 8000 ft). This advice is not very helpful when you are flown straight into, say Quito, Ecuador at 9000 ft: then you just have to gasp and bear it. Don't go higher until acclimatised.

If climbing, you should never sleep more than 1000 ft (320m) above where you slept the previous night (the motto is 'Climb High, Sleep Low'). You also need a lot more rest days, the body is making do with a rough running, inefficient engine after all, and to eat high energy, high carbohydrate foods. Avoid a high protein diet, as it increases your water requirements.

Dehydration is one of the more subtle effects of altitude. Because the air is dry, moisture is lost from the lung surfaces, and the extra exertion will pump out sweat, which will readily evaporate. Drink **at least** 4–5 litres of fluid a day. Fluid does not mean alcohol; for some reason not fully understood, drinking at altitude can be a cheap and fast route to oblivion.

The colour of your urine is again a guide; if it looks like a cup of tea that has just gone straight through you, you are losing far too much water and your kidneys are having to reclaim it.

There are drugs, such as Diamox (acetazolamide), Lasix (frusemide) and nifedipine, that are sometimes prescribed to prevent or treat AMS (and other drugs, such as dexamethasone, used if cerebral oedema threatens).

There is no consensus on such prophylaxis/remedies. Dr Charles Clarke of the UIAA Mountain Medicine Centre told me: 'The use of Diamox is a personal thing. Some people swear by it, others simply do not like drugs or the side effects. And remember, the condition can be relieved by descent.' Dr Clarke admits that the drug makes him feel 'off colour'.

On the other hand, Dr Jon Dallimore, who has lead many a Nepal trek, is a confirmed Diamox fan: 'I always use it and give it to my group for a few days before they ascend. I have never had a case of severe sickness on any of my treks.' A.J. Pollard writing in the *British Medical Journal* in May 1992 was equally forthright: 'Acetazolamide (500 mg slow release daily) provides protection against acute mountain sickness and should be started on the day of ascent above an altitude of 3000 m.'

How Diamox works is unclear. It is a diuretic, increasing the frequency of passing urine which will help reduce the oedema or fluid retention (which means it is not a good idea to take just before turning in), but it also makes breathing faster and deeper, giving you more oxygen. It can cause nausea and unpleasant tingling sensations of the fingers, and it also makes carbonated drinks taste strange. It cannot be used by anyone allergic to sulphonamides.

If you are trekking with an organised group, you should ask about medical standards. Do they carry oxygen (which can be given during the descent to help diminish symptoms, but is not a cure)? Is there a doctor on the team (some companies give discounts to encourage medical personnel along)? Do they use portable hyperbaric chambers (the Gamow Bag) which can be used to temporarily repressurise the victim? Companies such as Himalayan Kingdoms are impressed enough by Igor Gamow's invention to shell out £1800 on each one; other outfits are yet to be convinced.

More importantly, are they prepared for the disruption to the schedule if someone says, rather breathlessly, 'I think I'd like to go back now'?

The UIAA Mountain Medicine Centre is run by Dr Charles Clarke, a consultant neurologist, and offers advice to climbers, skiers and trekkers. It produces a useful series of information brochures on high altitude topics. See Useful Addresses

9 Road safety

Moving around any unfamiliar country has its risks. You may be robbed on the local bus or train, ferries are often overloaded and lack decent safety equipment, and the world is full of two-bit airlines. However, the items of transport most likely to cause you grief are the motor car and the moped. Unless you know what you are doing and can get a crash helmet, avoid the latter in many places. The hospitals at Koh Samui in Thailand see more moped-maimed *farangs* than anything else.

Road accidents

The figures from health insurance claims bear out that you should be a road worrier, and accidents are also the main reason for repatriation of VSO volunteers and the commonest form of death for Peace Corps workers. A straightforward accident is bad enough, with the threat of AIDS, a bad smash can take on a whole new dimension of horror. I know of one man in Nigeria who rammed an unlit truck, which was stopped in pitch dark in the middle of the road, and who then needed a blood transfusion. He was lucky, he did not develop antibodies to HIV, but he had a worrying 6 months.

Avoiding road accidents in places like Africa is easier said than done. Wearing a seat belt will help reduce the injury should you have an accident, and therefore the need for a blood transfusion and stitching. Larger vehicles are generally safer than small ones, though this does not apply to the open trucks which act as public transport in many parts of the world – an accident involving one of those can cause carnage.

Avoid vehicles which have obviously not been serviced for a long time. I have been in the situation of declining a 'loan' of a car because braking seemed to consist of sticking your feet through the rust holes in the floor. Also, don't go with obviously reckless or drunk drivers and don't be afraid to terminate a trip if you are worried for your safety.

4x4s

Four-wheel drive vehicles used to be the preserve of the aid and governmental agencies. These days you can hire Suzuki jeeps across the world. Anyone who has never driven one should heed a warning from journalist Jonathan Futrell:

> 'It was a great inviting patch of sand, and I was in a brand new Shogun. We went roaring across it, but suddenly started sinking. I tried to drive out, but it just dug us into the foul mud that was under the sand. I got out, and *I* started sinking, up to my waist. A Land Rover offered to give us a tow, but our chain wouldn't reach and his rope snapped. We sank deeper. The tide started coming in. I suddenly realised that I was going to have to put a marker buoy on it and leave it to the sea . . .'

Eventually a couple of odd characters in a two-engined, three axle mutant Land Rover straight out of *Mad Max* came along and, for a fee, snatched the Shogun out of the sinking sand just before the Irish Sea claimed it.

Jonathan admits he was suffering from the delusion most people embrace when they first get in a 4x4 – invulnerability. Having once gently rolled an Isuzu Trooper on its side while negotiating some very deep ruts from an earth-mover, I can sympathise. Off-road driving is a skill as much as, say, racing driving, and though you can learn by experience, that experience is probably not best gained in the middle of the African Bush. 'I have since been on a course,' says Jonathan, 'and I realise I knew absolutely nothing. We were lucky I didn't have to call Mitsubishi and tell them I had lost their Shogun. Well, not lost, I knew where it was, it was just under 2 fathoms of water.'

There are dozens of centres in the UK who will give you tuition in driving off-road. Ideally you want both theoretical tuition, followed by set pieces of increasing difficulty to illustrate the points, such as what to do if you fail a hill climb (the answer is: try again, you have no option). Costs range from £65–£250. A list of centres that offer courses can be found in the Useful Addresses section.

What such centres don't usually teach you is what happens when you break down. You should not go driving off into the bush without checking the tool-kit (people tend to borrow wrenches and screwdrivers without mentioning it, especially from 'pool' vehicles), the jack and the spare tyre, making sure that the vehicle is properly serviced and has plenty of fuel and lots of water (enough to keep topping up a haemorrhaging cooling system). You will need other spares according to conditions, but bad fuel is common in developing countries, as are fuel pump and radiator problems. Unlike medicine, a little knowledge in motor maintenance is not a dangerous thing, simple diagnostics are straightforward, though if the answer is 'broken drive shaft' the cure may be tricky.

If anything does go wrong miles from anywhere, remember the old game used on executive training courses. It postulates a plane crash, and gives you a choice of one or two items you can have to aid survival: compass, maps, plastic sheeting, mirror, walking boots, matches, hat, etc. The answer, we were told, is the mirror, not for checking your coiffure, but signalling. Staying with the broken down vehicle is your best bet.

The acknowledged UK expert on off-road expeditions is Jack Jackson, who has written *The Off Road Four Wheel Drive Book* (Haynes, £19.95).

10 Diarrhoea and how to avoid it

The list of ailments and invaders you can catch from food and water are, to say the least, impressive. My all time favourite is probably the guinea worm *Dracunculus*, a worm that can grow to 100 cm (39 in) in a limb, and discharges its eggs through a blister, which blows itself apart when the ulcer hits water. The traditional way of curing it was to gradually wind the nematode out round a small stick, though drugs are now available. All in all, it is pretty gruesome.

Fortunately your chances of catching it (by drinking water that contains the intermediate host, a small crustacean called Cyclops) are very low, even though it is endemic in Pakistan, India and Africa. The same is true of cholera, typhoid and tapeworms. You may be unlucky, but the odds are that, among all the biological exotica on offer, you will only suffer from the humble travellers' diarrhoea, which is why I shall deal with that first.

Gut wrenching problems

Very few travellers have not been there. Your companions are getting ready to leave, you struggle to your feet, make a few feeble packing motions and suddenly your insides undergo another huge churning, and the sweat appears on your forehead. Your mental destination board clicks round and stops at 'nearest lavatory'. You move towards it in that odd rushing-but-not-rushing, buttock-clenched gait of the colonically challenged, sighing with relief when you make it, convinced the end is not too far away now.

It isn't, of course. That is not to say diarrhoea shouldn't be taken and treated seriously, or that it may seriously damage your holiday schedule, just that the Angel of Death is actually very unlikely to be hovering over the tiny cubicle you will call home for next few days.

It doesn't have to be a particularly vicious microbe that gets you. Emma Tully, who has led many a tour through India for Cox & Kings says, 'It isn't food poisoning or bad water that gets people early on, it is the richness of the food. If you come and order something steeped in ghee, clarified butter, your stomach is going to wonder what's hit it. I advise people to stick to vegetarian food, dhal and rice for the first few days. After that they can eat what they want, with a few common-sense rules, such as avoiding fish if you aren't on the coast – Indian refrigeration isn't always what it might be.'

Emma claims that treacherous guts are not inevitable in India, but the problem is that most of us drop our guard sooner or later. It could be a tasty jumbo prawn or perhaps that after a few drinks, you forgot rudimentary precaution and brushed your teeth with local tap water.

Attack rates vary from country to country, but it isn't hard to guess from the nicknames it has (e.g. Montezuma's or the Pharaoh's revenge, Delhi belly) which countries have a 60–70 per cent chance of an attack within the first 2 weeks. On average, according to Professor M.J.G. Farthing of St Bartholomew's Hospital, approximately 30 per cent of people travelling abroad will suffer some form of stomach upset (and it isn't just the tropics, there has been a high number of cases of *Giardia* infection in the former Soviet Union).

The average length of attack is around 3–4 days, though 10 per cent of cases last over a week, 2 per cent longer than a month, and less than 1 per cent – not a nice thought this – longer than 3 months. About 15 per cent of people will vomit and 2–10 per cent will have blood in their stools (see below).

Note that there are several types of diarrhoea and you may have to judge for yourself just how serious it is. At the risk of making you feel queasy, here is a version of the classification adopted by the American Public Health Association:

Simple diarrhoea: Symptoms similar to the home variety. This can be caused by a wide number of organisms, such as *Campylobacter* or one of the many *Eschericia coli* strains, or a rotavirus. What is causing it is not too important. It can be treated generically (see below).

Dysentery, with stools containing blood or mucus: This might be caused by a bacterium called *Shigella*, or a protozoan (amoebic dysentery, caused by *Entamoeba*). Bacteria tend to cause a fever, amoebae don't. Either way, this is serious.

Diarrhoea lasting more than 14 days: You should have sought treatment long, long before. This could be caused by something like *Cryptosporidium* (which throws in debilitating abdominal cramps to boot), or one of the rather persistent little protozoans, such as *Giardia* (which causes, not surprisingly, giardiasis, complete with bloating and 'foamy-fatty' diarrhoea and flatulence – sounds great, doesn't it?), or again *Entamoeba*. Note that amoebae can migrate to the liver and cause major problems.

Severe purging, with watery stools: As seen in classic cholera (a little beastie called *Vibrio cholerae*). However some recent strains are quite mild and indistinguishable from 'ordinary' diarrhoea.

Mainly vomiting with some diarrhoea: Viral gastroenteritis.

Watery stools containing gross blood (as in large rather than hideous): Probably a strain of *E. coli* identified as living in cattle, and possibly transmitted through poorly cooked beef (the American Public Health Association point their finger at minced beef, burgers in other words).

It must be said that such classifications are simplistic, mainly because organisms don't know how they are supposed to behave, and may not act accordingly. But the chances are that if you get diarrhoea, it will be of the simple variety, and will go of its own accord within a few days (the average is 3.6) providing it is managed properly. You may think you have *Entamoeba* or *Giardia*, but they are estimated to cause less than 4 per cent and less than 1 per cent of travellers' diarrhoea respectively. However, they can take up to a couple of weeks to manifest their presence, so you may be at home before the full force hits you.

Prevention

There is a mass of advice on how to avoid travellers' diarrhoea, to the point where it could end up being the dominant aspect of your trip. A favourite is to avoid local hospitality, when food prepared in suspect conditions may be served. This is often easier said than done. You can plead a slight stomach upset, eccentric diet or bizarre medical condition, but there are times when no excuse will do. Times, indeed, that you should probably run the risk.

My mother-in-law was faced with this problem in a remote village in Kenya recently, where she had 'adopted' one of the children through a charity which was providing a new water supply. The boy's family invited her into their hut, where it was obvious that the meal represented a very large investment both in time and money. There on the table, in various dishes, was the family's Most Favoured Chicken.

The normal ploy in these circumstances is to fake it, moving food around, and hiding the bulk of it under the large leaf on the left, but she felt she had to sit down and consume everything offered, even though much of it looked, well, unappetising. Her reward was a stomach that stayed strong and true.

The other advice I have seen is to avoid street food all street food. Yet this can be the culinary highlight of any trip. OK, so crispy kebabs raw in the centre are a risk, but many foods freshly fried (i.e. while you watch) in hot oil will be safe, and at least you know it hasn't been sitting around acting as a breeding ground for the local fly population. Anyway, it is the **type** of food being cooked that should guide you, with shellfish and crustacea being the most suspect. I think, though, that you should probably lay off the street vendors when, as they do in Mexico City, the government puts up signs warning the locals of the dangers to their health.

However, dining in the hotel is not necessarily leagues ahead of eating alfresco. After all, you cannot see what is going on back there, nor who is preparing your food (it could be the street vendor's brother or sister). Hotels will often tend to go for elaborate non-local dishes, and attempting them, even something as seemingly simple as mayonnaise, in hot climates is asking for trouble. Then there is the problem of plates and cutlery: there is no escaping the fact that flies may well have walked up them, or the cleaning process may have been seriously flawed (I have seen the dishes being washed in Hong Kong harbour by those little touristy boat-restaurants). Wiping off damp plates, knives and forks may help, flaming with a lighter is sometimes suggested, but this is getting ridiculous: how long before someone invents the portable travel autoclave?

However, it does make sense to take precautions, and here are some suggestions to try and keep your insides where they belong. Inside

Water

It isn't just diarrhoea that is spread by water, there is also hepatitis A, typhoid and the likes of my old chum *Dracunculus* to contend with. Whereas you nearly always have the option of skipping a meal, remember you may have to keep your fluid intake as high as 4–5 litres per day or more under extreme conditions.

- **If in *any* doubt about public supplies, drink bottled water.** Make sure it is opened in front of you, to prevent proprietary brands being re-filled from the tap. Heavily chlorinated public water may be rendered drinkable by letting it stand overnight in a clean jar, covered with something to keep the bugs out, but not stoppered.
- **Do not use ice cubes,** use an ice bucket if you must. All those bacteria and protozoa in water are in the cubes, just waiting for your body heat to thaw them out.
- **Don't brush your teeth with tap water.** You'll swallow it.
- **Don't sing in the shower.** You'll swallow some.
- **Don't drink from isolated lakes and rivers:** you never know who or what is dumping into it. And there is a risk of leptospirosis from animal's urine in the lake.
- **If in doubt and there is no bottled water available, purify local water** with iodine, chlorine or iodine-resin water purifiers/filters (see below) or bring to a boil.
- **If you want to drink something other than water,** bottled and canned

carbonated drinks are fine, but they are sometimes kept under water as primitive refrigeration. It is easier to wipe the top of a bottle than a can. Generally safe are hot tea or coffee (try and take both black unless the milk is boiled, as it is in the preparation of *chai* in India). Alcohol does not quench your thirst; coconut milk does – straight from the coconut, of course. Note that bottled water does not always mean mineral water; in India what you get is treated municipal supplies.

Food

Food poisoning may have several culprits, including *Salmonella* species (the bacterium which causes typhoid), *E. coli*, *Giardia*, and *Shigella*. There is the added bonus of the risk of hepatitis A and a variety of unwelcome worms. Basically you want food that has been stored properly, cooked fresh (not re-heated) and served HOT and quickly. You don't want:

- **Salads.** Remember how many parts of the world fertilise their fields with human waste.
- **Uncooked vegetables/fruit that you have not peeled yourself.** If you can, wash fruits etc., even melons, in clean water before peeling, as you could contaminate from skin to inside with the knife or your hands.
- **Any western-style food involving elaborate preparation.** The chef may not be up to it; the climate certainly isn't conducive.
- **Food chilled on ice:** butter curls are often kept solid on ice, and bacteria are big on cross-contamination.
- **Anything exposed to flies,** which may include bread and sauces left on the table or opened bottles
- **Buffets.** Personally I hate buffets anywhere, but in hot climes they can be lethal thanks to flies and the heat. Ask yourself how long has the food been sitting there? The answer is always 'too long'.
- **Dairy food.** This is a rich source of bacteria. Ice-cream is often left to melt and refreeze (Louise Nicholson in her excellent India guide books make an exception for the ice-cream in Gujarat, where demand outstrips supply). Unpasteurised milk should be boiled or avoided. (There is a risk of brucellosis, and tick-borne encephalitis, from unpasteurised milk and cheese.)
- **Prawns, lobster, oysters, mussels, etc.,** all of which can efficiently

remove and harbour bacteria from contaminated water. They need to be cooked very thoroughly if they are to be safe. Skip unless you witness the cooking or are cooking them yourself. Even then, it will be a gamble.

- **Undercooked meat.** It may contain tapeworms and the like, or may have live *Salmonella* in it. If it is raw or distinctly pink, think twice.
- **Fish.** You have a (small) risk of catching fish tapeworms or intestinal nematodes from raw fish, though properly cooked fish is usually safer than meat. However, reef fish, such as snapper, grouper and barracuda may have concentrated toxins from microorganisms and may cause ciguatera, a numbness and tingling around lips and limbs, with vomiting thrown in for good measure. It is rarely fatal, but there were 200 cases reported in the Caribbean in 1992. It is also common in the Pacific. Disturbances to the ocean floor seem to throw up the micro-organisms, so the risk is greatest after storms or construction work. The effects hit 2–6 hours after eating the fish, and may last a week or more (one weird symptom is that hot and cold sensations are reversed so people feel as if they have burnt themselves on cold objects). There is another disease called sombroid poisoning which comes from poor refrigeration of fish such as tuna, mackerel and mahi-mahi. If a histamine-type reaction occurs within 30 minutes of eating such a fish – vomiting, rashes, etc. – you've got it.

Other things to think about:

- **In many countries the left hand and water is used for bottom-wiping instead of paper.** This means you will spend a lot of time examining street vendors' finger nails. Remember also to eat with your right hand.
- **Make sure you yourself adhere to good hygiene;** wash hands frequently. Antiseptic baby wipes can be used on both you and your cutlery.
- **Don't let all this paranoia put you off eating:** a liquid/fruit diet is also going to play havoc with your bowels.

Now here is an interesting thing, as reported by Dr James Le Fanu in *The Times*. Dr Raj Bhopal, Professor of Public Health at Newcastle University, asked travellers in India to fill out a questionnaire about the precautions they took against travellers' diarrhoea. When he analysed the results he found that those who instituted precautions 'at all times' were as likely to get diarrhoea as those who took 'none at all'. Dr Le Fanu also reports a couple who took every single measure to prevent problems on their round-the-world trip, down to eating only in tourist restaurants and wiping every dish with their own dishcloth. The woman had nine separate episodes of diarrhoea, the husband caught giardiasis plus two less life-threatening variations.

Michael Farthing, writing in the *British Medical Journal* in 1993, commented: 'The standard advice for travellers nearly always fails.' This is perhaps due to the organisms being very resilient and maybe because it is impossible to block every single route of infection. I am not suggesting that you ignore every piece of advice given above, just recommending you take on board the luck-of-the-draw aspect.

Cure

I still remember the years when I packed my Entero-Vioform for any stomach problems, in the days before it was discovered to cause eye problems. Recently, management of diarrhoea has moved away from a reliance on drugs.

Little homilies such as 'time is a great healer' don't go down very well when some vile bug is eviscerating you, even though it is often the truth. Trying to protect against an attack is best done by following the basic rules above. Dosing yourself up with proprietary brands, such as Pepto-Bismol, is not a good idea. Anyway if it is a long trip there won't be much room in your luggage for anything else, quite apart from the fact that such drugs are not recommended for much more than 3 weeks. Pepto-Bismol (bismuth subsalicylate) should be avoided by anyone with an aspirin intolerance, a bleeding disorder or peptic ulcers, and side effects include the very irritating tinnitus (ringing in the ears). It can also make treatment more difficult if you should come down with an infection, because it messes up absorption of some antibiotics.

If you do have any stomach problems, the most important thing is to replace lost fluids. Don't worry about the food you probably won't feel much like eating, and you can't starve to death in 72 hours. Hey, you wanted to lose that spare tyre anyway. If you can eat, it will help; soups, crackers, toast, pasta and rice are all good while you feel a little tender.

- **If it is a relatively mild bout, you can replace fluids just by drinking soft drinks** (though very sweet fizzy drinks may inhibit water absorption by the gut), tea, good water, but not alcohol.
- **If it is more explosive, then you should consider oral rehydration.** This is a combination of liquid plus electrolytes to replace the various salts and minerals that you are also losing. It is available from pharmacies (e.g. Dioralyte), where it is mainly sold for rehydrating babies, who are in the habit of having frequent diarrhoea. You can make your own version by combining a litre of boiled or filtered water with 8 level teaspoons of sugar (or honey) and half to one level teaspoon of salt. The latter should be adjusted to taste – you do not want to drink salty water, there should be just a hint of it (no saltier than tears it the usual rule of thumb). Nor do you want too much sugar. If you can find it, include half a teaspoon of baking soda to add bicarbonate, and a pinch of cream of tartar for potassium. You need to take in 3–4 litres per day minimum, more if it keeps coming out.
- **Several of the specialist companies mentioned in the Useful Addresses section produce a double-ended spoon which enables you to measure out salt and sugar exactly for a predetermined amount of water.** Particular care must be taken by anyone on diuretics for heart conditions or high blood pressure, which will exacerbate any dehydration. Consult a GP before you leave, and ask if, in the case of severe diarrhoea, you should temporarily halt the course.
- **If vomiting, take frequent, small sips** to try and keep fluid down.
- **The usual advice to sit and wait it out may be a problem.** You may have a plane or train to catch. The rest of the group may be tired of waiting around while you evacuate your bowels. 'In my experience,' says Hilary Bradt, who has had to contend with all these situations, 'people will take anything to stop it and get on with their trip.' So brands such as Imodium, Arret and Lomotil are taken. These will simply stop the symptoms without killing the bug, but if they work, fine (they will give usually temporary relief at best). But as it says on the packets in front of me: 'If symptoms

persist for more than 48 hours, consult your doctor'. Note these drugs should NOT be given to children.

- **If you have giardiasis or shigella or something else altogether more muscular than regular diarrhoea,** then powerful (read dangerous) drugs are available, which should not be taken casually, as they all have side effects, including increased photosensitivity and nausea. Doxycycline (not for children) and ciprofloxacin are often prescribed for bacilli, metronidazole for amoebae (in the absence of a stool test, telling the difference between the two dysenteries often hinges on whether you have a fever or not, see above) or giardiasis.
  Note that indiscriminate and unecessary use of antibiotics is antisocial, as there is a risk of encouraging the rise of drug-resistant strains, which could come back to haunt you. But I have to admit such considerations seem very remote when you actually get afflicted (see below).
- **While suffering from diarrhoea eat bland, non-spicy foods and avoid alcohol.**
- **If you have had a serious bout, consider getting a posttrip check-up,** in case something is still lurking.

Now here is another interesting thing. There is evidence from the work of Professor Michael Farthing of St Bartholomew's Hospital with marine commandos in Belize that a single dose of ciprofloxacin (Ciproxin) given within 24 hours of the onset of diarrhoea reduces the average length of most attacks, from 3 down to 1 day. Ciprofloxacin is available on prescription. Note such antibiotics should not be taken by children or pregnant women, and not by anyone for longer than 2 weeks.

Liquid gold

Once you have contemplated a glass of dirty, scummy water, for all you know alive with all manner of unsavoury organisms, and known you will have to drink it because you are in the first stages of dehydration, it would be nice to think you will never take the public supply in the UK for granted again. This is nonsense, of course. You'll be as careless and accepting of it as you ever were within 5 minutes of your return.

However, the above list of misfortunes should make you aware of how vital a good watersupply is away from home. You will not always be able to rely on a ready supply of bottled water if, for instance, you are trekking or travelling away from big cities in, say, Central America. And in hotter climes you will need at least 4–5 litres a day, and possibly up to double that. To ensure it is safe to drink you must adopt one of several methods.

Boiling: More or less infallible, cheap and requires no chemicals. Oh, and a complete pain most of the time. All agree that to be effective the water must be brought to a rolling boil; some authorities claim this is enough, others suggest boiling for 5–10 minutes to ensure you get the hardier specimens lurking within. Either way, the time needs to be increased at altitude, because the lower air pressure means water boils below 100°C, making the sterilisation less efficient. (The usual approximate guide is one extra minute per 300 m above sea level.) The water must be cooled, and then stored in a sterile, covered container.

Chemicals: If you cannot boil, there are chemical methods of wiping out most of the biological impurities. One is iodine, in the form of tablets (crush first as they don't dissolve well) or tincture of crystals. Anyone who has ever failed to put the cap back on a bottle of the tincture properly knows that the tablets are easier to use, though they too must be kept in an airtight container. Both liquid (4–6 drops per litre) and tablets are added to the water. If the water has suspended solids in it, double the recommended quantity. The water is than left to stand for 30 minutes before consuming. (I would always filter any water that had suspended solids in it if I could, but filter first then treat, not vice versa.)

The preparation for a tincture from crystals is a fag, but Dr Jon Dallimore, who leads treks in Nepal, and has had to purify a small reservoir's worth of water in his time, swears by it. Once prepared, it also gives you a reusable source. Take a 30 ml bottle of water, put in 6–8 g of the crystal and shake. Allow to settle. Use the liquid (not crystals) in a ratio of 12–15 ml per litre of water and allow to stand for 20–30 minutes. You can refill the crystal bottle and repeat, as only a small amount of iodine dissolves. Reckon on up to 750 top-ups before the crystals are exhausted.

A couple of drops of tincture can always be added to suspect restaurant water. Incidentally, some people hate the taste and prefer chlorine, or vice versa, although 'detasters' are now available for both.

Note, iodine is an important chemical in the functioning of the thyroid gland. Do not use constantly for long periods (i.e. over 6 months). Pregnant women should use something else.

Chlorine: Tablets (e.g. Puritabs) or bleach (5 drops to one litre) can be used. The water must be left to stand for 30 minutes. The drawback here is that chlorine probably does not inactivate some cysts, such as those that cause giardiasis (iodine is more effective at this), though the longer you can leave treated water before drinking, the better.

Filters/purifiers: Filters are often unfairly denigrated – the technology has come a long way since water was trickled through a bit of paper to remove the mud, and the rest was trust in God. Filtering followed by iodine or chlorine treatment will give you almost as much protection as boiling water. The problems start when people rely on (or manufacturers make claims for) filters that are not up to the job.

Activated carbon filters, for instance, mainly make the water more potable. They do not remove micro-organisms; a simple filter must be followed by sterilisation with tablets.

Otherwise look for units that both filter and purify (with an iodine resin complex for instance) and will remove all particles down to around 0.2–0.4 microns, which should remove most things except viruses (and it will probably remove most of those because they are usually in or on something larger than themselves). One drawback of filter/purifiers is that they are more bulk to carry around, so unless you are going well off the beaten tracks, tablets will probably be enough.

SafariQuip offers a wide range of purification systems, from the simple filter bag (£7.99) useful for filtering out debris prior to boiling or sterilisation, up to the excellent, Swiss-made Katadyn at £199. MASTA has the Trekker Travel Well (£25), activated charcoal coupled with iodine-resin, which can give 100 litres of safe water, or a pocket version (£9.95) which will give 25 litres. Explore Direct also has a variety of tablets and filters in its catalogue. Nomad is very good at going through the pros and cons of different treatments.

With any filtration unit you should check it is not flimsy, difficult to use or liable to shatter (durability and lack of clogging is what makes the Katadyn so expensive). Ask also what the filtration rate is – the catalogues always tell you how much clean water you can get, but not how fast you get it. The filter will also clog eventually: how easy are they to replace? All filtered water must be stored in sterile containers and untreated water should never be added. Re-treat water that has been left uncovered, you never known what has slipped in. And don't rely solely on a filter, they break, clog up (particularly with silt-laden water) and get lost or stolen. Always have tablet back-up.

I am afraid that if you are in the wilderness and waterless, hoping to make a survival still, extract water from a barrel cactus or suck up ground water, then you are in for trouble. They are all beyond the scope of this book. You should have packed a copy of *Stay Alive*, by Maurice Dunlevy, an Australian handbook on bush survival, *Survival* by Xavier Maniguet or the *SAS Survival Guide* by John Wiseman. Sorry, but I did mention it earlier.

11 Parasites

It isn't only diarrhoea that food and drink can give you. The number of parasites you can (but probably won't) pick up would, and does, fill several text books. The following are just a few of them.

Schistosomiasis

'We started getting reports at the end of 1993 that bilharzia was present in Lake Malawi,' says Jennifer Cox of the *Lonely Planet Guides*, 'mainly because the locals were warning travellers not to swim. This meant we had to put a stop press slip in our new guide to the area, because it hadn't previously been there.' The Liverpool School of Tropical Medicine has seen a similar pattern: suddenly, there was a new focus of bilharzia in Lake Malawi, and returnees were coming in with a puzzling infection their doctors had not seen before.

The cause of bilharzia, or more accurately schistosomiasis, is a little fluke or worm, which lays its eggs in either the bowel or the bladder (it depends on the species of worm, there are three types). The eggs then pass into fresh water, hatching out and hitching a ride inside a snail. There they mature, until they burst out as tiny cercariae, ready to infect a human by burrowing through the skin (there may be a rash). The male and females rendezvous at the liver, where, after maturing (for around 6 weeks) the male locks the female in a permanent embrace, and they decamp to their proposed site of egg production to complete the cycle.

The worms cause a variety of problems, not least painful bowel movements and urination. They can damage the liver and spleen, cause fever, blood in urine or sperm, and diarrhoea. They are extremely well adapted to humans, throwing off the body's defences with ploys such as molecular mimicry – their surface proteins copy our own. Treatment is with a single-dose drug, praziquantel (though there have been a few cases of resistance to this drug), but you really want to try and avoid getting it in the first place.

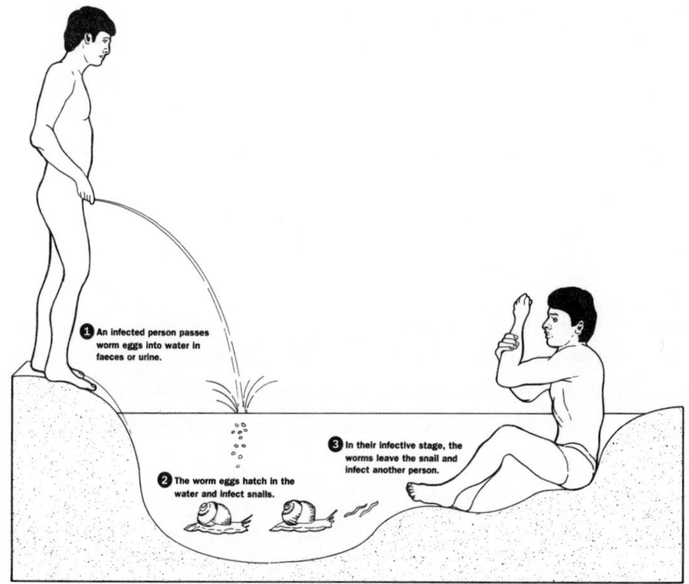

SIMPLE SCHISTOSOMIASIS LIFE-CYCLE

- **Do not swim, water-ski or splash about in fresh water in endemic areas, always check with locals.**
- **Do not wash clothes in untreated water.**
- **If you do have to wade, wear rubber boots.**
- **Chlorination kills the cercariae:** swimming pools are generally safe. Boiling or storing water for more than 3 days also destroys the infective stage.
- **If you think you have been exposed, vigorous towelling and 70 per cent alcohol rubbed on the skin will kill the burrowers if it is done in time.** Unfortunately this means minutes rather than hours, and 70 per cent alcohol is not something bathers usually carry with them.

Guinea worms

This nasty round worm lives subcutaneously and pops out through an ulcer to lay its eggs in water. The larval stage infects a small crustacean, which in turn will pass on *Dracunculus* to anyone drinking the water untreated. It is not common in travellers, who will normally be careful about their choice of drinking water. The main route of infection is stepped-wells, where locals wade into the water: the worm quickly pokes out through the ulcer and blows itself apart to release thousands of eggs, which then infect the drinking water. WHO has declared war on the worm.

Intestinal worms

Again, you would have to be very unlucky to get an intestinal worm. But it's not impossible. 'I did get infected, in Nepal, I think,' says Emma Tully of Cox & Kings. 'The problem was I had the cysts of a tapeworm developing in me, which migrated to my brain and started giving me blackouts. Luckily drug treatment got rid of them.'

The worms to watch for are:

Tapeworms from under-cooked pork, beef (often assumed to be OK rare, even though beef tapeworms are found in the UK) and fish. Symptoms are usually mild, and include diarrhoea, headache and lethargy. Tapeworm segments can occasionally be spotted in the faeces. Serious problems occur when the eggs pass not into an intermediary host (the pig or fish) but, through poor hygiene, back into the human, where it thinks it is in another host and migrates to the muscle or (as in Emma Tully's case) the brain (this is the pork tapeworm only). Raw fish in SE Asia may also carry liver flukes, a relative of tapeworms.

Hydatid cysts: These are what happens when again, hosts get mixed up. It is a tapeworm of dogs, and the eggs pass out in the faeces, normally to be picked up by another host (e.g. sheep). If a human gets them, the eggs develop as if that person were a sheep, growing in the liver or, rarely, the brain. Symptoms are mild, unless the nervous system is affected.

Round worm: More faeces-mouth contamination from *Ascaris* species. These are nasty long worms in the gut (via the lungs, where they may cause a cough or pneumonia) which are a hefty 20–30 cm long. They can cause intestinal blockage, but are easily treated with drugs.

Pinworm: Very common, even in the UK, this is thousands of little worms which live in the gut. They migrate to the anus at night to lay eggs, where they cause itching. Scratching re-infects. Again, they may be caught by bad hygiene, but they can also be thwarted by good hygiene. Even without drugs, the infection will be over in 6 weeks if the cycle of re-infection can be broken. Pinworms are particularly common in children, mainly because telling them not to scratch doesn't have any effect.

Hookworm: For once, pork or water is not to blame if you get this infestation. The worms live in the soil and do not mess around with intermediary hosts: they burrow into the skin directly. They may cause no symptoms, sitting there quietly in your small intestine supping blood, or, by sheer dint of numbers, they may cause anaemia. Eggs pass out in the faeces. You aren't at risk unless you go barefoot in tropical and sub-tropical countries. Flip-flops aren't good enough protection. Some hookworm larvae (of the dog and cat hookworm) wander around under the skin like lost souls leaving nasty red marks, like vapour trails. This is the colourfully named Creeping Eruption (or cutaneous larva migrans), and you catch it on beaches where dogs and cats have defaecated. The larvae usually die in 2–8 weeks, but there is a treatment.

Anisakiasis: Some raw fish contain nematodes, not tapeworms, but tiny round things that burrow into the stomach wall, causing, stomach-ache, vomiting and nausea. They may attack the small intestine and the lungs, causing a cough. However, to put this in perspective, there have been several hundred cases in Japan, which is not that many given the amount of uncooked fish consumed there. Cases have also been reported in the Netherlands (from raw herring), Scandinavia (gravadlax) and Latin America (ceviche). Best to use your judgement: if its a shack in the Laotian jungle specialising in sashimi, I'd pass.

Trichinosis

These are more worms from pork (is it worth it, you begin to ask yourself – have the chicken) that burrow through the gut wall and live in your muscle, causing soreness, fever, even bleeding in the whites of the eyes. The risk of getting it is low, especially if you avoid pork, suspiciously amorphous hamburgers and horsemeat. A drug called mebendazole works wonders, and is capable of knocking out a wide variety of worm infestations. Note that this worm occurs worldwide, except Australia.

Ring worm

Fooled you. This isn't a worm at all, but a fungal infection that just loves high humidity. Cleanliness, talcum powder and flip-flops (it is a disease of showers and changing rooms, too) all help defeat it. Daktarin or Canestan usually get rid of it.

12 Being bitten

Even if they don't carry disease, insects can make your life a misery, as anyone who has been driven off a beach by territorial sand flies can testify. Nor is the problem confined to the tropics: Scotland during the summer all but surrenders to the midges.

Just to convince you that prevention against insect bites is in your best interests, here is an arthropod rogues gallery. Lest this makes for terrible I-will-never-leave-these-shores-again paranoia, let me call upon Brenda, my intrepid mother-in-law. She has been to almost all the risk areas mentioned in this book, and has scuba-dived across the globe. With many thousands of nomadic miles under her belt, she recently had an enforced stay in hospital. Sunstroke? Sleeping sickness? Shark attack? Nope, she squirted herself in the eye with oven cleaner while at home in London.

The insect culprits

Mosquitoes

The obvious blight they bestow on mankind is malaria, which is a threat to one and a half billion people (1500 million). The WHO reckon that, worldwide, around 10,000 people catch it on holiday and return home with it, of which the UK accounts for about a fifth. To quote the WHO, 'the malaria situation is getting worse in many areas, and prevention and treatment of falciparum malaria (the most dangerous form) are becoming more difficult because the resistance of the parasite to anti-malarial drugs is increasing and becoming more widespread.'

However, it isn't only the *Anopheles* that packs a sucker punch in its bite. The virus that causes yellow fever is spread by the *Aedes aegypti* and relatives, and has a hefty form sheet – it is reckoned to have a 60 per cent fatality rate among non-immune (don't fool yourself, that means you) victims. And just in case you think that a few tabs of Lariam and a yellow fever jab are all you need, bear in mind that the American Public Health Association recognises a total of 60 viral diseases spread by mossies, from the Rift Valley fever of Africa, to the Snowshoe Hare encephalitis of the USA.

Dengue fever, a serious debilitating viral disease, is also spread by *Aedes* species (which feed early in the morning and late in the day). Because of the aches and pains it causes it is often known as breakbone fever. There is a lethal variation on the disease called dengue haemorrhagic fever, which has a high fatality rate in children. Neither disease is common in tourists (though I know of one travel writer who has had the relatively benign form, and the Liverpool School of Tropical Medicine is seeing an increase among backpackers to Vietnam and Thailand). Its relative rarity is just as well, as there is no immunisation and no treatment. It is endemic across much of Africa, South-East Asia and northern Latin America, and there have been cases in Australia: watch for fever and rash within 3 weeks of leaving an infected area.

Also on the mosquito menu is a little worm called *Wuchereria bancrofti*, which causes filariasis. The worms live in the lymphatic and blood systems, causing all sorts of problems, but most famously, in extreme cases, elephantiasis, where the blockage of the drainage system causes enlargement of extremities. I still shudder at the thought of a picture in the Wellcome Foundation's museum in London of a poor chap with elephantiasis of the scrotum. The worm is spread by several species of mosquito (including *Culex*, *Anopheles* and *Aedes*) endemic to warm, humid regions. The chances of travellers getting it are low.

And lest we get carried away, let us just remember that there are billions of mossies all over the world, including malarial zones, that do nothing other than give you a nasty bump.

Sandflies

More than just a nuisance, sandflies (phlebotomines) carry a little protozoan that causes the horrible leishmaniasis. This can either work its damage internally (visceral leishmaniasis or Kala Azar), causing fever anaemia and lethargy, and possibly death, or there is a disfiguring cutaneous version, known as desert sore or ulcer. It causes nasty skin lesions, which scar. It can affect the arms, legs and face or mucus membranes.

The chances of catching it are again low. 'I have seen four cases in 6 months,' says Doctor Emma Woolfenden of the Liverpool School of Tropical Medicine. 'all the cutaneous version and all from South America, although it does exist in the Middle East and beyond.' Beyond includes Pakistan, China, Ethiopia, Kenya and Namibia. Even parts of Texas. Any bite which seems to become inflamed and enlarged should be treated quickly.

Sandflies fever virus occurs in Sicily, Tuscany, Naples and the Middle East, and causes a headache lasting up to 3 weeks. You'll wonder what was in that Chianti.

Tsetse flies

This is the fly that causes sleeping sickness. Let's get one thing clear: just because you are in Africa and feel sleepy, doesn't mean you have sleeping sickness. It is probably just your normal indolence. The sleepy part comes late (probably too late) in the day when not only your blood, but also your central nervous system is full of trypanosomes, the protozoans that cause the disease. The first symptom is a hefty sore at the site of the tsetse fly bite. Fever, rash and enlarged lymph nodes follow. Death is inevitable without treatment (there are actually two forms of the disease, the main difference being that one kills you quickly, the other slowly), and though there is no immunisation it can be cured if caught early enough.

Cases among travellers are not common, though the risk is higher among those who go on safari (the disease tends to occur in small, well-defined 'hot spots' or foci within Africa). The fly is a strange beast, which is attracted to large moving objects (it normally feeds on game), so they will tend to follow Land Rovers and the like for many miles, often clustering around the windscreen or the spare wheel on the bonnet. Hence, being *in* a Land Rover does not necessarily mean you are safe from bites if the windows are open. According to Doctor George Wyatt of the Liverpool School of Tropical Medicine, they are also attracted to the colour blue, though I leave you to decide whether that should dictate your African wardrobe.

Kissing bugs

A very romantic name (though its alternative, Assassin bug, might be more accurate) for a bug that gives humans Chagas' Disease, which is basically a Central and Latin American version of sleeping sickness. They are properly known as triatomid bugs, and tend to live in poor housing, mainly mud or cane huts. The triatomids lurk in cracks in mud walls, behind loose canes and come out at night to feed. Oddly, it isn't the bite that infects you, it's the fact that bugs defaecate while feeding, and the bug crap contains the parasite. When you inevitably scratch the site, the parasites get rubbed into the skin puncture. Look for a nasty, swollen bite; with a fever following 1–3 weeks later. Seek treatment as the protozoans have a nasty knack of damaging heart muscle, with fatal results. Best of all, avoid mud huts. If you do have to use one, stay away from the other occupants and use a well tucked-in, treated mosquito net.

Blackfly

The *Simulium* is another little monster, transmitting a worm that causes severe skin problems and eventually migrates to the eyes causing corneal damage and river blindness (onchocerciasis). The flies breed in rivers, where the water flows over rocks and stones. Although present in South America, Simulium has had the greatest impact in Africa, particularly in the west. A heavy rash plus changes in pigmentation and elasticity of the skin are the first symptoms; little lumps then form, caused by females waiting for a roving male. The females then send out microfilariae which also migrate. The worms don't usually reach the eyes for some years. Drugs are very effective. It is recommended that you do not loiter near fast flowing rivers in remoter areas, where the *Simuliums* hang out, unless adequately protected by clothing and repellents.

Fleas and lice

Contrary to some newspaper reports, tourists are not coming down with plague. It does still exist in areas of great poverty, but although the fleas (brown, flattened, unmistakable to anyone who has ever owned a cat) you will meet will be capable of giving you a nasty nip, there will not be a red cross on your door the next morning. Well, probably not. (These days plague is treated with tetracycline, rather than a man with a cart and a bell.)

Lice, ticks and fleas may also carry typhus fever, which is going to make you very ill for a couple of weeks. It is only likely if staying in poor areas where infestations are common. Again, it can be treated with tetracycline.

If you are staying in a place suspect for fleas and lice, air all bedding and mattresses outside before sleeping. Treat sheets and mosquito nets with permethrin and douse yourself liberally with repellents. Creams and shampoos are available for the treatment of infestation.

Drastic treatment of yourself and beds and bedding is needed with scabies, which is caused by a burrowing mite that gets under the skin, and, as you might imagine, itches like mad. It can be caught by close body contact or from bedding. The offending bedding and clothing should be washed; people must be coated in a compound such as gamma benzene hexachloride (lindane) or similar, except for the head (and not children or pregnant women) and left on for a day before bathing.

More of a threat to tourists are jigger fleas, which burrow and cause infection in feet (wear shoes) in Central America and West Africa. You have to dig them out with a sterile needle, so try and avoid them. If the beach is full of locals, consider it safe. Otherwise ask.

Bed bugs

These days there is a natural fear of sharing bugs with a stranger, but there is no evidence that any bloodsuckers have transmitted HIV or hepatitis B. Bed bugs are therefore just a nuisance, the poor things don't

Biting insects and bugs

	MOSQUITOES			OTHER BITING FLIES			
	Anopheles	**Aedes**	**Culex**	**Tsetse fly**	**Black fly**	**Sandfly**	**Midge**
Description	Head and body in straight line and at angle to wall. Often have spotted wings.	Body parallel to wall with head bent down. Black and white	Brown	Large 6-15mm long Brown/greyish mouthparts stick out in front of head	Small 1.5-4mm Black, hunchbacked	Small 2-5mm Various colours, very hairy wings at 45° above body	Minute 0.2mm Dark spotted wings
Which Disease	Malaria Filariasis	Dengue fever, Japanese B encephalitis, yellow fever, filariasis, viral encephalitis.	Filariasis	Sleeping sickness	Onchocerciasis	Leishmania	Nuisance (often attack in swarms), filariasis
Where	Africa, Asia, Americas, Western Pacific	Africa, Asia, Americas, Western Pacific	Africa, Asia, Americas	Africa	Africa, Asia (Seasonal nuisance, e.g. N Canada)	Africa, Asia, Americas	Temperate (e.g. Scotland), Africa, Asia, Africa, Western pacific
When	Night, indoors and out Mainly rural	Day, indoors and out Urban and rural	Evening/night indoors and out Urban and rural	Day, indoors Rural	Day, outdoors Rural	Evening, indoors and out Urban and rural	Evening, outdoors Rural
Bite	Not usually painful, but normally produce local reaction lasting from a few hours to several days.			Very painful, usually cause allergic swellings	Painful, may cause pricking sensation followed by itching swelling and ulceration.	Immediately painful and cause itching. Similar in appearance to chickenpox, lasting a week	Sharp prick often followed by irritating lumps

FLEAS, TICKS AND BEDBUGS

	Cone nosed	**Bedbug**	**Tick**	**Flea**	**Louse**	**Mite**
Description	Very large 10-40mm long Many colours, winged or wingless, cone-like head, 6 legs	Large 10mm Brown, wingless, oval and flat when unfed, 6 legs	Large when fed 3-30mm Many coloured, wingless, pea-shaped when fed, 8 legs	Small 1-4mm Brown, wingless, flattened from side-to-side, 6 legs	Small 2-3mm Cream/brown, wingless, 6 legs with crab-like claws	a) minute - just visible to the naked eye Yellow/white b) quite easily seen by the eye Red and velvety
Which Disease	Chagas' disease	Hepatitis B Loss of sleep	Relapsing fever, typhus, Lyme disease, encephalitis	Bubonic plague, tungiasis	Typhus, relapsing fever	a) scabies b) typhus
Where	Americas	Africa, Asia, Americas. Western Pacific, Temperate	Africa, Asia, Americas, Western Pacific, Temperate	Africa, Asia, Americas, Western Pacific	Africa, Asia, Americas	Africa, Asia, Americas, Western Pacific
When	Night, in bed Rural/urban	Night, in bed Rural/urban	Day (long grass), night (e.g. caves) Rural	Night/day, indoors Rural/urban	Night/day, found on body hair/clothes Rural/urban	Night/day, indoors and out Rural/urban
Bite	Usually painless but may cause urticaria if host reacts to injected saliva	Extremely painful and lasting and sometimes causing skin problems due to secondary infection	Range from painless to extremely painful and venomous, with bleeding and ulceration	Range from no noticeable reaction to immediate pain and formation of rose-red pustules	Not usually painful, but may cause skin problems aggravated by scratching	a) is caused by the female scraping burrows in skin. Itching results from acid secretions and faeces b) mite causes intense itching

Reproduced with kind permission of Jane Miller

even have a decent disease to their name. Nets and repellents are again recommended if you are in doubt about your room (airing the bedding won't do any good, the bugs live in cracks in walls), as is insecticide powder liberally applied.

Ticks

After all this badmouthing of Africa, South America and Asia, it is something of a relief to find that Europe is not quite the disease-free bastion we sometimes assume. Tick-borne encephalitis (TBE) occurs in the undergrowth of forested regions in Russia, Austria, Germany, Poland and Scandinavia, and is caused by a virus transmitted by the bite of a tick called *Ixodes*. It is a summer disease, usually affecting foresters, but ramblers may be at risk. Shorts should be avoided, instead apply DEET or other repellents and go in for trousers with long socks over them. Yes, you will look like an Ovaltinee, but you are trying to prevent a serious bout of fever. Those at risk can be immunised against TBE.

Lyme disease is also transmitted by ticks, but is caused by a bacterium and, in addition to Europe, is found scattered in small foci across 46 states of the USA and in Canada. There were over 5000 cases in the USA in the first half of 1993. Lyme disease causes skin lesions and fever, followed by all sorts of complications, including heart problems and arthritis. So wear those socks and spray that DEET. Look initially for a rash developing around the bite, and seek medical attention. If you get a tick on you, don't panic – the vast majority of ticks worldwide will not be carrying a disease. But you should pull it off, vertically away from the skin surface, by grasping the head end, not the body, with tweezers, and gently twisting and pulling, then clean and disinfect the area. What do you mean you don't carry tweezers?

The intrepid Redmond O'Hanlon had some advice for the tweezer-less in Into *The Heart of Borneo*: 'There is no matching the strength of that irrational desire to find a means of . . . removing small, black, wild-boar ticks from your crotch with minimum discomfort (you do it with sell-otape).' Of course, not many of us would think to take sellotape with us to Borneo, in which case cigarettes (held near the tick) or alcohol (on the tick, not in you) are the next best thing. The tweezer method, incidentally, is the favoured approach by the Department of Entomology at the London School of Hygiene and Tropical Medicine.

Tumbu fly

Ah the horror. This is the granddaddy of all travellers' illness tales, just because it is so disgusting. The infection comes from a fly that lays its eggs on washing left to dry outside, on or near the ground. Ironing kills the eggs, though you have to be fastidious, and remember they like anything which has had sweat or other substances on them – take care with undergarments. If they are not killed, they hatch and the maggot burrows into the skin, leaving just two black dots at the top of the boil to breathe through. Blocking these two holes with oil drives the suffocating maggot to the surface. It was reported in the *Lancet* that covering the site with rashers of bacon works wonders in drawing them to the surface. Myiasis is mainly a problem in Africa, though such flies (Botflies) do occur in South America.

The unbitten law

It is generally agreed that the best way to prevent either the discomfort of insect bites or the relatively remote (except in the case of malaria) chance of contracting one of the above complaints, is to make sure you don't get bitten. The following precautions should be used.

- **Mosquito nets.** You may want to take a chance and rely on your hotels' or guesthouses' nets, but unless you are in a fairly upmarket establishment (which will probably have air-conditioning, which mosquitoes don't like anyway), you should take your own. They come in every conceivable shape, from bell-shaped ones which hang from a point on the ceiling (take your own nail or hook) to elaborate (and quite bulky) free-standing ones. Some individuals feel very claustrophobic under the single-point, bell-type tents, and you are more likely to touch the surface, where a lone raider can slip its proboscis through, so make sure the net is treated. Costs range from £16 to over £50. Suppliers include: Appropriate Applications, Clothtec, InterHealth, Mission Supplies, MASTA, Nomad, Oasis and SafariQuip.

- **Soak the net in an insecticide such as permethrin** (a 1 per cent solution), which should last for 6 months, when it should be re-soaked. The insecticide will kill, as opposed to merely repel, any mosquito that lands on it, making through-biting less likely. Some of the above companies, such as Oasis and SafariQuip, sell pretreated nets, and nearly all sell permethrin solutions for treating or retreating your own net. Smaller mesh cotton nets are the most effective at keeping all and sundry away from you, but they are more fragile than synthetic materials. If you treat the net, mesh size is less important, because anything trying to get you will die. The Long Road net (see Chapter 5) does not need treatment.
- **Use a repellent.** The vast majority of people swear by DEET (diethyl toluamide), which usually does do the trick. It is available as a spray or roll-on and as impregnated arm- and ankle-bands, and in several fancy flavours, including new long-lasting, slow-release. Clothing, arm- and ankle-bands can also be soaked in neat DEET, but you have to be careful about concentrations and allergic reactions (see below) and the fact it melts plastic. How long your application lasts does depend on many factors, such as absorption and 'sweat-off'. Dr Ron Behrens of the Hospital for Tropical Diseases has been conducting research into various repellent formulations for the last 5 years: 'My view is that the extended duration formulae are the most effective, which is why US and British armies have adopted them.' 3M's Ultrathon is one common version of these 'slow release' treatments. DEET should be washed off skin before retiring, when in theory the net takes over the job. Those worried about side effects and chemicals should try Mosi-Guard Natural, Mosi-Milk, Gurkha or X-Gnat, bearing in mind that they will sacrifice some repellent action for safety/peace of mind (see below). Clothing can also be sprayed with permethrin.
- **Use coils or those little plug-in heaters which evaporate pads of insecticide.** Coils are widely available, but if using overnight you have to make sure they will burn all night (remember that draughts and fans accelerate their combustion), otherwise dawn may herald a fresh wave of

assault. Plug-in types depend on a reliable electricity supply, not always available.

- **Make sure rooms are properly screened;** if there is air-conditioning, keep it chilly enough to deter mosquitoes. Spray the room just in case with a 'knock-down' insecticide (e.g. permethrin), particularly door and window frames.
- **Have a quick visual inspection before retiring,** both of the net, for tears or a mosquito that slipped in earlier (gaffa tape repairs these), and of the room.
- **Cover up arms and particularly legs at danger times** (which may vary according to the insect). Dark colours are supposed to attract mosquitoes, but don't think being the Man or Woman in White will save you: if they are hungry enough, they have no sartorial preferences.

The trouble with DEET

Insecticides and repellents are usually powerful chemicals which may well have side effects. Children seem to be particularly vulnerable to DEET, and there have been reactions using formulations with concentrations as low as 20 per cent. The US Department of Health and Human Services recommends that nobody use concentrations of greater than 30 per cent, as the increased efficiency in repelling insects is offset by toxicity considerations. (Autan Fresco, for instance, contains 10 per cent DEET, the roll-on version 20 per cent.) The figures are slightly misleading, of course, because people tend to reapply weaker concentrations as soon as they are bitten, and as the carrier solution evaporates, so the amount on the skin builds up.

Some DEET is inevitably absorbed through the skin (between 9 and a whopping 56 per cent), and you may get a reaction to this. According to a report in the *Lancet* (10 September 1988), a man who applied 70 per cent DEET daily and then took a sauna, developed acute manic psychosis after 2 weeks. *Which?* in July 1991 reported that there have been two deaths due to the extensive application of DEET onto the skin of under-fives, and there have been reports of fits. Less seriously, it attacks plastics and also this is no joke when you accidently lean on someone's furniture – strips varnish.

However, though there may be some skin irritation, particularly if the concentration is high, it must be stressed that most people find DEET effective and safe, and it remains the first choice of many experts for deterring biters.

There are some non-DEET repellents around, such as citronella oil-based soaps, though these are far less effective, and Gurkha (which claims to soften the skin as it repels, anodd benefit of the product being a descendent of Avon Skin So Soft). I have not yet tried the latter.

MASTA has invented and is marketing Mosi-Guard, a 'natural' formulation, claimed to be safe for babies and children. It is based on eucalyptus oils and certainly, judging by a demo I saw of protected and unprotected arms being put into cages of blood-crazed *Aedes aegypti*, is fairly effective.

A relatively new compound is X-Gnat, which has been developed by Tony Pisacane in Scotland, and consists of a chemical which is sprayed or brushed onto clothing, nets, hats, etc., and keeps mosquitoes away from nearby exposed skin. It looks very promising, though the clothes need to be something you don't want to keep: the resin complex which adheres so firmly to the surface is permanent. The active compound is claimed to last for 2–3 weeks before re-application is needed, and to be non-toxic. At the time of writing a skin product was also about to be released. Mosi-Milk and a variety of DEET sprays and liquids are available from SafariQuip.

A combination of DEET or Mosi-Guard on skin and DEET, permethrin or X-Gnat on clothing/hats would seem to be the ideal solution (in both senses of the word), though regular travellers usually find their own preference after trying a range of products.

Arachnids and annelids

Remember that any bite, venomous or not, is more likely to become infected in hot and humid regions. Disinfect and dress it immediately.

Scorpions

Painkillers and time are the best treatment for most scorpion stings. They cause painful swellings and numbness, but are rarely fatal (though scorpions are common in Australia, there have been no fatalities). The Arizona Poisons Unit are notified of over 2000 scorpion stings per year, but again deaths are very infrequent, the last was over 30 years ago. More recently the US Army division had 56 stings when they were stationed near Riyadh, Saudi Arabia during the Gulf War. Once more, there were unpleasant symptoms, but all those stung survived. Get medical attention anyway.

Spiders

The psychological damage done by spiders far outweighs their actual danger to travellers. There are over 50,000 species of these arachnids, and only around a dozen are genuinely dangerous to man. However, that danger grows in the telling: I seem to remember when I was young visualising Australia as a land where a trip to the lavatory had only a fifty-fifty chance of survival, thanks to the red-back spider. It turned out, of course, to be a somewhat exaggerated version of the truth.

In fact more lethal than the red-back is the funnelweb (*Atrax robustus*). Large (25 mm long), hairy and dangerous, it can cause death in 90 minutes (15 in children). Its bite can penetrate clothing, and leaves a double-puncture like a snake bite. The bite is painful, there is sweating, delirium and possibly death due to respiratory failure. For once, the male is deadlier than the female, particularly as it goes walkabout during the mating season (they can fall into swimming pools and bite the careless swimmer during their protracted death-throes). Ninety minutes is not a long time: the usual advice is to keep the limb and the person still and to wrap a tight roller bandage and splint around the affected limb. The idea is to stop the venom moving, but do not use a tourniquet, and then GET HELP. There used to be 2–3 deaths per year from bites, but there has been a immunisation since 1980, with no reported deaths since then.

Australia's other Most Wanted, that dunny-dwelling red-back (*Latro-*

dectus hasselti), lives in sheds, rubbish dumps, under tin cans – anywhere shady. The male is harmless, but the larger female has a relatively light bite, which will redden, followed by shivering and weakness. Adults rarely die, children may, but none have recently.

The black widow spider of North America (*Latrodectus mactans*) is supposedly recognised by a red, hour-glass mark on its underside, though I would be loathe to turn it over to check. Up in the mountains above Palm Springs, California, I saw enough of them to be able to testify to the red markings, though as the bite causes very painful muscle spasms, I wasn't close enough to check the exact shape.

Other well known villains include the tarantula (*L. tredecemguttatus*) of southern Europe and North Africa, the banana spider (*Phoneutria keiserlingi*) and the violin spider (*L. reclusa*) of North and South America, which has a particularly evil bite which fails to heal.

If bitten, seek medical attention. This may sound silly, but try to get a description of the spider, as there are anti-venoms for many of them.

There is one other danger from spiders that I can only report second-hand from Patricia Morse of Passage to South America who, while living fairly rough in Peru, had a spider lay its eggs in her leg. Doesn't bear thinking about really.

Leeches

If you have trouble placing leeches in their correct place in the animal kingdom, think of them as earthworms with a difference, because they are a relative of the common-or-garden worm. The only difference is, they have acquired a taste for bodily fluids.

Many people's perception of leeches comes from the film *African Queen*. Humphrey Bogart gives a good rendition of the horror when you look down and see this creature busy pumping itself up on your blood. But you probably won't *feel* anything because they squirt a little anaesthetic in with the anti-coagulant. Leeches, however, are more disgusting than dangerous unless the bites get infected.

Leeches are a problem mainly in the jungles of South East Asia, where they cling to vegetation, waiting for a passing pair of legs (there are also aquatic leeches, so think twice about swimming – they can slither up noses, among other things). Their mouthparts can penetrate clothing, and they often squirm their way into boots. No exposed spot will be left untouched. David Wickers recalls being in the Borneo jungle with a bald chap who suddenly found he had acquired a toupee of leeches. High concentrations of DEET are meant to deter them, as is Mosi-Guard (I am beginning to think you can cook with this stuff).

Removing leeches is tricky. The received wisdom is to use vinegar, lemon juice, cigarette ends, hot pins and matches to shift them, which leaves non-smokers and those who don't carry a ready supply of salad dressing ingredients at a disadvantage. And anyway, the consensus seems to be that the remedies don't always work, though trek-leader Dr Jon Dallimore always carries a lighter to torch the more stubborn ones, even if he does lose a little leg hair in the process.

If you can't shift them, leeches do fall off when full, but if you can't wait that long you can, despite dire warnings of tropical ulcers, pull them off. There is a slight risk of infection, so some sort of antiseptic cream is a good idea.

The vertebrates

Snakes

Ah yes, it all comes flooding back. I know how to treat a snakebite. You tear off a strip of material, often your shirt, or some ladies' undergarment, wrap it tightly around the top of the limb, open a bottle of whisky, give it to the victim, and then either (a) suck out the venom or (b) heat up your Bowie knife and cut out the affected site. Well that's what happens in the movies.

OK, so it is totally wrong, but it makes for good cinema. Snake bites are quite rare (indeed *seeing* a snake is quite rare), and only happen when the snake is panicked and defending itself, so do not antagonise them.

The rattlesnake rattle, after all, translates as 'bugger off, I don't want to bite you'. If you are in snake country, you should not go poking around in undergrowth or trees, and you should wear stout boots and trousers and carry a flashlight after dark. If bitten you should not apply the tourniquet, suck the wound or get to work with your Bowie knife. What you should so is:

- **Don't panic.** As with scorpion stings, the perceived danger is much greater than the actual threat, even if it is a poisonous snake. It is likely, also, to be a defensive strike rather than a vicious attack, hence only a fraction of its venom will be in the wound. (Note that only poisonous snakes leave fang marks at the top of the bite pattern; if there are no fangs, it is probably harmless. But you should still find an expert quickly.)
- **Keep the victim still.** Moving propels the venom.
- **Wash and clean the bite** to get rid of venom on the surface or in the wound.
- **If you can, splint the limb,** and wrap a crepe bandage or similar round it. If you don't have a splint, just use a firm bandage.
- **Remove watches, rings, etc.** in case of swelling. Identify the snake if you can, but don't try and catch it, you will end up with (a) two snake bites or (b) two people with snake bites, depending on who goes after it.
- **Get medical help.** An anti-venom may be available. Symptoms usually develop within 12–24 hours.
- **All sea snakes are poisonous,** with no anti-venom available. Get medical attention quickly.
- **Don't drink alcohol,** it will make things worse.
- **Similarly aspirin will increase any bleeding tendency;** go for paracetamol instead.

Dr David Theakston of the Liverpool School of Tropical Medicine is encouraging on your chances of having to instigate any of the above actions. 'Really snakes are a problem for farmers, herdsmen, huntsmen and so on of the rural tropics. I suppose walkers are at a slightly higher risk, but snake bites among visitors are very, very rare.' The Arizona Poisons Unit nominated another category: 'Over 50 per cent of the snake bites we see are what we call illegitimate bites,' said a spokesperson. 'That is, it was not the snake's fault. People have a few drinks and go out to try and catch or taunt them. It's a potent mixture of alcohol and testosterone that makes them do it.'

So, although many catalogues feature various venom extractors, only the most incorrigible of herpetophobes or those who fancy having a drink and then catching their own pair of rattlesnake boots should consider packing one.

The hair of the dog

The risk of catching rabies for the traveller is sometimes exaggerated (though with estimates that between 4 and 7 per cent of street dogs are infected in Thailand, and 1–3 per cent of visitors bitten by dogs, more being just licked, these are quantifiable odds). A few years ago an Englishman bitten by a friend's dog in Thailand kept a diary of the disease's progress. It made terrifying reading, as the hydrophobia (which is caused by spasms of the throat muscles – victims even gag on their own saliva) took hold.

However, rabies can come from the most innocuous source. Hilary Bradt had a friend in Peru who was infected by what seemed like a playful puppy. He only knew what he had when fever and headache gave way to hydrophobia. By this stage it was too late to treat it, and death followed. In early 1994 a farmer was infected in the USA by a rabid cow; a year earlier an 11-year-old girl in New York State mysteriously died. Rabies was only diagnosed when a vigilant pathologist noticed tell-tale blood clots in the brain: she had no bite marks. She probably caught it from a raccoon (though there have also been cases in the USA of people going into caves and catching it from inhaling dried bat urine).

If you are bitten by (or even get a nasty lick from) a dog, bat, jackal, wolf, raccoon, fox, or even, given the farmer above, a suspiciously-acting cow, then treat the wound quickly, by cleaning under running water for 5 minutes and applying 40 per cent alcohol or irrigating with iodine solution. The virus is actually quite fragile.

You will then need two further rabies jabs **even if you have had a pre-**

exposure immunisation. (If you haven't had a pre-exposure immunisation you will need a course of seven injections, including a dose of rabies-specific gammaglobulin – rabies antibodies – half in your arm, half around the wound over a period of several months).

Even without the pre-exposure immunisation, it will still take time to move along to the brain (unless you are bitten on the face), so don't panic, just head straight off for medical help. Symptoms usually take at least 10 days to appear, normally 20–90, but treatment **must** begin before that.

Advice about caging the dog and waiting to see if it dies are not practicable for most travellers. Don't forget, even if the animal isn't rabid, there is a risk of tetanus unless you are protected.

Other mammals

Tetanus and other bacterial infection is the main risk from bites from camels and horses, and usually these occur when you have hired the animals. Camels in particular have vile mouths: and, of course, they are remarkably accurate spitters. And their saliva is decidedly unpleasant.

Note that there is always a risk of animal attack on safari, and not necessarily from those animals you anticipate being vicious. Lions and leopards rarely go for humans unless antagonised or startled. However, water buffaloes may have silly hairstyles, but they are extremely truculent. Their preferred method of killing is to knock you to the ground, stand on you, and use a sharp horn to open you up. Do not antagonise. If you leave your tent at night, always carry a torch, it will dissuade most animals from charging.

Similarly, hippos are not the cuddly creatures they seem: there have been instances of white-water rafting and canoeing going horribly wrong when hippos have surfaced under a craft. And remember, as the old safari hands say: 'Never come between a hippo and its water.

Other threats depend on the quality of your guide: choose carefully, particularly on the increasingly popular walking safari. You will find out why that long grass hiding God knows what is called adrenaline grass.

Note that in 1993 VSO lost a volunteer who was trampled to death by an elephant: it does happen.

Some animals can even get you when they are dead. There is a risk of anthrax from some goatskin handicrafts: spores were found in some drums from Haiti some years ago. However, it has to be said that the risks are very low.

Sea hazards

'My boyfriend stood straight onto a sea urchin and got a huge amount of spines in him. I started to panic, when a local came over and started pointing rather rudely. It took a few moments to realise he was suggesting I urinated on Mark's foot.' TV researcher Amelia Dare eventually retreated modestly behind a hut, where she filled a small bowl and brought it back to the scene of the accident.

Whether urine works or not, it is a common remedy for softening the spines of sea urchins, one of the most likely forms of holiday disaster at sea. The first few times it happened to me, I tried to dig the spines out, a frustrating experience because, first your leg and twisted foot aches after a while and second they splinter into little pieces rather than coming out whole. Although something of a nuisance, they do eventually get rejected by the body (the urine is supposed to speed up the process). They rarely go septic unless you are one of those people who have to keep worrying at them with a sharp instrument until infection sets in.

Pieces of coral embedded in you are much more likely to fester. These you *should* worry, removing even the smallest slivers and disinfecting the area. I remember I used to scoff at people who wore rubber sandals or flip-flops while in the sea. Having soles like pin cushions eventually changed my mind.

Sharks

It is hard to remember if sharks were quite so emotive a subject before *Jaws*, but I suspect they were. There is something fascinating and repellent about these primitive machines with soulless eyes, the very antithesis of the dolphin we invest with so much understanding.

In fact there are less than 30 shark deaths around the world per year, with only 100 reported attacks in total. (Of course, there may be a few others who never get the chance to report anything.) There are 350 species of shark. Only ten are recognised as likely to attack humans. Even in Australia, which most of us regard as a Swim-Thru snack bar for the Great White, there are only two deaths per year. The trouble is those two can be hideous. In 1993, Terri Cartwright's husband and five children watched from a boat while she was attacked and killed by a shark while preparing to dive off the Tasmanian coast. Such images tend to stick in the mind. If you are diving, you should always take local advice on what species are present and the chances of them liking humans.

Other fish

There are other fish which, instead of coming to get you, lie there waiting for you to find them and reap the consequences. These include weever fish (which occur in the UK and Europe), stonefish, lionfish, scorpionfish and stingrays. They may be in sand, they may be cunningly camouflaged across stones. Either way, they all hurt like hell, to the point where you may pass out. Vomiting, sweating and diarrhoea are not unusual. Removing the spines if discharged or broken off into the skin, putting the affected region in hot water and bathing with ammonia (which can mean our old friend urine again) are all said to relieve symptoms. Seek medical help. There is anti-venom available for some fish stings, but antibiotics may also be needed.

The usual advice if you have to go in the sea and you suspect something may be lurking, is to shuffle forward, kicking up the bottom or prodding with a stick to scare them off. My advice is, if you suspect they are out there, find a bar instead: your rubber flip-flops probably won't be much help against a thrashing stingray.

Jelly-fish

You don't have to see jelly-fish to be stung by them. In the last couple of years there has been an outbreak of 'sea bather's itch' or 'eruption' off the Florida Keys. This is caused by the larvae of the thimble jelly-fish, *Linuche unguiculata*, which when trapped inside bathing costumes panic, insofar as a coelenterate can panic, and discharge their nematocysts, the stinging cells that all jelly-fish come armed with.

Being small, these stings cause irritation and rashes. The best advice is not to wear tshirts or one-piece swimming garments, to shower after swimming and to wash bathing costumes in hot water and detergents.

The real danger from jelly-fish comes from the thimble's, uglier, meaner, brothers and sisters (sexing a jelly-fish isn't easy – they are often colonies of individuals). The most lethal is the box jelly-fish which lurks around Asia and the Pacific. Its sting can cause paralysis of the breathing muscles and, though an antivenom is available, first-aid, including mouth-to-mouth resuscitation and a tourniquet on the affected limb may be necessary. In Australia, there are 3–4 deaths per year from the box jelly-fish, more than from sharks, so treat it with respect.

Almost as horrible is the Portuguese Man O'War, which is widely distributed and pops up off the UK coast. It is distinguished by the big air sac above the water, and again, stinging is very severe. After a sting undischarged nematocysts can still be on the skin, and these will fire if rubbed or rinsed with fresh water. It is usually suggested that vinegar or alcohol are used, but sea water will do if they are not available.

Even dead jelly-fish can sting – the nematocysts are just little capsules with pressure triggers so don't mess with them on the beach, and take the mass presence of them washed ashore as an indication that there are plenty of live ones out there.

Other marine hazards

There are poisonous octopi (don't go shoving your hand into crevices), sea snakes (all venomous), cone shellfish (coloured tropical molluscs, again, all toxic) and sea slugs, not to mention barracuda and moray eels. Is this a good time to mention you are more likely to be run over by a bus than . . .?

13 Recreational hazards

Given the exotic nature of travel these days, it is surprising that the commonest causes of death among travellers remain so stubbornly mundane. The biggest cause of death among young people on holiday is trauma, that is various physical injuries to the body. Perhaps they dived into an empty swimming pool, or into the shallow end, or larked about on a low-railed balcony and fell off, or they went off on a hired moped without a crash helmet. Dr Marianne Janosi, Medical Advisor to the VSO, sees it all the time: 'About 10 per cent of our volunteers end up coming home for at least a short time. The vast majority of them have been involved in road accidents.'

People lower their guard while abroad, they think the normal rules don't apply, that coming off a bike on a Greek road is somehow less dangerous than one in Gloucester; that drink-driving is suddenly OK, when in fact it is more, not less dangerous, because you are driving in unfamiliar surroundings. And the statistics show that driving is often more erratic abroad: Italy was losing so many of its own and other countries' young people in late night car smashes a few years ago, it tried to introduce a 2am curfew on clubs; Portugal has 1008 deaths per million registered vehicles every year, the UK has 207. Anyone who has ever taken a Lisbon taxi will believe this.

Also, quite naturally, people on holiday want to try something more adventurous than they can get on a wet Saturday night in Slough, such as white-water rafting or paragliding. Fine, but be aware that adventurous sports may well not be covered by your insurance policy, so if you need airlifting or hospitalisation, you could end up with a very large bill. Commercial Union define a 'hazardous sport' as anything other than: surface water sports, golf, fell walking, fishing, parascending (over water), pony trekking, rambling, tennis, badminton, archery or beach games.

This chapter is not meant to put the dampeners on fun, just point out some of the ways in which it can backfire.

The water

In the UK drowning is the third most common cause of death from accidental injury for all age groups, following road accidents and burns. In 1993, 496 people drowned in the UK, with lakes, rivers and canals presenting the most hazardous swimming environments.

Being abroad introduces a fresh set of hazards into the equation: unfamiliar surroundings, alcohol (it is estimated that 60 per cent of all boating fatalities involve raised alcohol levels), parasites and large carnivorous animals. Rebecca Kirkwood of the Royal Society for the Prevention of Accidents (RoSPA) summed up the main problem: 'It's usually, although not exclusively, the 15 to 30-year-old male, and alcohol is usually involved.'

Swimming pools

In a survey of a Midlands spinal unit, it was found that 10 per cent of admissions were from people who had dived into pools, many of them breaking their necks. In 1989, for instance, Glen Wawman saw people frolicking in his hotel pool in Cyprus, and dived in to join them. The frolickers knew there was a hidden ledge, but newly-arrived Glen had never been in before. He broke his neck and is paralysed.

In 1992, 17-year-old Joanne Todd went swimming in the hotel pool in Crete in the early hours after a party; 12 hours later her body was found on the bottom of the hotel pool (the pool was clean, but the dark green tiles reduced visibility). Swimming alone, at night, especially after alcohol is not recommended. It is not a uniquely British problem; one report from a Pittsburgh hospital (Journal of Trauma, 36: 349-51) looked at 46 men and 12 women who had spinal injuries due to diving into water. The average age was 23, and 41 had major cervical injuries, 22 had blood alcohol levels of more than 100 mg/100 dl, and only one in 15 had no trace of alcohol in their blood. 'Miscalculating the water's depth' was given as the main cause of accidents.

RoSPA have warned about inadequate pools in Corfu, the Algarve, Cyprus and across the developing world, where resorts are being built in areas with few local safety standards. Things to watch out for include:

- **Paddling pools built adjacent to the deep end of the pool:** toddlers go from 6 inches to 6 feet of water in no time at all.
- **No depth markings on the pool.** Ask someone; don't use yourself as a human dipstick by diving in. In fact, on your first exploration, always go in feet first (where there are depth marks they are often woefully inadequate).
- **Turbidity.** Can you see the bottom? Every year toddlers are discovered lying at the bottom of murky pools, where nobody has spotted them.
- **Is it adequately chlorinated?** Is it cleaned regularly?
- **For a poolside dive you need at least 1.5 m of water.** If there is a 1 m springboard the pool should be 3 m deep, and that depth should extend forward for more than 5 m, unlikely in some of the tiny pools hoteliers put in.
- **Are there lifebelts or poles?** Important if you have kids running around.
- **Just because there are lifeguards, don't rely on them.** Lifeguards are often there to preen, rather than keep a proper look out. I blame *Baywatch*.
- **Check the poolside tiles.** If they are broken or rutted or slippery, keep children away. Keep away yourself if there are any sharp surfaces.
- **Don't go out for that secret midnight dip,** chances are it will last a lot longer than you are expecting.

The sea

You may think it is the Great White Shark that is going to get you, but the chances are that it will be the undertow. Don't swim alone, or from beaches where there is nobody to check safety with, even if it is just someone who has swum from that particular beach before. And check that the person understands what you are asking: they may be nodding vigorously, thinking you have enquired if this is the Great White's breeding ground, where Portuguese Men-O'War and stonefish also gather.

Don't swim after a big meal (much of your blood will be around your alimentary canal, dealing with the food, rather than in your muscles, so cramp is more likely), or after alcohol, and don't think your crawl is any better in Thailand than it was at home – don't swim beyond your ability. Make sure you understand the local flag system.

Unfortunately, there are other dangers than currents and tides. Many of the world's seas are dumping grounds for industrial and human waste. An estimated 200 million gallons of sewage are dumped each year off Bondi Beach. The UK has 1000 sewage outlets around its coast, and 40 per cent of them pump out completely untreated human waste. It is little wonder that 1 in 20 bathers is likely to pick up something from the water around our shores. The problem has got so bad that an organisation called Surfers Against Sewage was formed when the surfers got tired of eye, ear and stomach problems ruining their sport.

The Mediterranean has similar problems, exacerbated by the fact that to all intents and purposes it is a closed environment – things kick around the Med for decades before it is their turn to be shunted out through the Straits of Gibraltar. However, much has been done to cut the amount of pollution; the water around the Balearics is noticeably cleaner than a decade ago, and the islands have 69 blue flags. Most Greek islands are OK; there was a problem in Lindos, Rhodes a few years back, but coincidentally, the same month it was highlighted in the *Sunday Times*, a new sewage plant was given the go-ahead (which, unfortunately, at the time of writing had not even been started).

There are still problems. In 1992 the sea water around Naples was found to contain levels of pollutants 150 times higher than recommended under Italian law; though the French Riviera has 129 blue flags, Cannes still fails the tests miserably; the cities and resorts of the Med pump out 2 billion tons of sewage annually; and busy Rimini has but one sewage plant to try and cope with its influx of summer visitors.

Italy has also suffered badly from algal blooms, such as those off the Adriatic Coast in the 1980s. The 'blooms' are not as pretty as the name suggests, they are an explosion in the population of microscopic organisms due to high levels of nutrients from sewage and/or industrial run-off. Contact can cause nausea, headache, vomiting, itchiness, and eye and skin problems. Avoid swimming where there is visible algal scum.

The toxins produced by such blooms are also concentrated by shellfish. There is disease called paralytic shellfish poisoning, which does sound like you have eaten too many molluscs while drunk, but is somewhat more serious than that. If you are in an area where blooms are reported or self-evident by scummy water or evil looking deposits on the beach, go carnivorous or vegetarian for a while.

Fresh water

It is another Hollywood cliché, the dip in the remote pool, clothes piled high next to a cascading waterfall. I blame Johnny Weissmuller, Paul Hogan and Levis ads. However, unless you have good local knowledge, avoid spur-of-the-moment dips in rivers and lakes. In Africa it isn't worth the risk of bilharzia or schistosomiasis (or swimmers' itch, when larvae from the avian version burrow into the skin and die) or antagonising the local hippo, water buffalo or crocodile population. Use chlorinated pools. Similarly take local advice in South and Central America, Asia and India. And just in case the legend of the candiru fish is true, don't wade into the Amazon to urinate. (Redmond O'Hanlon during his Venezuelan trip clearly believed it, fantasising: 'You have to get to a hospital before your bladder bursts; you must ask a surgeon to cut off your penis.')

It isn't just the tropics. Leptospirosis (Weil's disease), a bacterial infection carried in animal urine, is a risk worldwide. It is caused by a spirochaete that lives in dogs, pigs, cattle, rats and raccoons. Naturally there is some ignominy about catching a disease caused by rat urine. It is a hazard to workers in rice and sugar-cane fields, abattoirs and dairies. There were 29 cases in the UK in 1988, 15 in 1990. Travellers who are camping and bathing in local streams are the most likely to get it; if the water is polluted with infected animal urine, the organism can enter the bloodstream through the skin, particularly if there are cuts. The most bizarre cases I have heard of were British servicemen and women who contracted it while taking part in the annual mud-wrestling festival on the island of Lantau, Hong Kong. It causes recurring chills, fever, muscle ache and eventually jaundice and anaemia. Doxycycline treats it, just get to a doctor. It can be mis-diagnosed as meningitis.

Watersports

Scuba-diving is one of the great growth sports around the world, as people learn you do not have to practise for hours on end in your local pool and some freezing gravel pit, but can be taught at Eilat in Israel, Cairns or the Cayman islands. There are all sorts of environmental concerns with diving, including destruction of reefs by dive boats and by sheer pressure of numbers, but as far as safety is concerned make sure you chose an outfit that is recognised by an international diving association, such as the British Sub-Aqua Club or PADI (Professional Association of Diving Instructors).

White-water rafting is another popular add-on to holidays, and one that has no international regulatory body to allay your concerns. A few years ago the *Sunday Times* received a letter from a father whose daughter had died during a rafting expedition in Africa. It highlighted the misconception that because a sport or activity is 'packaged', people often don't realise it can be dangerous, until, as they are getting into the raft, a waiver is presented absolving the company of all responsibility if you should drown (and again your own insurance may be void). The woman in this case was worried, but peer group pressure got her into the raft. She drowned attempting to swim to shore when the crew and passengers abandoned the raft, after it had become trapped in a whirlpool.

There are, of course, many reputable adventure outfits, and many thousands of safe trips are undertaken every year, it is just worth noting that, like bungy jumping or mountain climbing, there is a substantial element of risk.

Canoeing would seem to have just the one major risk associated with it – drowning. In fact, in the UK the British Canoe Union also recognise that there is a one in 200,000 chance of a canoeist developing Weil's disease (see above); the chances are much higher in areas such as the Caribbean.

The trouble with sex

You can bring back more from your holiday romance than a broken heart . . .

HIV and AIDS

One estimate I was given suggested that over 30 per cent of male visitors have sex with locals in Thailand which, given that 20 per cent or more of all Thai prostitutes are believed to be HIV positive, is a daunting statistic. Whether accurate or not, Thailand certainly now has the highest AIDS rate in South-East Asia.

At one time casual sex carried with it the risk of a dose of gonorrhoea, or, if you were really unlucky, syphilis or a lifetime of herpes to carry around with you. Nowadays, there is the risk of infection with HIV, with hepatitis B as the second prize. However, as with all the potential problems in this book, the danger has to be put in perspective. The average traveller can, by simple actions, avoid 'high risk behaviour', and it is certainly not worth avoiding a country because of its HIV/AIDS statistics. Remember, too, that AIDS is a global disease and the advice applies just as much in the UK as it does on the road.

It is hard to believe that it is only just over a decade since most of us first heard of this mystery virus which was first identified in 1983. At first of course it was dubbed the 'gay plague', but it soon became apparent that drug users, people with haemophilia, organ transplant patients and Haitians were getting it too. And soon there were cases among heterosexuals who were contracting the virus through sexual contact. These days it is recognised that heterosexual transmission is responsible for the majority of the world's HIV infection.

If you are infected with the virus, your body develops antibodies to it, which are detectable after a few months (HIV positive). We now know that the virus weakens the bodies' defence (immune) system and this allows some other infections and cancers to become life-threatening, though someone with HIV may be asymptomatic for many years. The good news is that the virus is very fragile, HIV is not as infectious as, say, hepatitis B, and there are only a very few ways that the virus can gain access to your bloodstream. Block those, and HIV is no longer a threat.

HIV prevention

The WHO estimates that there are 14–15 million people with HIV or AIDS worldwide. It isn't just a disease of the developing world. It was, of course, first discovered in the USA, and the number of people infected with HIV is growing in Europe and Asia as well as Africa, where the lack of good health systems or money for prevention escalates the scale of the problem. In some African countries infection rates are estimated to be a quarter of the population (it may even be more some countries do under-report their cases). However, as the transmission routes are well understood, a few simple precautions can diminish the risk considerably.

- **Make sure any penetrative sex you have (vaginal or anal, homosexual or heterosexual) is safer sex,** that is you or your partner using a condom where appropriate. It is, of course, easy, but unrealistic, to simply say avoid sex with anyone who is infected with the virus – it is impossible to tell from appearances, and they may not know themselves.
- **The condom figures large in protection against HIV, so make sure you buy from a reputable source and that, if possible, they have a British Standard kite mark or other national equivalent.** Condoms that have been exposed to UV light (e.g. on market stalls) become brittle and fragile, so get them from chemists or family planning clinics. Condoms are not infallible: you should check the expiry date or, if there isn't one, the date of manufacture; it is probably best to discard condoms over a year old. Store them in a cool place (yes, a fridge will do). Given that the size also varies around the world, it is probably best that men, for their own comfort if nothing else, should take a good supply of the make they trust, know and love. Men (well, really, everyone) should know how to put one on. A report in France concluded that the vast majority of 41 brands tested had inadequate directions. If you don't know how to use one, it is probably best to practise at a less pressured moment than when they are actually needed.
- **Use condoms every time you have sex,** put the condom on before things

hot up too much (i.e. before the penis gets anywhere near a vagina or anus). If it breaks at any stage, replace it with a fresh one. After ejaculation, withdraw the penis, holding the condom at the base, then remove condom.

- **To quote from the UK NGO AIDS Consortium for the Third World** (though, again, it is worth noting that AIDS is not exclusively a problem for developing countries): 'Reducing partners reduces the risk of unknowingly being infected by a person who does not know, and probably has no special reason to suspect he or she is infected.' Of course, prostitutes have numerous sexual partners, and their behaviour may put them at high risk infection rates among female prostitutes in some cities are estimated to top 80 per cent. Just be aware that you are shifting the odds if you have sex with multiple partners or sex with someone who has had multiple partners.
- **Don't rely on someone's word that they don't have HIV,** even if they have recently had a test. It is estimated that about half the people with HIV in the UK do not know they have got it. Use that condom.
- **Non-penetrative sex is generally a very safe alternative.** Kissing, masturbation, mutual masturbation, etc. are all relatively risk-free as long as there is no broken skin or damaged gums, etc. Only an exchange of bodily fluids (blood, semen, vaginal fluids) can transmit the virus. Oral sex is thought to be less risky than vaginal or anal sex, but still carries some risk.
- **Avoid sharing injecting equipment such as needles and syringes.** If this is not possible make sure that they are sterilised by washing through with bleach and rinsing with water.
- **While the risk from sharing toothbrushes and razors is fairly low, it is good general health advice to avoid sharing them,** mainly because of the risk of other infections.
- **Do not consider body piercing, tattooing or acupuncture unless you are certain needles are sterilised.**
- **Blood transfusions should be avoided if at all possible.** The most likely reason for needing one is road accidents. The VSO say that road accidents are the commonest reason for expatriates needing blood transfusions and that simply wearing a seat belt considerably reduces the chances of sustaining an injury serious enough to require one. You may,

of course, be in a country where seat belts are not usually worn: try not to slip into their ways.

If you are in an accident you can lose up to 20 per cent of your blood without needing to be topped up. Above that volume you need volume as much as blood, which is why the WHO recommends, where possible, that synthetic 'plasma expanders' be used in place of blood. These carry no HIV risk, and do not need group matching. However, they may not always be available.

- **If you do need blood and have time, the Blood Care Foundation offers a service** (£5 per month, £30 per annum, plus family and corporate deals) whereby they will courier screened blood to you. This is not much use, however, if you have just had a car smash, lost 40 per cent of your blood and need an immediate transfusion to live. Make sure you know your blood group, and try to get someone to contact the nearest embassy or consulate (or your medical assistance company), who will probably know a source of screened blood. Even if the blood you are given is not screened, it is by no means certain it will be infected, and it will probably be needed to save your life.
- **Dental procedures are also a risk factor:** have a check-up before you leave, or check out sterilisation procedures at the dentist. Ask for your own syringes and needles to be used for injections (though you are unlikely to be travelling with dental burrs and drills, which may be contaminated). Sometimes, toothache may seem the better option (there are dental first aid kits, but unfortunately they are not going to help much if you need root canal work).
- **There is *no* evidence that HIV can be spread by mosquitoes or leeches,** nor are you at risk from normal social intercourse, such as handshakes, with someone with HIV. So unless you share a needle with them, or have unprotected sex, you can treat anyone with HIV as you would anyone else.
- **Alcohol screws up your judgement:** try to remember to use that condom.

Note that some countries are demanding an 'AIDS certificate' (or, more accurately, an 'HIV-free certificate'), before allowing long-stay aid workers and the like in. The WHO along with a number of governments have taken the line that there are no health reasons to 'discriminate solely on the basis of a person's HIV status', and that there is no public health risk. However, you don't want to be arguing the fine print of WHO policy with some stroppy border official; check whether your destination requires a certificate. Unlike yellow fever, there is no standard certificate, so you must also check what sort of paperwork they require. Also note that some countries will not accept outside testing: again, insist on your own syringes and needles. And it is worth re-iterating that you should not trust someone waving a certificate as a means of protection: use a condom, not a piece of stamped paper.

The HIV-prevention kit

'I was in Phuket, Thailand. I cut my thumb in the bathroom, almost to the bone. I started to pass out and staggered into the bedroom, grabbed a syringe and needle, and called for help. I woke up in a gleaming new medical centre, much more sterile than anything at home, all stitched up, with my syringe neatly laid, unused, next to me.'

Rob Follis, a globe-trotting scuba diver, was lucky his accident happened in a well-developed tourist area with good medical facilities and because, if it hadn't been quite so squeaky clean, he was near his sterile syringe. It illustrates one of the main problems with so-called 'AIDS kits' (really 'HIV-prevention kits') you must have them with you when the incident occurs if they are to be any use. If you are in a car accident and unconscious, you can hardly say, 'The transfusion kit is under my socks in the drawer. Room 101.' If you are unsure of local medical facilities should anything go wrong, **carry the kit with you**. You cannot predict things such as road accidents.

The advantage of commercially available kits is they don't make you look like you are a drug user. Some kits have customs letters with them, or the clinic gives a covering letter, which may be uncharitably interpreted as: 'This traveller does not trust your unclean Third World medical provisions', but that's better than 'Big Time Smack User', which may well be the spin some irascible officials will put on a selection of needles in an unmarked bag.

Expect to pay around £7–20 for a kit containing syringes, needles (you want a drip needle intravenous canula – as well), sutures, dressings and swabs, and some also contain sterile gloves, plastic tubing and bags. The dressings and sutures are just as important as the syringes as you are more likely to need treatment for cuts and grazes than anything else. Explanations to doctors in several languages are also a good idea.

SafariQuip offers a basic kit with two syringes and five needles plus swabs, dressings etc., neatly packaged, for £7.99. Homeway adds dental needle and gloves and three syringes/five needles for £12, and MASTA has ten needles, four syringes and dressings, etc. for £13.50.

Although larger kits with plasma expanders are available, it is rather impractical and unnecessary for most travellers to take synthetic bodily fluids with them, unless it is a large expedition. SAFA offers an expedition kit with plasma expanders, as well as less extreme supplies. All the other clinics and mail-order firms mentioned throughout the book have kits, and you can also try InterHealth, Call of the Wild and Travel Medical Centre.

Other STDs

After HIV and AIDS everything else seems like a reprieve, but there are other sexually transmitted diseases (STDs) that can blight your stay. On offer are hepatitis B, gonorrhoea, chlamydia, herpes, trichomoniasis, and a few others including pubic lice. Note that having an STD increases the chances of passing on or picking up HIV because of the various sores and blisters, etc. The usual rules about choosing sexual partners, washing genitals and urinating after intercourse (whatever happened to lighting a cigarette?) may help prevent STDs, though the only foolproof way is abstention or monogamy.

If you do catch an STD, avoid sexual activity during treatment, and make sure you inform anyone you have had sex with (they may have caught it and not know, which can be dangerous). If you are travelling with a regular sexual partner you should both be treated, even if one is asymptomatic, otherwise you could be locked into a cycle of re-infection, with the STD bouncing back and forth.

Note that STDs are often difficult to detect in women, where they can very quietly cause pelvic inflammatory disease and infertility.

Never try and self-treat STDs, its not worth playing around with the antibiotics.

There are over 20 known STDs. These are the commonest:

Hepatitis B is a nasty liver disease, similar to hepatitis A, but more chronic. It gives rise to jaundice and lethargy, possibly death. You can be immunised against it, but once you have it there is no real cure other than letting the disease run its course. In many countries 20 per cent or more of the population may be carriers. Note that there is also a hepatitis C (from intravenous drug use, transfusions and sexual contact), D and E (from contaminated water) for which the immunisation is not effective, so take care even if you have received the A and B immunisation. There is also probably F, G, H, etc. out there.

Gonorrhoea: Look for pain on urinating and penile discharge of pus (in women it may be asymptomatic for some time). If untreated it rolls out a cavalcade of symptoms including swelling, rashes and sterility. It can be treated with antibiotics (though some strains are a bit more tenacious than others).

Chlamydia is not only similar to, but often concurrent with gonorrhoea. It may lead to PID (pelvic inflammatory disease) in women, but again the symptoms of discharge and pain are more likely to be seen in males. Antibiotics will do the trick.

Herpes was the last major sexual horror story before AIDS, mainly because you have it for life. It starts with small fluid-filled blisters, more noticeable in males, which turn into sores. They are accompanied by flu-like symptoms. The first attack is usually the worst (and may be the last) episode. Drugs can relieve the symptoms, but will not cure it. Note that there can be oral-genital cross-infection from cold sores.

Syphilis: Big before antibiotics, this begins with a chancre (sore) on the genitals, followed by rash and fever some time later, followed by insanity and death. Antibiotics can cure as long as you know you have it.

Trichomoniasis: Much more symptomatic in women, giving a nasty discharge and painful urination and possibly itching (men get off with light discharge). 'Trich' is a protozoan, and can be treated with Flagyl, the same drug as for amoebic dysentery (again, do not self-treat).

Nongonococcal urethritis (NGU): This used to be called non-specific urethritis (NSU). This is anything that gives symptoms similar to gonorrhoea, but is not caused by it. Get treatment, as there can be complications in both men and women.

Other STDs include *Lymphogranuloma venereum*, which causes lesions and probably ulcers; chancroid; and *Granuloma inguinale* (also known as Donovanosis – and is a common STD in Papua New Guinea). Have any odd new growths or lesions investigated.

Other urinary/genital infections are, according to travel insurance medical claims, very common. These are bacterial, yeast or protozoan infections *not* caused by sexual intercourse, which may cause burning, itching or blood or pus in the urine in severe cases. Thrush is probably the commonest, though it is unlikely that most cases show up on medical claims, and can be treated with Canesten. There are a number of other bacterial and protozoan infections which need to be treated with drugs if they persist. Keeping clean and drinking plenty of fluids (for that all-important 'flushing' action) are recommended.

Drugs

Try and avoid even thinking about illegal substances where the tourist board literature says in the small print 'The penalty for drug smuggling is death'. Singapore, Malaysia, China and Thailand all frown upon free enterprise when it comes to narcotics. No Briton has been acquitted of a drugs offence in Thailand for more than 20 years.

There are places where it is legal to experiment: in cosmopolitan cities such as Amsterdam, or if the drug is in its legal native form, such as coca-leaf tea in South America (in Bolivia you can even get a primeval form of cola drinks – with the cocaine left in) or chewing khat or qat in the Yemen and parts of Africa.

Your prudence should also apply to Muslim countries and alcohol. Expats have their way around alcohol-hating regimes, but even they occasionally get caught out, resulting in imprisonment or corporal punishment. (In May 1994, a Briton was given 50 lashes in Qatar for alleged alcohol offences.) When it comes to breaking local mores, just say no.

14 Special cases

There are some cases where travel needs to be modified to take account of special circumstances, some permanent, some temporary.

Travelling with disabilities

There is no doubt that some countries make far better provision for travellers with a variety of physical disabilities: wheelchair-users are brilliantly catered for in many parts of the USA and Canada, to an extent that puts Europe to shame. Elsewhere, provision ranges from patchy to non-existent. However, whether the country is full of ramps or not, it seems little deters the more determined disabled from getting out there. For evidence read *Nothing Ventured*, a *Rough Guide* book devoted to the globe-trotting adventures of disabled travellers. It is enough to make the most fit, able-bodied person feel like a total wimp in comparison. Another series of books called Smooth Rides (FT Publishing, £9.99) looks at the provision for wheelchair travellers in various countries, including Australia and New Zealand, the USA and Canada, with more on the way.

A good place to start planning your assault on the world is the Royal Association for Disability and Rehabilitation (RADAR), who produce two useful books, *Holidays for Disabled People* and *Holidays and Travel Abroad.* The Disabled Living Foundation not only offers leaflets, but gives advice and contacts for further advice. Try also the Holiday Care Service. The Disabled Drivers' Association advises on driving holidays and access to car parks and buildings in towns and cities. The Spinal Injuries Association is also a good source of information.

Pregnancy

When I discovered my wife was pregnant, I cancelled our two forthcoming trips, one to India and the other to out-of-the-way Mexico. This wasn't a typical 'Sit down and take the weight off your feet' reaction, just a case of risk management.

I knew there were all sorts of problems, for example that malaria was much more dangerous in pregnancy, that certain live immunisations are proscribed, that various antibiotics and anti-diarrhoea treatments are untenable during pregnancy. That, plus the thought of being in the Baja California desert when something went wrong (miscarriages are more likely during the first 3 months) persuaded me that, all things considered, this was an exciting enough event without gilding the lily.

In fact, we did eventually travel, to Miami South Beach and to the Everglades, where it turned out the mosquitoes well, not all of them – were carrying eastern equine encephalitis.

Having said that, I know of women who have happily travelled to Pakistan, India, Africa and South America while pregnant and thought very little of it (though the one who gave birth prematurely in Caracas said her mother wasn't too pleased to miss the happy event).

Generally speaking, the following rules apply:

- **If you must travel great distances, try and make it between 18 and 26 weeks,** when the worst of morning sickness has worn off, and before the airline seats seem even smaller than usual. Note that most airlines will not permit travel after a certain date (32, 34 or 35 weeks depending on route and airline). If you just *look* as if you are about to give birth any minute, take a doctor's letter to checkin. Note that many insurance policies insert various disclaimers regarding pregnancy, e.g. with Commercial Union's you are not covered for 'any event which is the result of pregnancy or childbirth, where the pregnancy has extended for more than 28 weeks'.
- **In August 1990 *Conde Naste Traveler* carried a piece on the risk of radiation exposure to pregnant women, or more accurately, the unborn child, during long-haul flights.** It highlighted the fact that exposure to cosmic radiation at 35,000 feet is 100 times greater than at ground level. As with any radiation risk, there are differing opinions on this. One doctor I spoke to dismissed the advice not to take long flights

in the first 3 months of pregnancy (when the foetus is most vulnerable) as alarmist. British Airways pointed out to me that the International Commission on Radiological Protection suggest a maximum dose for pregnant women of 2 millisieverts to the abdomen during the entire 9 months. BA estimate that on a very long flight, say Narita (Tokyo) to London, passengers receive 0.12 mSv on average (solar flare activity can increase this, as can flying on Concorde). The risks may be low, but there are no absolutes in this area, just one more statistical gamble to add to the list.

- **Malaria prophylaxis is essential,** as the disease is more serious in pregnancy, and substantially increases the risk of complications and miscarriage. However, the current wonderdrug mefloquine (Lariam) as a prophylactic is out of the question for the first trimester (and don't get pregnant for 3 months after taking a course). Chloroquine and proguanil are considered safe, as is Maloprim (though a folate supplement will be needed if taking proguanil or Maloprim). Remember no regime is 100 per cent effective, so there is still a chance of getting the disease. Avoid being bitten: use nets and a natural repellent such as Mosi-Guard, Mosi-Milk or Gurhka. Better still, go somewhere non-malarious. It's a big world.
- **Avoid anti-diarrhoeal preparations such as Pepto-Bismol, which may cause bleeding.** Do not use powerful drugs such as Flagyl or antibiotics unless the illness is more threatening than the drug.
- **You need to ensure your immunisations for measles and rubella were up to date before you got pregnant.** These diseases are more prevalent in developing countries. Live immunisations, which include measles and rubella, are not generally given to a pregnant woman. Other live immunisations include oral polio (though some authorities are happy to recommend this, as there is an alternative, an injection, which is not a live immunisation), BCG, oral typhoid and yellow fever. Try and avoid high altitude holidays. The dehydration, lack of oxygen, etc. can be dangerous to mother and child.
- **Good food and water hygiene is more essential than ever.** Hepatitis E appears to be widespread across sub-Saharan Africa, Asia and has appeared in Mediterranean countries and central America. Though relatively uncommon, it is lethal in about 15–20 per cent of cases of

women who catch it in the second two-thirds of their pregnancy. Drink bottled water. Avoid unpasteurised milk/cheese (danger of listeriosis).

- **If travelling late in pregnancy try and identify a hospital with decent maternity facilities,** including emergency resuscitation facilities for newborn babies. The British Consulate should be able to advise. If it is your first child, think again.

Travel with kids

There is one irrefutable argument for starting your children off travelling young: up until the age of two they go free on airlines. Even better, get them moving while they are still being breast-fed: it saves on all that sterilisation equipment, and of course, immunity to many diseases is conferred through mother's milk. Airlines such as Virgin will let you pre-book bulkhead seats and offer 'Skycots' to lay the baby in.

That is not to say that every trip is perfect. When the *Sunday Times* asked for opinions on travelling with children, an awful lot of replies were very succinct: 'Don't'.

While ways of avoiding the 'Are we nearly there yet?' syndrome is beyond the scope of this book, health considerations are not.

Apart from boredom, the only health threat on flights is the pressure change at take-off and landing, which can cause distress, particularly in children too young to understand the 'swallow' command. Use sweets to get them to equalise their inner ears unconsciously.

Bear in mind that, as with adults, you will have visions of entomological horrors invading your child's body, but the most crucial thing to watch out for is accidents. Safety standards of swimming pools and balconies (low rails, or with big enough gaps for them to crawl through are not uncommon) may not be what you expect. Holiday apartments have a nasty habit of being separated from the beach by a mini-Monaco grand prix circuit, with inadequate underpasses (though this has improved in Spain, along the notorious Costa del Sol coastal road).

The chances are that what children get at home (coughs, diarrhoea, slight fever, toothache and, very commonly, sunburn) they will get abroad, only you will worry more because it might be something alien.

If venturing out of main tourist resorts in developing countries, make sure your child is fully immunised. Regardless of your destination they should be up to date with diphtheria, pertussis (whooping cough), tetanus, Hib, polio and mumps, measles and rubella (MMR). In addition, if staying for a lengthy period in a country where TB is common, consider the BCG immunisation (normally given at 12 years, but can be done at birth: there is strong evidence to suggest it is at its most useful in childhood). The Japanese B encephalitis and meningitis immunisations can also be given if required (the latter especially if attending local schools or mixing with the population in any way; it only protects against A & C, and B is the most common, though Hib dominates in the Indian sub-continent).

Children can be immunised against typhoid (18 months), yellow fever (9 months) and rabies (1 year; toddlers, being at dog level, may be vulnerable). There is junior Havrix immunisation for hep A, which can be given from 12 months (though it is a relatively mild disease in childhood, and infers lifelong immunity). Hepatitis B is a disease that infects children by some unknown route in many developing countries, so your child should be immunised if mixing with locals (but not under 3 years). It should be stressed that most holidaymakers will not need to pump their kids with this entire battery of immunisations (though those going deep expat may), and careful consultation with the clinic about countries and types of resorts is advisable.

One disease that should be taken seriously is malaria, which is much more dangerous in children than in adults. Unlike many diseases, breast-feeding offers no protection, so preventative measures must be taken from birth. Note that babies and children have a large surface area to volume ratio compared to adults, so be careful about applying repellents. DEET is not recommended for undersixes because a high percentage of it will be absorbed: use something like Mosi-Guard, X-Gnat or Gurkha instead.

Use also insecticide-impregnated nets, room sprays and malaria prophylaxis. All the major drugs can be used on children (though mefloquine is not recommended for under-twos, doxycycline not under 12 years) at a fraction of the dose calculated by weight and age. Chloroquine is available as a syrup, which can be mixed with sugar-free fruit drinks to help take away the bitter taste; it is also easier to measure than the alternative of trying to sneak in crushed tablets. People who have no experience of giving tablets to children, may be familiar with trying to fool cats into taking worming tablets. Well, its equally challenging. As with adults, the regime must be started one week before departure, continuing for four afterwards. Malaria must be eliminated if any flu-like symptoms develop within 3 months of return (or while away if extended stay), and should be considered a possibility up to one year later. (See Chapter 5 for more information and details of children's malarial prophylaxis.)

Other infections/diseases to watch out for include meningitis, which can be very difficult to recognise: the early signs mimic flu, or it can come on quickly. Nor do all the symptoms appear at once.

In babies watch for:

- **high temperature**
- **fretfulness**
- **vomiting**
- **refusing feeds**
- **high-pitched moaning cry**
- **child being difficult to wake**
- **pale or blotchy skin colour.**

In older children watch for:

- **headache**
- **fever and vomiting**
- **stiffness in neck**
- **pains in joints**
- **drowsiness or confusion**
- **dislike of bright lights**
- **rash of red/purple spots or bruises.**

Toddlers are at slightly greater risk of rabies because of their height, and their tendency to pet animals. Swimming in anything other than chlorinated pools may carry risks of parasites (e.g. bilharzia) in many countries.

Of all these, diarrhoea is the most likely to strike. It is essential to treat the fluid loss, using oral rehydration salts (ORS), which should be part of your travel health kit. Anti-diarrhoeal drugs are not a good idea, and may be potentially dangerous. Most are not recommended under the age of 12.

Diabetes

There are two forms of diabetes, one which requires insulin injections and one which can be controlled by tablets. The former presents more of a problem when travelling, because of the need to transport and store insulin, but none of the problems are anything like insurmountable, unless you insist the itinerary includes a long spell in the Nullarbor Plain. (Note that VSO and some other organisations will not take insulin-dependent diabetics in most cases, because of the risk of diarrhoea etc. upsetting dosages).

The first thing to do is ensure you have identification as a diabetic, such as a card from the British Diabetic Association (BDA) or the Medic Alert bracelet. The BDA ID will take up to 28 days to arrive. Check your travel insurance, many standard policies have exclusions for pre-existing medical conditions, and you could find yourself having to pay a hefty chunk – or even all – of any medical bills. (Douglas Cox Tyrie and Leisurecare both have policies for diabetics.)

When flying you must also order your meal in advance – allow at least 72 hours. Remember to pack plenty of spare needles, syringes, test strips, glucose and glucagon and, of course, enough insulin to allow for breakages. (If you do have to obtain insulin abroad, which is widely available, do check the strength carefully – 80 and 40, rather than 100 units per ml may be on offer).

Do not pack your insulin in your suitcase. There may be delays at the airport, and you will need it, or it may be damaged by the low temperatures in the hold. Insulin keeps fine for up to 3 months (check manufacturer's recommendations) as long as it is below 25°C. On arrival, try and store it in a fridge (not freezer – make sure there is no language confusion over this) or a cool dark place. Special insulated containers are available. Discard any insulin which becomes cloudy or lumpy over time.

The main concern on a long journey will be the change in time zones, which is confusing enough for the body, without the added complications of timing injections. The BDA's advice is simple: stay calm. A slight rise or fall in blood sugar is likely, but this is fine over a short period. 'Hypos' are very uncommon on planes. There is plenty of food on offer, and little chance to burn up your sugar. (Note that vomiting, due to motion sickness perhaps, may cause a hypo: test regularly if being sick, and use motion sickness tablets. Similarly anti-diarrhoeal preparations may be, for once, a good idea).

Check your blood sugar levels frequently. You need to find out flight and arrival times to work out the duration of the flight, and whether you will need insulin during it. If you are worried about calculations, leave your watch on local time and take and test as usual. You can always adjust to destination time over a period of days, lengthening time between injections on travelling west (when a small additional dose may be required), shortening if travelling east.

Again, on arrival test frequently: the change of climate and diet will affect your blood sugar level, making it more likely to go down. Carry glucose.

Guidelines for diabetic travellers are issued by the BDA. They also have information sheets on insulin availability (60p each) and translations of common questions for 78 countries.

Backache

People in the USA takes the curse of back pain more seriously than we do in the UK. The Arthritis and Back Pain Centre at the Swezey Institute in Santa Monica runs a course on 'packing mechanics' and other preventative measures for the traveller with back trouble. The main advice appears to be, make sure you get a firm mattress, which isn't always easy. The institute also recommends you:

- **Try and maximise legroom on planes so you can stretch.** If you can't wangle business class, try for bulkhead seats or ones by emergency exits (though airlines insist you be fit if you are the nearest to the way out). You may be able to pre-book your seat before check-in.
- **Get up and move around every 45–50 minutes** (an aisle seat may be preferable if you don't want to seriously rile your neighbour).
- **Use two lighter suitcases rather than one heavy,** it will help in balance. Use trollies.
- **Unpack clothes, toiletries, etc. on to high shelves** to minimise the amount of bending you have to do.
- **Adjust driving positions.** Advice varies. I am more comfortable with arms stretched out, but some experts suggest back sufferers almost hug the wheel. Whatever your position, stop the car and stretch every hour.
- **If you have an attack, lie down.** Use ice to cool the back, followed by pain killers or anti-inflammatory drugs.
- **If you have difficulty urinating or numbness or shooting pains in one or both legs, be very careful,** this could be a sign that a disc has gone (or is about to go) or that this is a sciatica attack. Seek medical advice; don't lift that suitcase.
- **Various cushions and back supports may help:** try The Back Shop.

15 If you are ill

The first thing to remember is that, should you get ill in Europe, your E1-11 form gives you cover in EC countries. It does not, however, give complete cover: in France you get 75 per cent of medical bills refunded, in Portugal patients have to pay for their X-rays, laboratory costs and their food. Refunds may be obtainable abroad, but often reimbursement takes place upon your return. The form should have been filled in and stamped at the post office prior to leaving, and you should read the booklet *Health Advice for Travellers*.

But these days, the normal traveller is not too concerned about illness within Europe. The true nightmare is finding yourself halfway along the Orinoco/Annapurna circuit or the trans-Siberian Railway and falling ill, far from the familiar cosseting of the NHS. Lonely Planet suddenly takes on a whole new meaning.

Experts will advise you to stay calm and not panic, but lying in a developing country on a mattress that is more alive than you are, with a temperature of 102°, feeling as if a Gila monster is trying to get out of your stomach, it is hard not to succumb to the odd bout of God-help-me-I-am-about-to-die depression. So, get the panicking out of the way early on, and decide that if you really are going to die, you better do something, even if it is only making decent funeral arrangements.

What's up doc?

It is worth reiterating at this point that the most likely problem you are going to face is travellers' diarrhoea, caused either by a bacterium or one of the more persistent protozoa, such as *Entamoeba* or *Giardia*. Treacherous guts afflicts between one-third and half of all travellers to the developing world and, as discussed earlier, even the most fastidious hand and food washer/water steriliser can succumb. Most symptoms go after a few days, and rehydration is the most essential treatment. (You may, having read all the evidence, decide to travel with a broad spectrum antibiotic such as ciprofloxacin, which will certainly kill most gut pathogens, but does wipe out the good guys as well; however, many doctors are not keen to let laypersons routinely dose themselves with such powerful compounds). If the diarrhoea does persist for more than a few days, then seek medical advice.

Of the more serious diseases, a Europ Assistance survey found that of the 13,000 medical cases they handled in 1993, 60 per cent of calimants needed hospitalisation (the rest were minor accidents, cuts, flu and gastroenteritis, minor chest infections and childhood illnesses). The main reasons for a stay in hospital were heart disease (and suspected heart attacks), respiratory conditions, accidents, strokes and orthopaedic problems. There were 240 people with heart problems serious enough for them to need repatriation.

Heart problems give rise to a variety of symptoms, such as pains in chest, shoulder or down the left arm, which may be due to angina; difficulty in breathing after strenuous exercise, with an asthma-like attack that worsens if the person lies down. If you experience any of these, catch a cab to the local hospital. If there is one, that is (a cab or a hospital).

Is there a doctor in the house?

The second part of the nightmare is going to the local doctor and finding out that Dr Mengele didn't perish in the Paraguayan jungle after all, just took up practice in your local village. Or you find that the language barrier is stuck firmly in place, despite your best medical charades. How can you find a reliable, English-speaking practitioner (this is no time to practice your Gujerati)?

One thing you could do is join the International Association for Medical Assistance to Travellers (IAMAT), which publishes a booklet of hospitals and English-speaking doctors. The charges are standardised worldwide at $45 for an office visit, $55 for home/hotel and $65 for weekends and holidays. There is no membership fee for IAMAT, but donations are suggested.

American Express has a Global Assist emergency service, and the company provides free 24-hour advice on doctors, dentists, lawyers, etc., though you obviously have to pay locally for their services. You should check whether your credit/charge card has a similar service: it varies depending on class of card and issuing bank.

Failing the helpful plastic, large international hotels have probably had their fair share of heart attacks, accidents, and bad backs on the premises, and they may be able to suggest an English-speaking doctor. There is a risk, here, of course being referred to someone who 'touts' the hotel with commissions. Ask for a choice.

A better bet might be the nearest British Consulate (numbers are given in the health advice section of this book): ask who they would go to. If you are in a country for more than a few weeks it is worth registering with a consulate: should the emergency be an earthquake or civil unrest, at least someone knows to count you in or out, and get you a seat on the last plane out.

If there is no UK consulate, try the US one: they usually keep lists of English-speaking doctors, medical centres and hospitals. If your American accent is up to scratch the State Department run an Overseas Citizens' Emergency Center which offers 24-hour advice on medical, financial or legal problems. There may also be a mission hospital/clinic or an outpost of Oxfam, Save the Children Fund, VSO, a Medical Research Council project, or the US Peace Corps in the area, all of whom have good, solid medical back-up for their field staff (and usually have well-stocked emergency medical supplies). The Field Officer is the person to contact, he or she will have access to the medical supplies, and a well practised route to any doctors/clinics in the area. Local expats will also have good inside knowledge.

Hilary Bradt suggests in her *Backpacker's Africa* that travellers to East Africa join The Flying Doctors' Society of Africa; contact the African Medical & Research Foundation. A month's cover costs £10 (£25 a year), and when your Toyota coughs its last in the middle of the Serengeti, you might just consider it money well spent. Even if you don't use it, the cause is a good one.

All of this drama might be avoidable if you have travel insurance with medical assistance. Medical assistance means just that, it does not mean you have to fork out the cash and then hustle the insurance company at home. A good assistance company will deal directly with doctors/hospitals, etc., find your companions hotel rooms if required, approve charges, approve or recommend surgical procedures, arrange transportation to a better hospital if necessary, and even evacuate you home by air ambulance or commercial airliner.

A good assistance company (such as Europ Assistance, Worldwide Assistance, Travellers' Medical Service, etc.) not only has 24-hour manned phones, a doctor (preferably on site rather than on call), multi-lingual operators, keep a database of local hospitals, and will be able to tell whether the one you are in is up to the job in hand, and move you if not. Insurance companies are listed in the Useful Addresses section.

Local remedies

If something goes wrong in the UK, we expect there be a hospital nearby. That is why we make a fuss when a hospital closes and it takes an extra 10 minutes for an ambulance to get to the nearest A&E department. It is easy to forget that the vast majority of the world's population do not have the luxury of a local hospital. Nor an ambulance. As Dr Marianne Janosi of VSO tells all her volunteers: 'If you are involved in an accident, the only way you will get to a hospital is if somebody kindly stops and loads your dripping carcass into their car.'

So in many destinations, for all practicable purposes, there just might not be a hospital to take you to. Hence, it could be possible that you are laid up, far from a phone, unable to call your assistance company, waiting for a slow-moving help message to get through, and a helpful local practitioner of a somewhat, shall we say, ad hoc nature, offers you one of the local cures.

In the useful *Where There Is No Doctor*, author David Werner points out that in Mexico, rural villagers have a number of cures for snakebite, including 'Guaco' leaves, the skin of a poisonous lizard, tobacco, snake's bile and, the ultimate eye-for-an-eye, biting the snake that bit you. None of these actually work.

However, he also points out that, extreme examples apart (e.g.smearing cow dung on the head for ringworm or tying a crab to a goitre), many medicinal plants do exist that may be beneficial. After all, quinine and artenam are examples of 'natural' malaria cures, papaya and garlic can be used to get rid of worms, papaya calms mosquito bites and coca leaf tea does seem to alleviate altitude sickness.

You have to use your judgement as to how much you get involved in some shaman's kill-or-cure schemes. If the suggested remedy involves an external application, as an ointment or a compress, anything but a live scorpion in your trousers, it is unlikely to do any harm. Whether you drink some unknown liquid is likely to depend on (a) how much you trust your hosts, (b) how much you don't want to upset them and (c) just how desperate you are for a cure.

However, one old hand at health care in foreign countries had some words of warning. 'You should always treat the local medicine with respect, as they often have a completely different way of looking at medicine and diseases and their causes, as the Chinese and Indians do, but which may be just as valid. But the people to avoid are the local bone setters: if you have broken something, or been in an accident, get to a hospital if you can.'

Of course when you do get your broken bones to a hospital/doctor, there are in theory all sorts of things you should ask, like are the syringes disposable or autoclaved or at the very least bleached? Is the blood screened for hepatitis B, C and HIV? Do they have X-rays, NMR scans? Unfortunately, by the time you need such services, you are usually too far gone to ask about them. However, if you are compos mentis, you should stall on having injections/blood transfusions if you can (plasma expanders are a safe substitute for blood, but they are hard to come by unless you bring your own, or have access to an aid organisations' supplies) and you should also ensure you know your blood group (though it *should* be redetermined before any transfusions). Mismatched blood can cause no end of problems, including death. (The Medic Alert bracelet has already been mentioned. It is a stainless steel bracelet engraved with a warning of any allergies, rare blood groups, diabetic status, etc., plus a 24-hour emergency phone number.)

However, I have one friend who was involved in a car crash in Africa who did receive a transfusion, which saved his life. He didn't pick up anything (in fact, he was too frightened afterwards to ask whether the blood supplies were screened), but now says, 'If they hadn't done it, I would have died in the hospital, so given the choice I probably would have said, well, go ahead anyway. Luckily, I was completely out of it and didn't have to make the decision.'

The best bet of all, of course, is not to get ill, and not to have an accident. But who can guarantee that?

Medicines abroad

You may well be sent to the pharmacist with (or very often without) a prescription for a drug. It may be identified by a brand or proprietary name (such as Lariam for mefloquine, or Bactrim for the less handy co-trimoxazole). The active ingredient will be on the label somewhere: check you are being given the right remedy. The estimable Dr Richard Dawood, editor of Travellers' Health, exposed one of the largest problems with pharmaceuticals in the developing world in his regular column in *Conde Nast Traveler*, that there is a big market in counterfeiting, mainly of the more popular proprietary brands. He suggests looking out for badly printed labels, or colour variations from one batch to the other. If suspicious, try another outlet (if there is one). If you are unsure that the dosage/drug is correct, you can call your medical assistance company, or your own doctor, bearing in mind that the received wisdom of how to treat conditions varies from country to country.

Some countries also have over-the-counter remedies that contain substances that are potentially dangerous, and this is particularly true of cold and fever remedies. Treat them with care, they sometimes make Night Nurse seem like an amphetamine.

16 Volunteers' special needs

There are numerous reasons why your stint abroad may be something more than a holiday. Some people just find a beach, sling their hammock and decide to do a Robert Louis Stevenson. But for the vast majority of the long-term Britons abroad they are working, either for an agency, such as the Overseas Development Administration (ODA); a charity, such as Voluntary Service Overseas (VSO) or Save the Children Fund (SCF), or for a commercial organisation. Multinationals often move families rather than individuals, and have a very slick system of housing, educating children and health care, and it is unlikely they will face quite the same problems as volunteers.

For those without a BP or Barclays Bank behind them, it is to be hoped that the organisation who sends them does a sufficiently thorough job in warning/preparing them for the complexities of settling down abroad, but just in case, here are some basic guidelines.

Fit for the job

'We have hundreds of enquiries from people wanting to help,' says Helen Daly, Health Officer of SCF, 'but many of them are unsuitable because they lack overseas experience and relevant skills. We recruit engineers, nurses, doctors, teachers, administrators and managers all, however, with previous experience of working in a developing country.'

Dr Marianne Janosi of VSO has similar problems. 'Thousands apply every year, and the first criterion is, have they the correct skills? And are they up to date, or did they qualify 50 years ago? If they have the qualifications, we send them a simple medical form to fill out – have you a major medical condition, have you ever suffered from schizophrenia, that sort of thing – and that helps us eliminate some early on, before they give up their job and so on.'

The selection process is strict in most reputable agencies. As Helen Daly lightheartedly points out: 'When I first went abroad as a volunteer to Thailand with an Irish agency, it was much more casual than now. I was naive, I knew nothing, I wasn't even sure where Thailand was I think my atlas said Siam. One of the major changes now is that people who donate money to charitable organisations want to know how it is being used. The countries we work in want much more say in how money is utilised and what programmes we get involved in. So we have to make sure we select the right people with the appropriate skills.'

At VSO if you pass the first postal stage, there is a day of selection, with a panel, a onetoone interview, and what Dr Janosi calls 'mind games'. 'And then we ask them to have a medical with their GP, and I look at the results and, if they seem to be medically suitable, I hope I am doing the right thing by saying they are fit to go.'

Dr Janosi recalls too, that in her first forays into the field she had no training. 'These days they have several weeks of preparation. They are taught about change of working patterns and practices, adjusting to new countries, and they are given the names of volunteers who have returned from the country they will be posted to. I also give them a 3-hour medical lecture. I frighten the life out of them.'

The frightening consists of confronting them with the ugly facts: that 10 per cent of them will be repatriated home during their service (though half will return once they have had their minor medical problems sorted), and that the vast majority of problems are due to road accidents. 'It is also the commonest cause of death. We have about two a year, nearly always road traffic accidents ... although we did have one poor man trampled to death by an elephant last year.'

It is easy to assume that something as romantic as death by rogue elephant is a likely contender for second place after road accidents, but the runner-up in the repatriation stakes is a little more prosaic. 'Depression. Psychiatric problems are something that worries everyone, Oxfam, SCF, the Americans, the French, anyone who sends people abroad to work, we all worry about it. We have more trouble with the mental aspects than all the physical illnesses combined.'

Screening gets rid of the manic depressives and the schizophrenics, but it is the borderline groups that sometimes slip through. 'There are some people who are ... well, inadequate,' says Dr Janosi. 'They get depressed every time the wind blows. Many of those we catch, but sometimes they get through. People are very silly, they leave girlfriends and boyfriends behind, and it just doesn't work. But then, sometimes the very best people break down, some dramatically with a suicide attempt, other times, they lose weight, they cry a lot. But I think it is the second commonest reason for repatriation, psychiatric problems.'

So ask yourself before applying: could you stand to be away from friends, relatives, TV, bars, pubs, that new trendy Polynesian-Italian restaurant and the latest Quentin Tarantino movie for two whole years?

Shock treatment

VSO also tries to prepare for that other sudden impact, culture shock. Apart from the arranged chats with previous volunteers, they have a resource centre with books and videos about each country, the social mores (are uncovered arms, knees, chests offensive? What is acceptable as swimwear? Should you bring presents when invited into a house? And lots more besides), the climate, style and pace of life. Agencies such as ODA send out detailed briefing sheets, under the following headings: First impressions; Country background, geography and climate; Travel; Baggage and freight; Accommodation; Health (including what medicines to bring); Schools; Clothing; Food; What else to take; Sport and leisure; Banking/money; Communications; Spouse employment opportunities; Vehicles. Most government agencies provide similar documents.

Listings such as these are available from the Women's Corona Society, a charitable institute which provides information for all travellers (not just women) posted overseas. A briefing costs from £3.50–£5, depending on the country.

There is also a series of books from Kuperard (available through bookshops) on culture shock, covering individual countries, and also one for the particular problems of wives (or should that be partners? I suppose political correctness has yet to penetrate the expat world to any great degree), and another aimed at children.

Your local library may also keep the *World Travel Guide* (Columbus Press), a hefty tome mainly aimed at the travel trade, but with a helpful breakdown of each country, much like the ODA sheets.

Luckily, most agencies don't let you get away with just stepping off the plane and plunging into an alien land. Often they insist on a 1, 4 or 6 week course before you are unleashed on the local people, which will incorporate language, culture and health matters. It will soften the blow (for the locals if nothing else).

Arriving

The chances are that the culture shock won't hit immediately. People on short-term contracts and those who have not yet been assigned or rented homes are usually put into temporary accommodation. This may be something like the British Aid Guest House in Dhaka, Bangladesh, or it may be an international standard hotel.

One expat warned me of the seductive qualities of these temporary billets, which may make the eventual shock all the more profound. It seems for a number of workers, the hotel becomes an oasis or bolt-hole, where they can cut off the outside world. For a start it will probably have air-conditioning, possibly a bar when much of the country is dry, and you won't have any language problem.

It also means guards are dropped, and the volunteer can forget they are in a developing country, and drink the water, order the salads, suck on those raw prawns, do all the things that we travel nags suggest you don't do. Retreating back there at every opportunity becomes a way of life, but is a foolish option because the chances are that this cocoon will eventually be taken away, and the next stop is a house, or perhaps a hut.

'Actually a mud hut isn't as bad as it sounds,' one old hand told me, 'modern western houses weren't designed for some of these climates, we just like them because they are familiar. A mud hut is the coolest place to be in summer if you haven't got air-conditioning. And in a hut you can just light a fire to drive out all the things that live in the roof. That and a tame gecko takes care of most of the insects.'

Living in a mud hut isn't quite as fanciful as it sounds. Some government agencies do provide houses, either local ones, or in a western 'enclave', but charities (e.g. VSO) prefer their people to live close to the indigenous populations, which may mean a hut. Of course in a disaster/refugee situation, a hut may be a luxury it could all be down to tents and camp beds. In this situation, and perhaps in houses and huts, the biggest challenge is personal hygiene, particularly if there is threat of cholera or dysentery (see below).

Burn out

'One of our biggest problems,' said one SCF manager, 'is overwork. People feel isolated, they have lost the normal social support mechanisms such as sports facilities, theatre, etc. There may be no 'outlet' for staff, so they immerse themselves in work. We advise all our people on how to identify and manage stress and how to prevent such burnout.' Several returning volunteers have told me of days starting at 7am and finishing late in the evening, and being on-call through the night. It may be just more than a heavy work-load: volunteers on a first posting often feel they have something to prove, to themselves or to the people who arrived before them. They also want to make a difference, something which, if they feel they have failed, can itself lead to problems.

Most agencies (and the majority of expats I have spoken to) recommend some sort of relaxation skill, from running to bird-watching through to learning to play the guitar. Or you could keep a diary for the article or novel you may well write.

Ted Lawson spent a year for VSO in Papua New Guinea, and kept a diary which he eventually published as *A Village in New Guinea: The Realities of Life With VSO*. The sub-title is something of a misnomer, as the majority of volunteers, as Lawson admits, do not find themselves up the

Boze River without a boat. That said, his claim that his book reflects 'the frustrations, anger and depression and also the times of happiness, excitement and pure contentment, that is the lot of volunteers everywhere' may well be true. It certainly is a bizarre journal, with the constant problems of cannibals (retired) falling behind with their tractor payments.

Learning the local language is another essential, but the most important thing, to modify a favourite term of abuse, is to 'get a life', one as close to being multi-layered as the one at home. And take time off, even if it only means taking off into the hills for a day.

It also takes some people time to slow down from UK speed, an exaggerated version of the feeling of returning from, say, New York, to an English village, where life seems suddenly parochial and achingly slow. Times that by ten or 20, incorporating a baffling bureaucracy, where a day's queuing is the norm (particularly frustrating when it takes a few wasted days to realise that most locals hire someone to queue for them. This isn't only a developing world thing, it is common in Spain and Italy, where being a professional queuer can be a full time job), long mid-day closing, a vast array of religious holidays, bribery and a 12-hour drive or river journey to the nearest town.

Health and hygiene

The most important thing is to stay healthy. Dr Janosi reckons on four major problems for her volunteers abroad, if you survive the threat of road accidents: malaria (particularly as long-term prophylaxis is often tricky), diarrhoea problems, HIV and AIDS, and depression. Of these, the one most likely to affect all volunteers at some time is diarrhoea. The main ways of avoiding diarrhoea for the average traveller have already been covered, but the expat may face a whole new set of long-term problems.

Water, of course, will still have to be boiled, sterilised or filtered unless you are very sure of the supplies. Some places go overboard and put so much chlorine in you can almost see green fumes coming off. Water overdosed like this tastes a lot better if left to stand overnight, covered (but not stoppered) to prevent flies getting in.

However, you may not have a chlorinated or even a mains supply. WHO estimate that in urban populations, 65 per cent of the world have house connections and 20 per cent have public taps, often with intermittent supplies. Only a tiny percentage of rural dwellers have mains water, though 60 per cent can draw on a relatively safe water supply. The volunteers may find themselves in the other 40 per cent, having to deal with stepped-wells, pot chlorinators for wells, spring boxes for channelling natural springs, how to avoid contaminating wells, etc. The chances are that iodine/chlorine tablets and water purifiers are going to be invaluable in such situations.

But there will also be domestic waste to think of (another WHO figure claims that only one-third of the world can adequately dispose of their rubbish), waste which may well attract flies, rats and sundry crawling insects. It can also attract mosquitoes, many species of which will happily breed in a tin can or an old tyre, with the danger of diseases such as dengue fever, malaria or yellow fever.

In the absence of refuse collection and the local bottle bank, the choice is either to burn it or bury it. If burning, make sure that you don't incinerate batteries or aerosols, and remember that a lot of plastics give off highly toxic fumes when they ignite. If burying, make sure it is well away from the water supply, and covered by a good layer of soil, not a couple of inches that animals can easily excavate.

The best option is to separate waste into organic material for composting, combustible for burning and the remainder for burying. Compost heaps are fine, but must be protected against flies and rats, otherwise they cause more problems than they are worth.

There is also the matter of personal waste, which is even trickier and even more likely to present a health hazard unless disposed of properly. According to the WHO, only a third of the world's population has proper human waste disposal, and if you are in their midst you can't spend two years going off into the bush with a spade. This may mean using, building or modifying an outhouse/latrine.

These should be built well away, and not uphill, from any well or river and from dwellings – at least 25 metres if possible, with 10 as an absolute minimum – and arranged so that marauding animals cannot get the human waste (a classic way for the pork tapeworm lifecycle to be completed). This means a deep pit, with a simple structure over the top, with earth or ashes periodically thrown down to form a layer to cut down (you won't be able to eradicate) smells and flies. It should also have a cement floor, to prevent hookworm, etc.

A more sophisticated version is to build one with ventilation and a fly trap or screen. This is a classic outhouse, which involves a hole with a cover, plus a vent-pipe which extends higher than the hut, with the pipe top covered by a fine mesh fly screen, so odours can escape and flies can't. One way of using these is to alternate two ventilated improved pit latrines (VIPs), using one for 1–2 years, and then blocking it off to let the waste compost before emptying (if left for 1–2 years the vast majority of pathogens should have died) and re-using.

More sophisticated latrines are possible, such as a pour-flush with a U-bend, connected to a septic tank. Such considerations are covered in detail in Cairncross and Feachem's *Environmental Health Engineering in the Tropics*.

Watch the flies, watch the flies

Of course that wasn't really what Kevin McCarthy said at the end of *Invasion of The Body Snatchers*, but it would have been more valuable advice than watching the skies for alien pods. Actually it isn't only flies (though it is no coincidence that the evidence in Nepal shows that the rate of travellers' diarrhoea follows exactly the seasonal fluctuations in the local fly population), the main thing is to proof your house/shack/hut against mosquitoes, which means using very fine mesh over windows (and frequently checking for, and repairing, gashes), and also ensuring that there are no breeding sites for mosquitoes near the house (or, preferably, the whole village, though that may be over-ambitious). This means checking all sources of standing water, such as rain barrels, guttering and roof tanks, for mosquito larvae and pupae, killing any that are there (oil or paraffin poured on the surface suffocates them), and ensuring no more can enter, either by tight-fitting lids or mesh, and/or by floating expanded polystyrene packing chips on the surface. The same applies to any rubbish lying around, right down to small puddles in the bottom of jars, water in the saucer of plant pots – give them less than an inch, and they'll take it, thanks.

Back to the world

'Back to the world' was the phrase used by returning Vietnam vets. Aid volunteers, expats in general, often have a reverse culture shock (or 're-entry syndrome') upon their return. It can be because of a drop in the standard of living – what no servants? – but is more likely to be the change of pace. 'I remember standing in the middle of Bolton Marks & Spencer,' recalls one victim after some time in the remoter parts of the Yemen, 'and there were just *too many people*. I really couldn't cope, I had to go and walk around Queens Park to get some space. It took a few months before I could fit in again.'

Note that most agencies have an option for counselling if you need it for any reason. The best ones make this offer *before* you leave, so it is obvious this is a standard offer, and you aren't unique or cracking up under the strain.

17 Home again

Don't drop your guard

It is inevitable that the last few days or weeks of your trip may seem like the time to wind down. I have done it myself, woken up in a blur one morning, actually on top of my mosquito net, covered in bites (fortunately in a nonmalarious area). Similarly, I know of people who, blessed with bowels that had remained co-operative throughout their trip, let things slip for the last couple of meals.

The message is not to relax those safeguards. In some ways bringing biological souvenirs back is worse than suffering them while away. Most importantly, **keep taking the tablets**, you must finish the course of anti-malarials to kill off any parasites lurking in your blood (there may be some that can survive longer than the 4 weeks you need to take the drugs, but it is unlikely to be the lethal variant).

The once over

If you have returned from your trip, had no symptoms or suffered only a mild dose of diarrhoea, then you will be wasting everybody's time by having a check-up. However, if you had a fever, persistent diarrhoea or an unexplained rash, book an appointment.

Even if you had a trouble-free trip to the tropics or sub-tropics, if you develop flu-like symptoms upon your return, don't even bother booking an appointment, get on down there – *malaria needs to be excluded.*

If you have any fever, diarrhoea, cough, skin rash, itching, weight loss, lethargy, abdominal pain, muscular or joint pain within a few months of return (and some malarias can burst onto the scene 6–14 months after exposure), you should also be checked out.

Go along to your doctor with a list of the injections you received before leaving, your itinerary, the type of malaria tablets you took (or are still taking) and any incidents (swimming, eating that suspect raw fish, etc.) you think may have put you at risk. It may be that your GP thinks his tropical medicine is a bit rusty, in which case you will be referred to a specialist hospital.

There are a vast array of tests you can have, but careful questioning and examination of skin, liver, spleen, abdomen, etc., should narrow down the range of options. So full biopsies of skin, bone marrow, liver or a camera down the throat (I have had that – you don't want it, trust me), or up the bum are unlikely. However, a stool test for bacteria/protozoa/ parasitic worms is common (microscopic examination and cultures will be used), as is checking the urine for schistosome eggs.

Blood smears can show up malaria, sleeping sickness and reveal tell-tale signs of other parasitic infections. More complex antibody tests can be used for bilharzia, leishmaniasis, dengue fever, HIV and filariasis.

Treatment may include a course of anti-malarials, antibiotics or anti-protozoans. Doctors may prescribe the worm-busting mebendazole for returning aid workers, just in case. For certain gut infections, you may be required to quarantine yourself until stool tests show you are clear of the invaders. It's good to be back, isn't it?

Part II
A Country-by-country Guide

Abbreviations used in the Country-by-Country Guide

Chol	cholera
DF	dengue fever
Dip	diphtheria
Ech	echinococcosis
Fil	filariasis
Hep A	hepatitis A
Hep B	hepatitis B
Hep C	hepatitis C
JE	Japanese encephalitis
Leish	leishmaniasis
Men	meningococcal meningitis
MSF	Mediterranean spotted fever
Onch	oncherocerciasis
Pol	polio
Rab	rabies
Schis	schistosomiasis
TB	tuberculosis
TBE	tick-borne encephalitis
TD	travellers' diarrhoea
Tet	tetanus
Typh	typhoid
YF	yellow fever

All Visa requirements in the text refer to holders of British Passports.

18 Health needs by region and country

This section is designed to provide a quick source of reference to major health problems in a region or country, without the need to interpret complex or miniscule charts. The world has been split into its major geographical and political areas, and the countries arranged alphabetically within them.

A general introduction covers matters common to whole of the region. There is then a list for each country of the time difference, capital, embassy and tourist office in the UK (if applicable) and the local British Embassy/ Consulate (usually in the same place, but not always), which can help with lost passports etc. If in the country for some time, it is definitely worth considering registering with the Consulate or High Commission: should there be a natural disaster or evacuation because of war, the consulate a) knows you are there, and b) can pass information on to anxious relatives. Note, however, that consulates close not only on local holidays but also follow UK ones – it is very frustrating to find yourself hammering on a locked, silent door, only to be told by the gardener that it is August bank holiday back home.

This is followed by a run through of what specific precautions you should take in that country. Note that not every known disease is covered in either the general summary or under the specific country listing. There are innumerable parasites, tick fevers and viral infections that exist but are unlikely to trouble the visitor, and a second volume would be needed to even list them all. Worse, the list of diseases that **can** occur would put you off travel to most countries, including, quite possibly, your own.

There is only one compulsory immunisation, for the mosquito-borne viral disease yellow fever, which is considered to be endemic, but not necessarily active, in the following countries:

Angola, Benin, Belize, Bolivia, Botswana, Brazil, Burkina Faso, Burundi,

Cameroon, Central African Republic, Chad, Colombia, Congo, Cote d'Ivoire, Costa Rica, Ecuador, Equatorial Guinea, Ethiopia, French Guyana, Gabon, Gambia, Ghana, Guatemala, Guinea, Guinea Bissau, Guyana, Honduras, Kenya, Liberia, Mali, Mauritania, Nicaragua, Niger, Nigeria, Panama, Peru, Rwanda, Sao Tome and Principe, Senegal, Sierra Leone, Somalia, Sudan, Suriname, Tanzania, Togo, Trinidad & Tobago Uganda, Venezuela, Zaire, Zambia.

Travelling to or from any of these may require a yellow fever certificate. It is advisable to be immunised if your itinerary touches any of the above countries, because onward travel may become a problem. Note that countries vary in their interpretation of this list: some enlarge it, others consider countries such as Trinidad & Tobago not to be a threat. Check carefully. If in doubt, get a jab: it lasts 10 years. (It should not be given to children under 9 months.)

The situation with cholera is even more confused. Some African and South American countries, against WHO policy, demand to see evidence of immunisation if coming from an 'infected' area. Consider having just a single shot to get a piece of paper (the immunisation is not particularly effective, see Chapter 3).

In December 1994 the WHO considered the following countries to be cholera infected:

Afghanistan, Angola, Argentina, Belize, Benin, Bhutan, Bolivia, Brazil, Burkina Faso, Burundi, Cambodia, Cameroon, Chad, Chile, China, Colombia, Costa Rica, Cote d'Ivoire, Djibouti, Ecuador, El Salvador, French Guyana, Ghana, Guatemala, Guinea, Guinea-Bissau, Guyana, Honduras, India, Indonesia, Iran, Iraq, Kenya, Laos, Liberia, Malawi, Malaysia, Mali, Mauritania, Mexico, Mozambique, Myanmar (Burma), Nepal, Nicaragua, Niger, Nigeria, Panama, Peru, Philipinnes, Rwanda, Sao Tome & Principe, Sierra Leone, Somalia, Sri Lanka, Suriname, Swaziland, Tanzania, Togo, Tuval, Uganda, Ukraine, Venezuela, Vietnam, Zaire, Zambia, Zimbabwe. Plus Albania, Ukraine, Russia.

Cholera is not usually a disease of tourism, and in most of these countries it is easily avoided by good food and water hygiene.

Some countries also require an HIV-free certificate. The WHO does not approve of this action, but cannot stop it. There is no internationally recognised certificate, so you *must* check with the embassy what is required. Some countries will not accept test results from outside clinics. Consider taking your own supply of syringes and needles.

Note, in any country where there is civil unrest or a terrorism campaign, it is worth phoning the Foreign Office to check their latest advice to travellers.

There are various commercial agencies which will sort out visas for you. These include: Worldwide Visas, Visaservice and Thomas Cook.

The information in this section was compiled from a variety of sources, including travellers' clinics, MASTA, the Malaria Reference Laboratory, Travel Medicine International, the TRAVAX NHS on-line information service, WHO and the Centers for Disease Control publications. Such is the nature of travel medicine, that certain areas, such as the distribution of malaria, visa and yellow fever requirements, are subject to change. It is important to consult your travel clinic or GP for up to the minute advice. Or you can ring MASTA (calls 49p min peak/39p cheap).

Having said that, however, the chance of any one country eradicating malaria or becoming free of schistosomiasis by the time you have read this are slim.

Do not read the entry for any single country in isolation, look also at the regional pattern of diseases at the beginning of each geographical section.

18.1 AFRICA

NORTH AFRICA

North Africa includes Algtpgoto 223eria, Egypt, Libya, Morocco and Tunisia.

Note that by mid-1995 the code for telephoning the UK from these countries should begin standardising to 0044-. Check locally, as the date for changeover varies.

HEALTH RISKS THROUGHOUT THE REGION

Malaria: There is no risk in Tunisia, minimal risk in Algeria, Libya and Morocco. However, in rural areas of the Nile delta, the Sudanese border region, El Faiyum and the oases, the traveller should take prophylaxis (chloroquine or proguanil).

Yellow fever: North Africa is not a yellow fever endemic area. However, if travelling from one of the countries mentioned below to Algeria, Libya, Tunisia or Egypt, you are required to have a yellow fever certificate:

Angola, Benin, Bolivia, Brazil, Burundi, Burkina Faso, Cameroon, Central African Republic, Chad, Colombia, Congo, Cote d'Ivoire, Ecuador, Equatorial Guinea, Ethiopia, French Guyana, Gabon, Gambia, Ghana, Guinea, Guinea Bissau, Guyana, Kenya, Liberia, Mali, Mauritania, Niger, Nigeria, Panama, Peru, Rwanda, Sao Tome and Principe, Senegal, Sierra Leone, Somalia, Sudan, Suriname, Tanzania, Togo, Uganda, Venezuela, Zaire.

Note, Egypt also requires a certificate from travellers coming from Botswana, Malawi and Zambia. Morocco has no yellow fever requirements. Note that yellow fever immunisations should not be given to children under 9 months.

Other health risks: Include a variety of viral fevers transmitted by sandflies and ticks; leishmaniasis (sandflies) occurs in both forms, visceral and cutaneous. Travellers in rural areas especially should take care not to be bitten by insects, and should avoid dogs, which harbour the ticks that cause Mediterranean Spotted Fever. North African dogs may also carry rabies. Various worm infections are common in the population, e.g. roundworm (*Ascaris*), hookworm (from soil: wear shoes) and schistosomiasis (also called bilharzia, an infection carried by some fresh water snails, particularly in Egypt, Libya and Tunisia, but all fresh water should be considered suspect unless chlorinated). Echinococcosis (hydatid disease), caused by cysts from dog faeces, is also present.

Dysenteries, brucellosis, giardiasis and other food-borne diseases need protecting against. Except in the best hotels/resorts, implement food and hygiene precautions. Hepatitis B is endemic, hepatitis A is a risk, hepatitis C and E occur. There have been outbreaks of cholera (not a disease of tourism).

The incidence of HIV and AIDS is low in North Africa compared with other parts of the continent. Nevertheless, blood transfusions and dental procedures should be avoided where possible, as there is still a risk of both HIV and hepatitis B.

Just because a disease is present in a country doesn't mean the tourist will come into contact with it. Many are in specific foci, and only very adventurous travellers or aid/health workers are at any risk at all, and then not always. Malaria and intestinal bugs are dishonourable exceptions.

Immunisations to consider for the North African region include: hepatitis A, hepatitis B (for at-risk groups), rabies, tetanus, typhoid. Travellers outside main resorts and long-stay workers may want to ensure tuberculosis, diphtheria, and polio are up to date. There is a small risk of meningococcal meningitis (outbreaks in dry season: December to June, mainly Egypt).

Note, not all the recommended immunisations may be needed. Which others you have willvary with the type and duration of your trip. To avoid unnecessary immunisation discuss your itinerary with a travel clinic or your GP.

ALGERIA

+ 1 hours GMT
Capital: Algiers
Embassy: 53 Holland Park, London W11 3RS (0171-221 7800)
Consulate: 6 Hyde Park Gate, SW7 5EW (0171-221 7800)
British Embassy: BP 3 Residence Cassiopee, Batiment B, 7 Chemin des Glycines, Algiers. Tel: (2) 60 56 01 or 60 54 11; Fax: (2) 60 44 10
Visa required: Yes, if staying over 3 months
Yellow fever certificate: Yes, if older than 1 year arriving from infected area
HIV test: Yes, if intending to stay over one year

Recommended health precautions
Note, at the time of writing serious civil unrest has made tourism to Algeria a dangerous prospect. Seek advice before travelling (0171-270 4129)

Immunisations: Hep A; Typh; Pol; Tet. Consider also Dip; Rab; Hep B if extended stay

Malaria prophylaxis: Little risk in most areas, some reports of malaria in oases, though the severe Plasmodium falciparum is relatively rare. Chloroquine or proguanil should be considered for extensive travel in remote regions. Use nets and repellents

Mains water chlorinated, but high risk of TD away from best resorts: implement all food and water hygiene precautions. Schis, Leish local favourites. High rates of parasitic infections in local populations (e.g. hookworm). Always wear shoes

EGYPT

+ 2 hours GMT (+ 3 in summer)
Capital: Cairo
UK Tourist Office: Egyptian Tourist Office, 170 Piccadilly, London W1V 9OD (0171-493 5282)
Embassy: 26 South Street, London W1Y 6DD (0171-499 2401)
British Embassy: Sharia Ahmad Raghab, Garden City, Cairo. Tel: (2) 354 0852; Fax: (2) 354 0859
Visa required: Yes, available at airport on arrival
Yellow fever certificate: Yes, if arriving from infected area. Travellers from Sudan may need proof of immunisation against YF, Chol, Typh and Men
HIV test: Yes, foreign workers are required to have an HIV-free certificate. Certificates issued abroad not usually accepted

Recommended health precautions
Immunisations: Hep A; Typh; Pol; Tet. Consider also Rab; Hep B and, very occasionally, Men

Malaria prophylaxis: There is some risk in parts of the Nile delta, the oases, the El Faiyum area and the south. There have been cases around Luxor and Karnak. There is no reported drug resistance: chloroquine or proguanil are recommended for those at risk. Use nets and repellents

Mains water chlorinated, but v. high risk of TD, with reports of up to 60% affliction by some tour groups: implement all food and water hygiene precautions. Avoid dairy products. Parasitic infestations common around the Delta area (e.g. Fil: small thread-like worms spread by mosquitoes and midges; DF: viral disease spread by mosquitoes; Rift Valley fever: spread by mosquitoes). Avoid insect bites; wear shoes. Hep C endemic

Note that over the past few years there have been attacks on organised tour groups by extremist groups. The current Foreign Office advice is to avoid the area around Assiut, although attacks have occurred in Cairo elsewhere. In 1993, 250,000 Britons visited without mishap; the best advice here is that discretion is the better part of tourism

---

LIBYA

+ 1 hours GMT (+ 2 in summer)
Capital: Tripoli
Embassy: Diplomatic relations with UK frosty. Libyan interests through Royal Embassy of Saudi Arabia, 119 Harley Street, W1 (0171-486 8387); British interests through Italian Embassy, PO Box 4206, Sharia Uahran 1, Tripoli, Libya. Tel: (21) 31191

Visa required: Yes
Yellow fever certificate: Yes, if over 1 year old and arriving from infected area
HIV test: Yes, if seeking residence or foreign worker

Recommended health precautions
Immunisations: Hep A; Typh; Pol; Tet. Consider also Rab; Hep B

Malaria prophylaxis: V. slight risk to most travellers, mainly in oases in southwest, Feb to Aug. Chloroquine or proguanil recommended drugs. Use nets and repellents

There is risk of TD: implement all food and water hygiene precautions. Various parasites (e.g. Ech, roundworms) very common in rural areas

---

MOROCCO

+ 0 hours GMT
Capital: Rabat
UK Tourist Office: Moroccan National Tourist Office, 205 Regent Street, London W1R 5DF (0171-437 0073)
Embassy: 49 Queen's Gate Gardens, London SW7 5NE (0171581 5001)
British Embassy: BP 45, 17 Boulevard de la Tour Hassan, BP 45, Rabat. Tel: (7) 209 051/6; Fax: (7) 720906. Consulates in Casablanca, Tangier and Agadir
Visa required: No
Yellow fever certificate: No
HIV test: No

Recommended health precautions
Advised immunisations: Hep A; Typh; Pol; Tet. Consider also Rab and Hep B if extended stay

Malaria prophylaxis: V. slight risk in some rural areas and on the coast, May to Oct, not usually worth taking drugs (chloroquine or proguanil would be recommended). Use insect repellents and nets

Mains water chlorinated, but outside of best resorts/hotels there is risk of TD: implement all food and water hygiene precautions. Care with western-style buffets. Leish, a protozoan disease spread by sandflies (who also spread sandfly fever) and Schis present, as are soil parasites. Avoid bites; wear shoes

---

TUNISIA

+ 1 hour GMT
Capital: Tunis
UK Tourist Office: Tunisian National Tourist Office, 77a Wigmore Street, London W1H 9LJ (0171-224 5561)
Embassy: 29 Prince's Gate, London SW7 1QG (0171-584 8117)
British Embassy: 5 Place de la Victoire, Tunis 1015 RP. Tel: (1) 245 100 or 245 649; Fax: (1) 354 877
Visa required: No, if staying less than 3 months
Yellow fever certificate: Yes, all travellers over 1 year old arriving from infected area
HIV test: No

Recommended health precautions
Immunisations: Hep A; Typh; Pol; Tet. Consider also Rab; Hep B

Malaria prophylaxis: Slim chance of catching; avoid bites just in case

Outside of best hotels high risk of TD: implement all food and water hygiene precautions. Care with western-style buffets in hotels. Avoid sandfly bites – they carry both fever and Leish. Parasites common (e.g. Ech, hookworm), especially in rural areas.

CENTRAL AFRICA

Central Africa includes Angola, Cameroon, Central African Republic, Chad, Congo, Equatorial Guinea, Gabon, Sudan, Zaire and Zambia.

Note that by mid-1995 the code for telephoning the UK from these countries should begin standardising to 0044-. Check locally, as the date for changeover varies.

HEALTH RISKS THROUGHOUT THE REGION

Malaria: There is a high risk of catching malaria in this region. Furthermore the dominant form is the severe *Plasmodium falciparum*. A regime of prophylactic drugs essential, as is preventing mosquito bites. Any flu-like symptoms either while there or upon return should ring serious alarm bells.

Yellow fever: Central Africa is a yellow fever endemic area, and there have been reports of outbreaks in Angola, Sudan and Zaire. However, there is a risk throughout the region, and all travellers should be immunised.

Note that you **must** be immunised if travelling to Cameroon, Central African Republic, Congo, Gabon or Zaire. No certificate, no entry, no matter which country you have come from.

If travelling from one of the countries mentioned below to Angola, Equatorial Guinea, or Sudan, you are also required to have a yellow fever certificate:

Angola, Benin, Bolivia, Brazil, Burkina Faso, Burundi, Cameroon, Central African Republic, Chad, Colombia, Congo, Cote d'Ivoire, Ecuador, Equatorial Guinea, Ethiopia, French Guyana, Gabon, Gambia, Ghana, Guinea, Guinea Bissau, Guyana, Kenya, Liberia, Mali, Mauritania, Niger, Nigeria, Panama, Peru, Rwanda,

Sao Tome and Principe, Senegal, Sierra Leone, Somalia, Sudan, Suriname, Tanzania, Togo, Uganda, Venezuela, Zaire.

Note, restrictions usually apply to travellers over 12 months old. Children under 9 months should not be immunised unless absolutely necessary.

Other health risks: Include cholera – against WHO recommendations, some countries may ask for a cholera certificate, particularly if coming from a country where the disease is active. Independent travellers should consider getting a single shot and a piece of paper confirming their injection. The immunisation is not particularly effective, except against ignorant bureaucracy, and the best way to avoid cholera is by good food/water hygiene.

Also present is a whole variety of diseases spread by biting insects, including filariasis (small thread-like worms from mosquitoes), leishmaniasis (protozoa from sandflies), onchocerciasis (worms, cause river blindness, spread by blackflies), trypanosomiasis (protozoans, sleeping sickness, tsetse flies). Avoid insect bites and tick bites (the latter spread African tick typhus). The region is part of the meningitis belt across Africa, and an immunisation is available for types A & C. Schistosomiasis (bilharzia, flukes spread by snails) is widespread, so unchlorinated fresh water should be avoided for bathing or washing.

AIDS is endemic throughout the region, though the actual percentage of HIV-positive individuals varies from country to country. No country is completely free, some have very high numbers. It is important for travellers, if possible, to avoid medical and dental procedures involving unsterile equipment, and to avoid transfusions involving unscreened blood. Carry your own supply of sterile syringes and needles, etc. Unsafe sex (i.e. penetrative sex without condoms) should be avoided. By following the guidelines in Chapter 13, the average traveller is not at risk from HIV.

Hepatitis B, another blood and sex (and transfusion) problem, is hyperendemic, and both A and E are widespread, the latter a serious problem during pregnancy. There have been outbreaks of dengue fever (flu-like viral disease, day-biting mosquitoes) in Angola and Sudan. Cholera, typhoid and the bacteria/protozoans (e.g. *Entamoeba*, *Giardia*, *Shigella*) causing diarrhoea are all present. Parasitic worm infections are common in the local populations, particularly in rural areas, including Guinea worm (*Dracunculus*, from contaminated water), hookworm (from soil: wear shoes), roundworm (*Ascaris*), tapeworms and various flukes. Unpasteurised dairy produce may carry brucellosis. Rabies is present throughout Central Africa.

However, just because a disease is present in a country doesn't mean the tourist will come into contact with it. Many are in specific foci, and only very adventurous travellers or aid/health workers are at any risk at all, and then not always. Malaria and intestinal bugs are dishonourable exceptions.

Note that not all recommended injections may be required (though this is one region ofthe world where they probably will be). Check with your travel clinic or GP. Long-stay visitors may be required to have their diphtheria and tuberculosis protection brought up to date.

ANGOLA

+ 1 hour GMT
Capital: Luanda
Embassy: 98 Park Lane, London W1Y 3TA (0171-495 1752)
British Embassy: CP 1244, Rua Diogo Cao 4, Luanda. Tel: 334582/3
Visa required: Yes; tourist travel not permitted, business only
Yellow fever certificate: Yes, if over 1 year old and arriving from an endemic area
HIV test: No

Recommended health precautions
Immunisations: YF; Hep A; Typh; Pol; Tet. Consider also Rab; Hep B, Men. Note that a Chol immunisation certificate is msometimes demanded if entering from an infected area
Malaria prophylaxis: High risk of malaria, mainly P. falciparum, with chloroquine resistance reported. Mefloquine recommended (not children under 15 kg, during first trimester of pregnancy or if history of epilepsy or psychiatric disorders), or chloroquine/ proguanil. Use nets and repellents.

V. high risk of TD: treat all food and water as suspect. V. high rates of parasitic worm infections in local populations (e.g. hookworm): always wear shoes. There have been outbreaks of sleeping sickness. The years of war in Angola have made sure all the local disease/parasite specialities (Fil, Schis) can thrive.

CAMEROON

+ 1 hour GMT
Capital: Yaounde
Embassy: 84 Holland Park, London W11 3SB (0171-727 0771)
British Embassy: Avenue Winston Churchill, BP 547 Yaounde. Tel: 220545; Fax: 220 148. Plus Consulate in Douala
Visa required: Yes
Yellow fever certificate: Yes, travellers over 1 year from all countries

HIV test: No

Recommended health precautions
Immunisations: YF; Hep A; Typh; Pol; Tet. Consider also Men (esp. N. Cameroon); Rab; Hep B if extended stay. Note that a cholera immunisation certificate is sometimes demanded if entering from an infected area

Malaria prophylaxis: High risk (mainly *P. falciparum*), with drug resistance (inc. Fansidar) reported. Mefloquine recommended (not children under 15 kg, in first tri-mester of pregnancy or if history of epilepsy or psychiatric disorders), or chloroquine/proguanil. Use nets and repellents

V. high risk of TD: implement all food and water hygiene precautions. Treat water supplies as suspect. Full battery of local parasites, including sleeping sickness (patchy), DF (south), tick typhus plus high infection rates (e.g. hookworm, roundworm): always wear shoes; cook food thoroughly.

CENTRAL AFRICAN REPUBLIC

+ 1 hour GMT
Capital: Bangui
British Consulate: c/o Socacig, 13P 728, Bangui. Tel: 61030; Fax: 615 130
Visa required: Yes, obtain from Bangui immigration office
Yellow fever certificate: Yes from all travellers over 1 year old
HIV test: No

Recommended health precautions
Immunisations: YF; Hep A; Typh; Pol; Tet. Consider also Men; Rab; Hep B if extended stay

Malaria prophylaxis: High risk, mainly P. falciparum, with drug resistance reported. Mefloquine recommended (not in children under 15 kg, first trimester of pregnancy or if history of epilepsy or psychiatric disorders), or chloroquine/proguanil. Use nets and repellents.

V. high risk of TD: implement all food and water hygiene precautions. HIV risk high if medical/dental/sexual activity. Regional parasite specialities present (Fil, Schis), plus tick typhus, also Lassa fever, a nasty rat-borne viral disease, which occurs in rural areas.

CHAD

+ 1 hour GMT
Capital: Ndjamena
UK representation: Worldwide Visas Ltd, 9 Adelaide Street, London WC2 N4HZ (0171-379 0419)
British Consulate: Avenue Charles de Gaulle, BP 877, Ndjamena, Chad. Tel: 51 30 64

Visa required: Yes; travel within country needs special permit
Yellow fever certificate: Yes, from all travellers over 1 year of age (Chad does not seem to be consistent on this, having changed its requirements recently: check)
HIV test: No

Recommended health precautions
Immunisations: YF; Hep A; Typh; Pol; Tet. Consider also Men, Rab; Hep B if extended stay. Note that a Chol immunisation certificate is sometimes demanded if entering from an infected area

Malaria prophylaxis: High risk, mainly *P. falciparum*, also a showing by P. ovale; chloroquine resistance reported. Mefloquine recommended (not for children under 15 kg, in first trimester of pregnancy or if history of epilepsy or psychiatric disorders), or chloroquine/ proguanil. Use nets and repellents.

V. high risk of TD: implement all food and water hygiene precautions. Strong showing by Schis in the parasite stakes, also Fil (south) and usual suspects.

CONGO

+ 1 hour GMT
Capital: Brazzaville
Consulate: Livingstone House, 11 Carteret Street, London SW1H 9DJ (0171-222 7575)
British Consulate: c/o British Petroleum Development Ltd. ave Marien Ngouabi, Boite Postale, 1181 Pointe-Noire. Tel: 943 988; Fax: 943 990
Visa required: Yes
Yellow fever certificate: Yes, travellers over 1 year old from all countries
HIV test: No

Recommended health precautions
Immunisations: YF; Hep A; Typh; Pol; Tet. Consider also Rab, Men; Hep B if extended stay

Malaria prophylaxis: High risk of *P. falciparum*, with drug resistance reported. Mefloquine recommended (not for children under 15 kg, in first trimester of pregnancy or if history of epilepsy or psychiatric disorders), or chloroquine/ proguanil. Use nets and repellents

V. high risk of TD: implement all food and water hygiene precautions. Full range of parasites and insect vectors to be avoided

---

EQUATORIAL GUINEA

+ 1 hour GMT
Capital: Malabo
Embassy: Contact Embassy in Paris (1 47 66 44 33)
British Consulate: World Bank Compound, Apartado 801, Malabo. Tel: 2400
Visa required: Yes
Yellow fever certificate: Yes, if entering from an infected country
HIV test: No

Recommended health precautions
Immunisations: YF; Hep A; Typh; Pol; Tet. Consider also Men; Rab; Hep B if extended stay

Malaria prophylaxis: High risk of *P. falciparum*, with drug resistance reported. Mefloquine recommended (not for children under 15 kg, during first trimester of pregnancy or if history of epilepsy or psychiatric disorders), or chloroquine/proguanil. Use nets and repellents

V. high risk of TD: implement all food and water hygiene precautions. Parasitic infections in local populations (e.g. hookworm, roundworm). Recently reported outbreak of paragonimiasis, the oriental lung fluke, a lung infestation which comes from eating undercooked shellfish.

GABON

+ 1 hour GMT
Capital: Libreville
Embassy: 27 Elvaston Place, London SW7 5NL (0171823 9986)
British Embassy: closed. Call Foreign Office (0171-270 2516)
Visa required: Yes
Yellow fever certificate: Yes, travellers over 1 year old arriving from all countries
HIV test: No

Recommended health precautions
Immunisations: YF; Hep A; Typh; Pol; Tet. Consider also Men; Rab; Hep B if extended stay

Malaria prophylaxis: High risk of *P. falciparum* (over 90 per cent of all cases are this potentially lethal form), with chloroquine resistance reported. Mefloquine recommended (not for children under 15 kg, during first trimester of pregnancy or if history of epilepsy or psychiatric disorders), or chloroquine/proguanil. Use nets and repellents

V. high risk of TD: implement all food and water hygiene precautions. African tick typhus and Onch (blackflies, mainly in south) also a hazard: avoid bites.

SUDAN

+ 2 hours GMT
Capital: Khartoum
Embassy: 3 Cleveland Row, St James's Street, London SW1W 1DD (0171-839 8080)
British Embassy: PO Box 801, off Sharia Al Baladiya, Khartoum East. Tel: (11) 70760/6/9; Fax: (11) 144 4137
Visa required: Yes
Yellow fever certificate: Yes, if entering from an infected country
HIV test: No

Recommended health precautions
Immunisations: YF; Hep A; Typh; Pol; Tet. Consider also Men; Rab; Hep B if extended stay

Malaria prophylaxis: High risk of *P. falciparum*, with chloroquine resistance reported. Mefloquine recommended (not for children under 15 kg, during first trimester of pregnancy or if history of epilepsy or psychiatric disorders), or chloroquine/proguanil. Use nets and repellents

V. high risk of TD: implement all food and water hygiene precautions. Leish is very common: avoid sandfly bites; at the time of writing a visceral leishmaniasis epidemic had caused deaths. All other common regional afflictions present, including sleeping sickness (south).

Note, at the time of writing there is a civil war in the south of the country. Check with Foreign Office (0171-270 4129) if travelling to Sudan.

ZAIRE

+ 1 to + 2 hours GMT
Capital: Kinshasa
Embassy: 26 Chesham Place, London SW1X 8HH (0171-235 6137).
British Embassy: BP 8049, avenue de Trois Z, Kinshasa-Gombe. Tel (12) 34775/8
Visa required: Yes; check current entry restrictions with embassy
Yellow fever certificate: Yes, travellers over 1 year old from **all** countries
HIV test: No

Recommended health precautions
Immunisations: YF; Hep A; Typh; Pol; Tet. Consider also Men; Rab; Hep B if extended stay. A Chol certificate may or may not be demanded ; you may also need one for onward travel

Malaria prophylaxis: High risk of *P. falciparum*, with drug resistance reported. Mefloquine recommended (not for children under 15 kg, during first trimester of pregnancy or if history of epilepsy or psychiatric disorders), or chloroquine/proguanil. Use nets and repellents

V. high risk of TD: implement all food and water hygiene precautions. Just about all regional specialities are here, including patchy foci of active sleeping sickness; onchocerciasis; and plague (in the NE, outbreak 1991–2; carry tetracycline. Civil unrest has helped make Zaire somewhat unhealthier than previously

ZAMBIA

+ 2 hour GMT
Capital: Lusaka
UK Tourist Office: Zambia National Tourist Office, 2 Palace Gate, Kensington, London W8 5NF (0171-589 6343)
British Consulate: PO Box 50050, Independence Ave, Lusaka. Tel: (1) 228955; Fax: (1) 262 215
Visa required: No
Yellow fever certificate: Yes, all travellers over 1 year old entering from infected country
HIV test: No

Recommended health precautions
Immunisations: Hep A; Typh; Pol; Tet. Consider also Rab; Men; Hep B if extended stay
Malaria prophylaxis: High risk of *P. falciparum*, with chloroquine resistance reported. Mefloquine currently drug of choice (not for children under 15 kg, during first trimester of pregnancy or if history of epilepsy or psychiatric disorders), or chloroquine/proguanil. Use nets and repellents, seek advice if mefloquine unsuitable

There is a risk of travellers' diarrhoea, particularly outside Lusaka: implement all food and water hygiene precautions. There is some sleeping sickness risk in N, foci of other common nasties reported. Worm infestations (hookworm, whipworm) common in rural populations

EAST AFRICA

East Africa includes Burundi, Comoros Islands, Djibouti, Eritrea, Ethiopia, Kenya, Malawi, Mozambique, Madagascar, Mauritius, Reunion islands, Seychelles, Somalia, Tanzania (inc Zanzibar), Uganda.

Note that by mid-1995 the code for telephoning the UK from these countries should begin standardising to 0044-. Check locally, as the date for changeover varies.

HEALTH NEEDS THROUGHOUT THE REGION

Malaria: High risk throughout the region, including towns and cities, except in

Nairobi, Kenya and Addis Ababa, Ethiopia and at high altitude (over 2500 m). There is little risk in resort areas of Mauritius, no risk on the Seychelles and Reunion. Note that the very dangerous *Plasmodium falciparum* is the dominant form, often with rates of over 80 or 90 per cent of total cases (though *P. malariae*, *vivax* and *ovale* also present. Chloroquine resistance is widespread.

Yellow fever: Although most countries do not insist on travellers from the UK being immunised, yellow fever is endemic throughout the region. Rwanda insists on a yellow fever certificate for **all** travellers (over 12 months old), regardless of journey's origin. Otherwise those over 12 months old need an immunisation certificate if travelling on from an infected country.

If travelling from:

Angola, Benin, Bolivia, Brazil, Burkina Faso, Burundi, Cameroon, Central African Republic, Chad, Colombia, Congo, Cote d'Ivoire, Ecuador, Equatorial Guinea, Guyana, Ethiopia, French Guyana, Gabon, Gambia, Ghana, Guinea, Guinea Bissau, Kenya, Liberia,Mali, Mauritania, Niger, Nigeria, Panama, Peru, Rwanda, Sao Tome and Principe, Senegal, Sierra Leone, Somalia, Sudan, Suriname, Tanzania, Togo, Uganda, Venezuela, Zaire

to any country in East Africa (except Comoros) you will need a yellow fever certificate. (Note, children under 9 months should not be immunised.)

Other health risks: Cholera. Against WHO recommendations, some countries may ask for a cholera certificate, particularly if coming from a country where the disease is active. Independent travellers should consider getting a single shot and a piece of paper confirming their injection. The immunisation is not particularly effective, and the best way to avoid cholera is by good food/water hygiene.

Other diseases include: dengue fever (virus spread by day-biting mosquitoes), filariasis (roundworm infections spread by mosquitoes), hepatitis A, hepatitis B, hookworm (from soil: wear shoes), leishmaniasis (sandflies), meningococcal meningitis, rabies, schistosomiasis (not Reunion and Seychelles), typhoid, trypanosomiasis (sleeping sickness, tsetse flies), various intestinal parasites (e.g. *Ascaris*, roundworm) and traveller's diarrhoea. The latter may be caused by bacteria or a variety of protozoans, and may need drug treatment. Note that in some countries (e.g. Tanzania) multi drugresistant strains have appeared.

There is a whole battery of other diseases, from echinococcosis (hydatid disease, cysts caught from dog faeces) to plague that exist, but most travellers will not be at risk. To avoid schistosomiasis, which is carried by some fresh water snails, do not swim or bathe in fresh water. Always wear shoes to prevent invasion by soil parasites and observe the standard rules of food and water hygiene, drinking and brushing teeth in bottled or purified water where supplies suspect, peeling all fruit, cooking all meat well, etc. Avoid unpasteurised dairy products (risk of brucellosis). The most likely affliction for the visitor is the socalled travellers' diarrhoea, caused by organisms such as *E. coli*, *Shigella*, and *Giardia*.

However, throughout the region take care to avoid insect bites, including mosquitoes, sand flies and others. Ticks on dogs and bush ticks may carry typhus. Take malaria prophylaxis.

AIDS is endemic throughout the region, though actual numbers of HIV-positive individuals varies from country to country. No country is completely free of HIV, and some countries have very high rates of HIV infection among groups with high risk behaviour. It is important for travellers, if possible, to avoid medical and dental procedures involving unsterile equipment, and to avoid transfusions involving unscreened blood. Carry your own supply of sterile syringes and needles, etc. Unsafe sex (i.e. penetrative sex without condoms) should also be avoided. However, by following the guidelines in Chapter 13, the average traveller is not at risk from HIV.

In fact, just because **any** disease is listed as being present in a country, it doesn't mean tourists will come into contact with it. Many are in specific foci, and only very adventurous travellers or aid/health workers are at any risk of some of the more exotic infections, and then not always. Malaria and intestinal bugs are dishonourable exceptions.

Immunisations to consider for the East African region include: hepatitis A, hepatitis B (for at-risk groups), meningococcal meningitis, rabies, tetanus, typhoid, yellow fever. Travellers outside main resorts and long-stay workers should ensure tuberculosis, diphtheria and polio are up to date. Note, not all the recommended immunisations may be needed; only yellow fever is a compulsory immunisation. Which others you have will vary with the type and duration of your trip (e.g. travellers to socalled 'international' standard hotels are unlikely to need typhoid). To avoid unnecessary injections discuss your itinerary with a travel clinic/GP.

BURUNDI

+ 2 hours GMT
Capital: Bujumbura
Embassy: Contact the Embassy in Belgium (2-230 4535)
British Consulate: BP 1344, 43 Avenue Bubanza, Bujumbara. Tel: (2) 223711
Visa required: Yes
Yellow fever certificate: Yes, all travellers over 1 year old arriving from an infected area
HIV test: No

Recommended health precautions
Immunisations: YF; Hep A; Typh; Pol; Tet. Consider also Men; Rab; Hep B. Although no reported cases in tourists, there have been outbreaks of meningococcal meningitis (risk May-Oct)

Malaria prophylaxis: chloroquine resistant *P. falciparum* common. Mefloquine prophylaxis recommended (not for children under 15 kg, in the first trimester of pregnancy or where history of epilepsy or psychiatric problems), or chloroquine/proguanil. Use nets and repellents

All water suspect. V. high risk of TD: implement all food and water hygiene precautions. Schis lurks in some of the lakes. Leish and Fil also present

---

COMOROS ISLANDS

+ 3 hours GMT
Capital: Moroni
Embassy: Contact the Embassy in Paris (1 40 67 90 54)
British Consulate: Contact Madagascar
Visa required: Yes, obtainable on arrival
Yellow fever certificate: No (there have been some cases of certificates demanded upon arriving from infected areas, but this is not official policy)
HIV test: No

Recommended health precautions
Immunisations: Hep A; Typh; Pol; Tet. Consider Rab; Hep B

Malaria prophylaxis: The disease is found in all areas. Mefloquine (not for children under 15 kg, during first trimester of pregnancy or if epilepsy or history of psychiatric problems) is the current recommendation, or chloroquine/proguanil. Use nets and repellents.

High risk of TD outside better tourist hotels: implement all food and water hygiene precautions. DF present, along with patchy distribution of other local favourites, such as Fil.

DJIBOUTI

+ 3 hours GMT
Embassy: Contact the Embassy in Paris (1 47 27 49 22)
British Consulate: BP 81, Gellatly Hankey et Cie, Djibouti. Tel: 35 57 18; Fax: 35 32 9.
Visa required: Yes
Yellow fever certificate: Yes if over 1 year old and travelling from infected area
HIV test: No

Recommended health precautions
Immunisations: YF; Hep A; Typh; Pol; Tet. Consider Rab; Hep B; Men

Malaria prophylaxis: *P. falciparum* common, but drug resistance not reported. Mefloquine now first choice drug (not for children under 15 kg, in the first trimester of pregnancy or where history of epilepsy or psychiatric problems), with chloroquine and proguanil still recommended sometimes. Use nets and repellents

Mains water heavily chlorinated. High risk of TD: implement all food and water hygiene precautions. HIV risk low for region

---

ERITREA

+ 3 hours GMT
Capital: Asmara
UK Consulate: 96 White Lion Street, London N1 9PF (0171-713 0096)
Visa required: Yes
Yellow fever certificate: Yes, all travellers arriving from infected area
HIV test: No

Recommended health precautions
Immunisations: YF; Hep A; Typh; Pol; Tet. Consider Rab; Hep B; Men

Malaria prophylaxis: risk countrywide under 2000 m. Drug-resistant *P. falciparum* dominates over *P. vivax*, *ovale* and *malariae*, so mefloquine increasingly recommended (not for children under 15 kg, in first trimester of pregnancy, or where history of epilepsy or psychiatric problems) over chloroquine/proguanil. Use nets/repellents

Water highly unreliable. V. high risk of TD: implement all food and water hygiene precautions. Other diseases include Leish (avoid sandfly bites) and Schis (do not bathe/swim in fresh water). Wear shoes to protect against soil-borne parasites

---

ETHIOPIA

+ 3 hours GMT
Capital: Addis Ababa
Embassy: 17 Prince's Gate, London SW7 1PZ (0171-589 7212)
British Embassy: PO Box 858, Fikre Mariam Abatechan St, Addis Ababa. Tel: AA 612354; Fax: 610588
Visa required: Yes
Yellow fever certificate: Yes if over 1 year old and travelling from an infected area
HIV test: No

Recommended health precautions
Immunisations: YF; Hep A; Typh; Pol; Tet. Consider Rab; Hep B; Men

Malaria prophylaxis: Not in Addis Ababa or highlands. Elsewhere *P. falciparum* most common form, with *P. vivax* and *malariae* also present. Although traditionally a chloroquine and proguanil region, mefloquine now recommended (not for children under 15 kg, in first trimester of pregnancy or where history of epilepsy or psychiatric problems). Use nets/repellents.

Water highly unreliable. V. high risk of TD: implement all food and water hygiene precautions (there is Chol in east of country). Watch for Leish and Schis

---

KENYA

+ 3 hours GMT
Capital: Nairobi
UK Tourist Office: Kenyan National Tourist Office, 25 Brook's Mews, London W1Y 1LG (0171-355 3144)
High Commission: 45 Portland Place, London W1N 4AS (0171-636 2371)
British High Commission: PO Box 30465, Bruce House, Standard St, PO Box 30465, Nairobi. Tel: Nairobi (2) 335 944; Fax: (2)333 196
Visa required: No (yes for UK citizens of Asian origin)
Yellow fever certificate: Yes, all travellers over 1 year old arriving from an infected area
HIV test: No

Recommended health precautions
Immunisations: YF; Hep A; Typh;. Pol; Tet. Consider Rab; Hep B; Men

Malaria prophylaxis: Not in Nairobi or above 2500 m, but endemic elsewhere. *P. falciparum* is the common form (though *P. ovale* and the others present), with much chloroquine resistance. Mefloquine recommended (not for children under 15 kg, in first trimester of pregnancy or where history of epilepsy or psychiatric problems). Use nets and repellents. Seek advice if mefloquine not suitable. (Note that mefloquine resistance has been reported in the west of the country)

Mains water chlorinated. High risk of TD outside of good tourist hotels and resorts, moderate to low within. Stick to bottled water. Watch for bites from sandflies, tsetse flies and mosquitoes. Parts of the country have a high incidence of Ech (hydatid disease, cysts caught from dog faeces). In 1994 there was an outbreak of YF in the Lake Baringo and Elgeyo Marakwet districts, with 24 deaths.

MADAGASCAR

+ 3 hours GMT
Capital: Antananarivo
Consulate: 16 Lanark Mansions, Pennard Road, London W12 8DT (0181-746 0133)
British Embassy: BP 167, First Floor, Immeuble Ny Havana, Cite de 67 Hectares, Antananarivo. Tel: (2) 27749; Fax: (2) 26690
Visa required: Yes
Yellow fever certificate: Yes if travelling from, or having transitted through, an infected country
HIV test: No

Recommended health precautions
Immunisations: Hep A; Typh; Pol; Tet. Consider Rab; Hep B

Malaria prophylaxis: Low risk in the capital and resorts, but common elsewhere. *P. falciparum* common form (over 90 per cent), with reported chloroquine resistance. Mefloquine recommended where appropriate (not for children under 15 kg, in first trimester of pregnancy or where history of epilepsy or psychiatric problems), or chloroquine/proguanil. Use nets and repellents

Water suspect. High risk of TD outside of better tourist hotels. Schis present

---

MALAWI

+ 2 hours GMT
Capital: Lilongwe
High Commission: 33 Grosvenor Street, London W1X ODE (0171-491 4172/7
British High Commission: PO Box 30042, Lingadzi House, Lilongwe 3. Tel: 731544; Fax: 734163
Visa required: No
Yellow fever certificate: Yes, travellers entering from infected country
HIV test: No

Recommended health precautions
Immunisations: YF (for travel in rural areas); Hep A; Typh; Pol; Tet. Consider Rab; Hep B; Men

Note: TRAVAX reports that cholera certificates have been demanded at the border with Tanzania, with up to £20 being charged for immunisation (though I'd pay £20 NOT to be immunised, and you must use your own syringes). Consider being immunised before you leave

Malaria prophylaxis: The disease is widespread with chloroquine-and Fansidar-resistant *P. falciparum* the most common form Mefloquine recommended (not for children under 15 kg, in first trimester of pregnancy or where history of epilepsy or psychiatric problems). Use nets/repellents and seek advice if mefloquine not suitable

Unsafe water. High risk of TD, good food and drink hygiene essential. Most other regional diseases, with an exceptional showing by Schis and Leish. Risk of tick typhus

---

MAURITIUS

+ 4 hours GMT
Capital: Port Louis
UK Tourist Office and High Commission: 32–33 Elvaston Place, London SW7 5NW (0171-584 3666; 0171-581 0294)
British High Commission: PO Box 186, Curepipe, King George V Avenue, Floreal Tel: 686 5795/6/7; Fax: 686 5792
Visa required: No
Yellow fever certificate: Yes, all travellers over 1 year entering from infected country
HIV test: Yes, if working you must have an HIV-free certificate, and there may be retesting 3 months after arrival

Recommended health precautions
Immunisations: Hep A; Typh; Pol; Tet. Consider Rab; Hep B

Malaria prophylaxis: The disease is a risk in certain rural areas (but not Rodriquez Island). *P. falciparum* with some chloroquine resistance reported. Nevertheless, risk is low, though chloroquine and proguanil still often recommended. Mefloquine increasingly preferred, but only if travelling extensively rurally. Use nets/repellents

Water unsafe. Risk of TD outside of large hotels/resorts, good food and drink hygiene essential

---

MOZAMBIQUE

+ 2 hours GMT
Capital: Maputo
Embassy: 21 Fitzroy Square, London W1P 5HJ (0171-383 3800)
British Embassy: Caixa Postal 55, Av Vladimir I Lenine 310, Maputo. Tel: (1) 420 111/2; Fax: (1) 421 666
Visa required: Yes, independent travel restricted
Yellow fever certificate: Yes, travellers over 1 year old entering from infected country
HIV test: No

Recommended health precautions
Immunisations: Hep A; Typh; Pol; Tet.

Consider Rab; Hep B; Men (recent outbreaks in army camps)

Malaria prophylaxis: the disease is widespread, including urban areas, with *P. falciparum* the common form, with the other three less than 10 per cent combined. Mefloquine recommended (not for children under 15 kg, in first trimester of pregnancy or where history of epilepsy or psychiatric problems), or chloroquine and proguanil. Use nets and repellents

High risk of TD, good food and drink hygiene essential. Drinking water suspect. Schis common

---

REUNION

+ 4 hours GMT (+ 3 in summer)
Capital: Saint-Denis
Embassy: Contact Reunion Tourism in Paris (1 40 75 02 79)
Visa required: No
Yellow fever certificate: Yes, travellers over 1 year old entering from infected country
HIV test: No

Recommended health precautions
Immunisations: Hep A; Typh; Pol; Tet, consider Hep B

Malaria prophylaxis: No

Public water supplies unsafe: risk of TD, good food and drink hygiene essential. No real parasite threats to tourists

---

RWANDA

+ 2 hours GMT
Capital: Kigali
Embassy: Contact Brussels (2 763 0705)
British Consulate: BP 356, avenue Paul VI, Kigali. Tel: 75219/75905
Visa required: Yes
Yellow fever certificate: Yes, all travellers over 1 year old
HIV test: No

Recommended health precautions
Note, at the time of writing the aftermath of the civil unrest means it is impossible to assess the true health situation in the country. Suffice it to say, it certainly hasn't improved.

Immunisations: YF; Hep A; Typh; Pol; Tet. Consider Rab; Hep B; Men

Malaria prophylaxis: The disease is widespread (including urban areas) with *P. falciparum* the common form. Chloroquine and Fansidar resistance common. Mefloquine recommended (not for children under 15 kg, in first trimester of pregnancy or where history of epilepsy or psychiatric problems), or chloroquine and proguanil. Use nets and repellents.

V. high risk of TD, good food and drink hygiene essential. All other major local diseases present to some degree

---

SEYCHELLES

+ 4 hours GMT
Capital: Victoria, Mahe
UK Tourist Office and High Commission: PO Box 4PE 2nd Floor, Eros House, 111 Baker Street, London W1M 1FE (0171-224 1670/0171224 1660)
British High Commission: PO Box 161, 3rd Floor, Victoria House, 3rd floor, 161, Mahe. Tel: 225 225
Visa required: No
Yellow fever certificate: Yes, all travellers arriving from infected countries
HIV test: Yes, if working for the government or one of its agencies

Recommended health precautions
Immunisations: Hep A; Typh; Pol; Tet. Sometimes Rab; Hep B

Malaria prophylaxis: No

Risk of TD low, but stick to bottled water as mains supply variable in quality. Few indigenous diseases likely to affect tourists

---

SOMALIA

+ 3 hours GMT
Capital: Mogadishu
Embassy: 60 Portland Place, London W1N 3DG (0171-580 7148)
British Embassy: PO Box 1036, Hassan Geedi Abtow, 7/8, Mogadishu. Tel: 20288/9
Visa required: Yes
Yellow fever certificate: Yes, all travellers entering from infected country. Note: Somalia may also demand a cholera certificate if travelling from an infected area
HIV test: No

Recommended health precautions
Note, at the time of writing the country is still in a state of civil unrest. Contact the Foreign Office for travel advice: 0171-279 4129

Immunisations: YF; Hep A; Typh; Pol; Tet. Consider Rab; Hep B; Men

Malaria prophylaxis: The disease is widespread with *P. falciparum* the common form (the others constitute less than 10 per cent of all cases). Mefloquine recommended (not for children under 15 kg, in first trimester of pregnancy or where history of epilepsy or psychiatric problems), or chloroquine and proguanil. Use nets/repellents

V. high risk of TD, good food and drink hygiene essential. DF (patchy), Schis, Fil (south) and other diseases common

---

TANZANIA

+ 3 hours GMT
Capital: Dodoma (Admin) Dar es Salaam (Comm)
High Commission: 43 Hertford Street, London W1Y 8DB (0171-499 8951)
British High Commission: PO Box 9200, Hifadhi House, Samora Ave, Dar es Salaam. Tel: (51) 29601; Fax: (51) 46301
Visa required: No, but visitor's pass
Yellow fever certificate: Yes, all travellers over 1 year old
Note: Tanzania also often demands a Chol certificate if travelling from an infected area
HIV test: No

Recommended health precautions
Immunisations: YF; Hep A; Typh; Pol;. Tet. Consider Rab; Hep B; Men; Chol

Malaria prophylaxis: The disease is widespread with *P. falciparum* the common form (*malariae* and *ovale* make up the rest). This includes areas below 2000 m and Zanzibar and Pemba islands. Hefty chloroquine and Fansidar (treatment) resistance: mefloquine now preferred drug (not for children under 15 kg, in first trimester of pregnancy or where history of epilepsy or psychiatric problems). Seek advice if mefloquine not suitable. Use nets and repellents

Mains water none too clean. High risk of TD, good food and drink hygiene essential. Most other diseases of the region (Schis, Onch (patchy), tick typhus) present

---

UGANDA

+ 3 hours GMT (+ 2 in summer)
Capital: Kampala
High Commission: Uganda House 5859 Trafalgar Square, London WC2N 5DX (0171-839 5783)
British High Commission: 10/12 Parliament Ave, PO Box 7070, Kampala. Tel: (41) 257054/9
Visa required: No
Yellow fever certificate: Yes, all travellers over 1 year old entering from infected country
Note: Uganda may also demand a Chol certificate if travelling from an infected area
HIV test: No

Recommended health precautions
Immunisations: YF; Hep A; Typh; Pol; Tet. Consider Rab; Hep B; Men

Malaria prophylaxis: The disease is widespread, all year, all areas, with *P. falciparum* the common form. Due to widespread drug resistance, mefloquine is now recommended (not for children under 15 kg, in first trimester of pregnancy or where history of epilepsy or psychiatric problems) over chloroquine and proguanil. Nets and repellents essential

V. high risk of TD: good food and drink

hygiene essential. All other diseases present in some part or other of the country, though the sleeping sickness is very patchy

---

WEST AFRICA

West Africa includes Benin, Burkino Faso, Cape Verde Islands, Cote d'Ivoire, Gambia, Ghana, Guinea, Guinea-Bissau, Liberia, Mali, Mauritania, Niger, Nigeria, Sao Tome and Principe, Senegal, Sierra Leone and Togo.

Note that from 1995, the international dialling code to the UK from all these countries should be 0044-. Check locally, as the speed of standardisation varies.

HEALTH RISKS THROUGHOUT THE REGION

Malaria: A high risk of malaria exists throughout the year for all countries except the Cape Verde Islands. Malaria prophylaxis is essential, as is protection against mosquito bites. Resistance to chloroquine is widespread. The common form is the malignant *P. falciparum*, which may account for over 90 per cent of the cases.

Yellow fever: West Africa is a yellow fever endemic area. The following countries require a yellow fever certificate for entrance, regardless of where travelling from:

Benin, Burkino Faso, Cote d'Ivoire, Ghana, Liberia, Mali, Mauritania, Niger, Sao Tome and Principe, Senegal, Togo.

If travelling from one of the countries mentioned below to Cape Verde Islands, Equatorial Guinea, Gambia, Guinea, Guinea-Bissau, Nigeria, Sierra Leone you are also required to have a yellow fever certificate:

Angola, Benin, Bolivia, Brazil, Burkina Faso, Burundi, Cameroon, Central African Republic, Chad, Colombia, Congo, Cote d'Ivoire, Ecuador, Equatorial Guinea, Ethiopia, French Guyana, Gabon, Gambia, Ghana, Guinea, Guinea Bissau, Guyana, Kenya, Liberia, Mali, Mauritania, Niger, Nigeria, Panama, Peru, Rwanda, Sao Tome and Principe, Senegal, Sierra Leone, Somalia, Sudan, Suriname, Tanzania, Togo, Uganda, Venezuela, Zaire.

Note, restrictions usually apply to travellers over 12 months old; children under 9 months should not be immunised.

Cholera: Against WHO recommendations, some countries may ask for a cholera certificate, particularly if coming from a country where the disease is active.

Independent travellers should consider getting just a single shot and a piece of paper confirming their injection. The immunisation is not particularly effective, and the best way to avoid cholera is by good food/water hygiene.

Other health risks: The region is part of the meningitis belt across Africa. A whole variety of diseases are spread by biting insects, including filariasis (spread by mosquitoes), leishmaniasis (sandflies), onchocerciasis (river blindness, black flies), trypanosomiasis (sleeping sickness, tsetse flies). Dengue fever (from mosquitoes) occurs throughout West Africa, most recently in Burkino Faso, Cote d'Ivoire, Guinea, Nigeria, and Senegal. Take precautions against insect bites and tick bites (the latter spread African tick typhus), using nets, clothing and insect repellents.

Schistosomiasis, a parasitic infection from some fresh water snails, is widespread, especially in Burkino Faso, Mali, Niger and Nigeria. No unchlorinated fresh water should be used for bathing/washing/paddling.

AIDS is endemic throughout the region, though the percentage of HIV-positive individuals in the population varies from country to country. No country is completely free. It is important for travellers, if possible, to avoid medical and dental procedures involving unsterile equipment, and to avoid transfusions using unscreened blood. Carry your own supply of sterile syringes and needles, etc. Unsafe sex (i.e. penetrative sex without condoms) should also be avoided. However, by following the guidelines in Chapter 13, the average traveller is not at risk from HIV.

Hepatitis B is hyperendemic, both A and E are widespread, the latter a particular problem during pregnancy. Cholera, typhoid and the bacteria/protozoans causing diarrhoea are also very common. Lassa fever, a viral disease spread by rats, is found in the region, particularly Liberia and Sierra Leone, though the risk to most travellers is small.

Parasitic worm infections are common in the local populations, particularly in rural areas, including Guinea worm (*Dracunculus*), hookworm, roundworm, tapeworms and various flukes. You should wear shoes at all times, drink only sterilised water and cook all food thoroughly. Unpasteurised dairy products may carry brucellosis. Travellers' diarrhoea, caused by organisms such as *E.coli*, *Giardia* or *Entamoeba*, is the most likely cause of illness. Rabies is also present throughout West Africa.

Note that just because a disease is present in a country doesn't mean the tourist will come into contact with it. Many are in specific foci, and only very adventurous travellers or aid/health workers are at any risk at all, and then not always. Malaria and intestinal bugs are dishonourable exceptions.

Note also that not all advised immunisations may be required (though this is one region of the world where they probably will be). Check with your travel clinic or GP. Long-stay visitors may be required to have their diphtheria and tuberculosis protection brought up to date.

BENIN

+ 1 hour GMT
Capital: PortoNovo
Consulate: 16 The Broadway, Stanmore, Middx JA7 4DW (0181-954 8800)
British Consulate: BP147, SOBEPAT, Cotonou. Tel: 313342/312058
Visa required: Yes (only 15-day visas available)
Yellow fever certificate: Yes, travellers over 1 year of age from all countries
HIV test: No

Recommended health precautions
Immunisations: YF; Hep A; Typh; Pol; Tet. Consider also Men; Rab; Hep B if extended stay

Malaria prophylaxis: High risk of *P. falciparum*, with drug resistance (including mefloquine) reported. Mefloquine recommended (not for children under 15 kg, in first trimester of pregnancy or if history of epilepsy or psychiatric disorders), or chloroquine and proguanil. Use nets and repellents

V. high risk of TD: implement all food and water hygiene precautions. Protect particularly against Schis, and ticks from dogs, in rural areas, in case of African tick typhus.

BURKINA FASO

+ 0 hour GMT
Capital: Ouagadougou
Honorary Consulate: 5 Cinnamon Row, Plantation Wharf, London SW11 3TW (0171-738 1800)
British Embassy: Dealt with by Cote d'Ivoire
Visa required: Yes, can be obtained on arrival
Yellow fever certificate: Yes, all travellers over 1 year of age from all countries
HIV test: No

Recommended health precautions
Immunisations: YF; Hep A; Typh; Pol; Tet. Consider also Men; Rab; Hep B if extended stay

Malaria prophylaxis: High risk of *P. falciparum*, with widespread multi-drug resistance reported. Mefloquine recommended (not for children under

15 kgs, during first trimester of pregnancy or if history of epilepsy or psychiatric disorders) or chloroquine and proguanil. Use nets and repellents

V.high risk of TD: implement all food and water hygiene precautions. There have been DF epidemics; Schis infection common. Protect also against Fil, sleeping sickness, Onch. In fact, treat every insect as hostile

---

CAPE VERDE ISLANDS

-1 hour GMT
Capital: Cidape de Praia
Embassies: N/a, visas obtainable on arrival
Visa required: Yes
Yellow fever certificate: Yes, if over 1 year of age and arriving from a country that has had a yellow fever case in the last 6 years
HIV test: No

Recommended health precautions
Immunisations: Hep A; Typh; Pol; Tet. Consider Rab; Hep B if extended stay

Malaria prophylaxis: No risk of malaria, except perhaps on Sao Tiago, where chloroquine or proguanil is recommended

Water quality poor. High risk of TD: implement all food and water hygiene precautions. DF, Leish, Fil and tick typhus known

---

COTE D'IVOIRE

+ 0 hour GMT
Capital: Abidjan
Embassy: 2 Upper Belgrave Street, London SW1X 8BJ (0171-235 6991)
British Consulate: 3rd Floor, Immueble 'Les Harmonies', Angle Boulevard, Carde et Avenue Dr Jamot, Plateau, 01BP2581, Abidjan. Tel: 226 850/1/2; Fax: 223 221
Visa required: No
Yellow fever certificate: Yes, travellers over 1 year of age arriving from all countries
HIV test: No

Recommended health precautions
Immunisations: YF; Hep A; Typh; Pol; Tet. Consider also Men; Rab; Hep B if extended stay

Malaria prophylaxis: High risk of *P. falciparum*, with drug resistance reported. Mefloquine recommended (not for children under 15 kg, during first trimester of pregnancy or ifhistory of epilepsy or psychiatric disorders), or chloroquine and proguanil. Use nets and repellents

V. high risk of TD: implement all food and water hygiene precautions. Protection needed against most insect-borne diseases common to region. Schis present

---

GAMBIA

+ 0 hour GMT
Capital: Banjul
UK Tourist Office and High Commission: 57 Kensington Court, London W8 5DG (0171-937 6316/7/8)
British High Commission: PO Box 507, 48 Atlantic Road, Fajara, Banjul. Tel: 95133/4; Fax: 96134
Visa required: No
Yellow fever certificate: Yes, all travellers over 1 year old arriving from an infected country
HIV test: No

Recommended health precautions
Immunisations: YF; Hep A; Typh; Pol;. Tet. Consider also Men; Rab; Hep B if extended stay

Malaria prophylaxis: High risk of *P. falciparum*, with chloroquine resistance reported. Mefloquine recommended (not for children under 15 kg, during first trimester of pregnancy or if history of epilepsy or psychiatric disorders), or chloroquine and proguanil. Use nets and repellents

Water supplies generally unsafe. Risk of travellers' diarrhoea outside the better resort hotels on coast: take all food and drink hygiene precautions. Schis risk along the river that makes up the country: avoid swimming, etc. Risk of Fil

---

GHANA

+ 0 hour GMT
Capital: Accra
High Commission: 104 Highgate Hill, London N6 5HE (0181-342 8686). For tourist information ring 0171-493 4901
British High Commission: PO Box 296, Osu Link, Off Gamel Abdul Nasser Avenue, Accra. Tel: (21) 221665; Fax: (21) 224 572
Visa required: Yes
Yellow fever certificate: Yes, all travellers from **all** countries
HIV test: No

Recommended health precautions
Immunisations: YF; Hep A; Typh; Pol; Tet. Consider also Men; Rab; Hep B if extended stay

Malaria prophylaxis: High risk of *P. falciparum*, with chloroquine resistance reported. Mefloquine recommended (not for children under 15 kg, during first trimester of pregnancy or if history of epilepsy or psychiatric disorders), or chloroquine and proguanil. Use nets and repellents

There is a risk of TD, even where there is a piped water supply: implement all food and water hygiene precautions. The usual parasitic suspects are present, with a v. high incidence of hookworm and intestinal worms. Avoid insect/tick bites. There has been an outbreak of YF in the north and east in recent years; a programme of mass immunisation has been instituted

---

GUINEA

+ 0 hour GMT
Capital: Conakry
Embassy: Contact Paris (1 47 04 81 48)
British Consulate: BP 834 Conakry. Tel: 46 17 34 or 46 53 61; Fax: 44 42 15
Visa required: Yes; no tourist visas, business only
Yellow fever certificate: Yes, travellers over 1 year arriving from an infected country
HIV test: No

Recommended health precautions
Immunisations: YF; Hep A; Typh; Pol; Tet. Consider also Men (outbreaks in Kerowane and Kissidougou in 1993; deaths); Rab; Hep B if extended stay. Guinea, or its neighbours, may ask to see a Chol certificate if arriving from an infective area

Malaria prophylaxis: High risk of *P. falciparum*, with drug resistance reported. Mefloquine recommended (not for children under 15 kg, during first trimester of pregnancy or if history of epilepsy or psychiatric disorders), or chloroquine and proguanil. Use nets and repellents

V. high risk of TD: implement all food and water hygiene precautions. Take precautions against mosquito, blackfly and tsetse fly bites

---

GUINEA-BISSAU

+ 0 hour GMT
Capital: Bissau
Embassy: 8 Palace Gate, London W8 4RP (0171-589 5253)
British Consulate: CP 100, Mavegro International, Bissau. Tel: 21 15 29
Visa required: Yes
Yellow fever certificate: Yes, if travelling from an infected country
HIV test: No

Recommended health precautions
Immunisations: YF; Hep A; Typh; Pol; Tet. Consider also Men; Rab; Hep B if extended stay

Malaria prophylaxis: High risk of *P.*

falciparum, with drug resistance reported. Mefloquine recommended (not for children under 15 kg, during first trimester of pregnancy or if history of epilepsy or psychiatric disorders), or chloroquine and proguanil. Use nets and repellents

V. high risk of TD: implement all food and water hygiene precautions. Usual collection of insect-borne diseases, including sleeping sickness

---

LIBERIA

+ 0 hour GMT
Capital: Monrovia
Embassy: 2 Pembridge Place, London W2 4XB (0171-221 1036)
British Consulate: Contact Freetown, Sierra Leone
Visa required: Yes
Yellow fever certificate: Yes, all travellers over 1 year old (to be presented with visa application). Note: May still ask for cholera certificate
HIV test: No

Recommended health precautions
Immunisations: YF; Hep A; Typh; Pol; Tet. Consider also Men; Rab; Hep B if extended stay. (And perhaps a Chol certificate)

Malaria prophylaxis: High risk of *P. falciparum*, with drug resistance reported (including mefloquine and Fansidar). Mefloquine recommended (not for children under 15 kg, during first trimester of pregnancy or if history of epilepsy or psychiatric disorders), or chloroquine and proguanil. Use nets and repellents

V. high risk of TD: implement all food and water hygiene precautions. Lung flukes possible from raw shellfish. Full complement of insect-borne diseases present

---

MALI

+ 0 hour GMT
Capital: Bamako
Embassy: Contact Embassy in Brussels (2 345 74 32)
British Consulate: BP2069, Bamako, Mali
Visa required: Yes, 1 month only
Yellow fever certificate: Yes, all travellers over 1 year old from **all** countries
HIV test: No

Recommended health precautions
Immunisations: YF; Hep A; Typh; Pol; Tet. Consider also Men (particularly in south); Rab; Hep B if extended stay

Malaria prophylaxis: High risk of *P. falciparum*, with drug resistance to both chloroquine and mefloquine reported. Mefloquine recommended (not for children under 15 kg, during first trimester of pregnancy or if history of epilepsy or psychiatric disorders), or chloroquine and proguanil. Use nets and repellents

V. high risk of TD: implement all food and water hygiene precautions. Major parasites present, risk factors higher in south (e.g. for Onch)

MAURITANIA

+ 0 hour GMT
Capital: Nouakchott
Embassy: Contact Paris (1 45 04 88 54)
British Consulate: Contact Rabat, Morocco
Visa required: Yes
Yellow fever certificate: Yes, all travellers over 1 year old, unless arriving from a non-infected area and staying less than 2 weeks
HIV test: No

Recommended health precautions
Immunisations: YF; Hep A; Typh; Pol; Tet. Consider also Men; Rab; Hep B if extended stay

Malaria prophylaxis: Low risk of *P. falciparum*, high risk of *P. vivax* in most areas of the country. Chloroquine and proguanil or, increasingly, mefloquine recommended (not for children under 15 kg, during first trimester of pregnancy or if history of epilepsy or psychiatric disorders). Maloprim sometimes given as alternative regime (not widely used in UK). Malaria risk decreases in the desert areas of the north (risk mainly July–Oct). Use nets and repellents where appropriate

V. high risk of travellers' diarrhoea: implement all food and water hygiene precautions. DF and sleeping sickness risk low, more of a risk with others (e.g. Leish, Schis)

NIGER

+ 1 hour GMT
Capital: Niamey
Embassy: Contact Paris (1 45 04 80 60)
Honorary British Vice-Consulate: BP 11168, Niamey. Tel: 732015 or 732539
Visa required: No
Yellow fever certificate: Yes, travellers over 1 year old arriving from all countries
HIV test: No

Recommended health precautions
Immunisations: YF; Hep A; Typh; Pol; Tet. Consider also Men; Rab; Hep B if extended stay

Malaria prophylaxis: High risk of *P. falciparum*, particularly in south, with drug resistance reported. Mefloquine recommended (not for children under 15 kg, in first trimester of pregnancy or if history of epilepsy or psychiatric disorders), or chloroquine and proguanil. Use nets and repellents

V. high risk of TD: implement all food and water hygiene precautions. Most parasitic diseases of the region present (e.g. Fil, Schis, Onch, tick typhus and patches of sleeping sickness)

NIGERIA

+ 1 hour GMT
Capital: Lagos
High Commission: Nigeria House, 9 Northumberland Avenue, London WC2N 5BX (0171-839 1244). Consular section at 56–57 Fleet St EC4 (0171-353 3776)
British High Commission: PB 12136, 11 Eleke Crescent, Victoria Island, Lagos. Tel: (1) 619531/7
Visa required: Yes
Yellow fever certificate: Yes, if over 1 year old and arriving from infected country
HIV test: No

Recommended health precautions
Immunisations: YF; Hep A; Typh; Pol; Tet. Consider also Men; Rab; Hep B if extended stay

Malaria prophylaxis: High risk of *P. falciparum*, with multidrug resistance reported. Mefloquine recommended (not for children under 15 kg, during first trimester of pregnancy or if history of epilepsy or psychiatric disorders), or chloroquine and proguanil. Use nets and repellents

V. high risk of TD: implement all food and water hygiene precautions. High rural rates of parasitic infections including *Dracunculus* (guinea worm) and hookworm, and some areas of high Fil infection; DF active in the south. Avoid all insect/tick bites

---

SAO TOME & PRINCIPE

+ 0 hour GMT
Capital: Sao Tome
Embassy: 42 North Audley Street, London W1A 4PY (0171-488 1995)
British Consulate: Hull Blythe (Angola) Ltd, BP 15, Sao Tome. Telex: 220 (a/b HBALTD ST)
Visa required: Yes
Yellow fever certificate: Yes, all those over 1 year old, unless arriving from non-infected country and staying for less than 2 weeks
HIV test: No

Recommended health precautions
Immunisations: YF; Hep A; Typh; Pol; Tet. Consider also Men; Rab; Hep B if extended stay

Malaria prophylaxis: High risk of *P. falciparum*, with chloroquine resistance reported. Mefloquine recommended (not for children under 15 kg, during first trimester of pregnancy or if history of epilepsy or psychiatric disorders), or chloroquine and proguanil. Use nets and repellents

High risk of TD: implement all food and water hygiene precautions. Schis and Fil are the main diseases

---

SENEGAL

+ 0 hour GMT
Capital: Dakar
Embassy: 11 Phillimore Gardens, London W8 7QG (0171-937 0925)
British Embassy: BP 6025, 20 Rue du Docteur Guillet, Dakar. Tel: 237392; Fax: 23 27 66
Visa required: No
Yellow fever certificate: Yes, all travellers over 1 year old from all countries
HIV test: No

Recommended health precautions
Immunisations: YF; Hep A; Typh; Pol; Tet. Consider also Men; Rab; Hep B if extended stay

Malaria prophylaxis: High risk of *P. falciparum*, with drug resistance reported. Mefloquine recommended (not for children under 15 kg, during first trimester of pregnancy or if history of epilepsy or psychiatric disorders), or chloroquine and proguanil. Use nets and repellents

High risk of TD: implement all food and water hygiene precautions. Most regional diseases present, but sleeping sickness rare. TRAVAX reports cases of Schis flukes resistant to praziquantel (the drug usually used to cure it) an even more important reason not to mess about in unknown waters

---

SIERRA LEONE

+ 0 hour GMT
Capital: Freetown
UK Tourist Office/High Commission: 33 Portland Place, London W1N 3AG (0171-636 6483)
British High Commission: Standard Chartered Bank of Sierra Leone Building, Lightfoot Boston Street, Freetown. Tel: 223961
Visa required: Yes
Yellow fever certificate: Yes, all travellers arriving from infected country
HIV test: No

Recommended health precautions
Immunisations: YF; Hep A; Typh; Pol; Tet. Consider also Men; Rab; Hep B if extended stay

Malaria prophylaxis: High risk of *P. falciparum*, with drug resistance reported. Mefloquine recommended (not for children under 15 kg, in first trimester of pregnancy or if history of epilepsy or psychiatric disorders), or chloroquine and proguanil. Use nets and repellents

Risk of TD: implement all food and water hygiene precautions. Lassa fever risk in rural areas, possible sleeping sickness (patchy) plus the usual suspects in various locales

---

TOGO

+ 0 hour GMT
Capital: Lome
Embassy: Contact Paris (1 43 80 12 13)
British Consulate: BP 20050, British School of Lome, Lome. Tel: 214 606; Fax: 214 989
Visa required: No, up to 90 days
Yellow fever certificate: Yes, all travellers over 1 year old coming from all countries
HIV test: No

Recommended health precautions
Immunisations: YF; Hep A; Typh; Pol; Tet. Consider also Men; Rab; Hep B if extended stay

Malaria prophylaxis: High risk of *P. falciparum*, with chloroquine resistance reported. Mefloquine recommended (not for children under 15 kg, during first trimester of pregnancy or if history of epilepsy or psychiatric disorders), or chloroquine and proguanil. Use nets and repellents

Some safe water, but generally high risk of TD: implement all food and water hygiene precautions. Low but persistent levels of all regional afflictions (Fil, Schis, tick typhus, etc.)

SOUTHERN AFRICA

Southern Africa includes Botswana, Namibia, South Africa, Swaziland and Zimbabwe.

Note that from 1995, the international dialling code to the UK from all these countries should be 0044-. Check locally, as the speed of standardisation varies.

HEALTH RISKS THROUGHOUT THE REGION

Malaria: Malaria is patchily distributed in Zimbabwe (mainly in the north, Harare is malaria-free), South Africa (rural areas, including game parks, northern Natal, parts of the Transvaal), northern Botswana and northern Namibia. The dominant form (up to 99 per cent of cases) is *P. falciparum*.

Yellow fever: Southern Africa is outside the yellow fever endemic zone, so the risk of catching it is far lower than the central sub-Saharan countries. Botswana has no yellow fever entry requirements. However, Namibia, South Africa and Zimbabwe require a certificate if you are entering from an endemic yellow fever zone. These are: Angola, Benin, Bolivia, Brazil, Burkina Faso, Burundi, Cameroon, Central African Republic, Chad, Colombia, Congo, Cote d'Ivoire, Ecuador, Equatorial Guinea, Ethiopia, French Guyana, Gabon, Gambia, Ghana, Guinea, Guinea Bissau, Guyana, Kenya, Liberia, Mali, Mauritania, Niger, Nigeria, Panama, Peru, Rwanda, Sao Tome and Principe, Senegal, Sierra Leone, Somalia, Sudan, Suriname, Tanzania, Togo, Uganda, Venezuela, Zaire.

Note, restrictions usually apply to travellers over 12 months old. Children under 9 months should not be immunised.

Cholera: Against WHO recommendations, some countries, notably Zimbabwe, may ask for a cholera certificate, particularly if coming from a country where the disease is active. Independent travellers should consider getting just a single shot and a piece of paper confirming their immunisation. The immunisation is not particularly effective, and the best way to avoid cholera is by good food and water hygiene.

Other health risks: The region is **not** part of the meningitis belt across Africa, but there is evidence the belt is slipping and moving south. For instance Windhoek in Namibia, traditionally clear, has had cases. As 80 per cent of all cases are in under-25s, children in particular are at risk (remember, though, only A and C can be immunised against). Many of the other diseases found further north are still active in this region, though sleeping sickness is very sporadic, with little risk to tourists.

Schistosomiasis (bilharzia, fluke infection from some fresh water snails) is widespread, and there are cases of leishmaniasis, mainly in Namibia. Take the usual precautions against insect bites and tick bites (the latter spread African tick typhus), using nets, clothing and insect repellents.

AIDS is present throughout the region, though actual percentage rates of HIV-positive individuals varies from country to country. No country is completely free, though at the time of writing the rates do not approach those found further north. Nevertheless, it is important for travellers to avoid medical and dental procedures involving unsterile equipment, and to avoid transfusions involving unscreened blood. Carry your own supply of sterile syringes, needles, etc.,and avoid unsafe sex (see Chapter 13).

Hepatitis B is endemic, and both A and E are widespread, the latter is a problem during pregnancy. Cholera, typhoid and the bacteria/protozoans causing diarrhoea may be present, particularly away from major urban centres.

Parasitic worm infections are very common in the many rural populations, particularly in poor areas, including hookworm, roundworm (*Ascaris*), tapeworms and various flukes. You should wear shoes at all times, drink only sterilised water and cook all food thoroughly. Travellers' diarrhoea is the most common affliction for visitors.

Rabies is present throughout Southern Africa. Note that just because a disease is present in a country doesn't mean the tourist will come into contact with it. Many are in specific foci, and only very adventurous travellers or aid/health workers are at any risk at all, and then not always. Malaria (in those regions where it occurs) and intestinal bugs are dishonourable exceptions.

Note also that not all recommended immunisations may be required. Check with your travel clinic or GP. Long-stay visitors may be required to have their diphtheria and tuberculosis protection brought up to date.

BOTSWANA

+ 2 hours GMT (+ 1 in summer)
Capital: Gaborone
High Commission: 6 Stratford Place, London W1N 9AE (0171-499 0031)
British High Commission: Private Bag 0023, Garbarone. Tel: (3) 52841; Fax: (3) 56105
Visa required: No
Yellow fever certificate: No, not officially, but if entering from an infected area, it is a good idea, just in case
HIV test: No

Recommended health precautions
Immunisations: Hep A; Typh; Pol; Tet. Consider also Rab; Hep B

Malaria prophylaxis: The disease occurs Nov–Jun, mainly in the north. Drug resistant *P. falciparum* common. Mefloquine prophylaxis increasingly recommended (not for children under 15 kg, in first trimester of pregnancy or where history of epilepsy or psychiatric problems). Chloroquine and proguanil, or Maloprim sometimes suggested as alternative. Use nets and repellents

High risk of TD: implement all food and water hygiene precautions. The Okavango Delta is a very popular safari area; it has some sleeping sickness. Risk of tick typhus and TBE. Avoid bites

NAMIBIA

+ 2 hours GMT
Capital: Windhoek
Commission: 6 Chandos Street, London W1M OLQ (0171-636 6244)
British Consulate: 116A Leutwein Street, Windhoek 9000. Tel: (61) 223022; Fax: (61) 228895
Visa required: No
Yellow fever certificate: Yes, if over 1 year old and arriving from infected area
HIV test: No

Recommended health precautions
Immunisations: Hep A; Typh; Pol; Tet. Consider also Rab; Hep B. In 1994 there were cases of meningococcal meningitis in the north and in Windhoek. Not usually a prime risk area, but long-stay workers should consider immunisation.

Malaria prophylaxis: Risk usually from Nov–Jun, in northern areas (all year along Kavango river), though appears to be spreading. Unfortunately the form prevalent at this time is the chloroquine-resistant *P. falciparum* we have come to know and hate. Mefloquine prophylaxis often recommended (not for children under 15 kg, in first trimester of pregnancy or where history of epilepsy or psychiatric problems) with the usual chloroquine and paludrine alternative, or sometimes chloroquine and proguanil with a maloprim alternative (the latter is not widely used in the UK). Use nets/repellents

Risk of TD outside major urban centres and good hotels: implement all food and water hygiene precautions. Leish, sleeping sickness: avoid bites

---

SOUTH AFRICA

+ 2 hours GMT
Capital: Pretoria
UK Tourist Office: South Africa Tourist Board, 5/6 Alt Grove, Wimbledon, London SW19 4DZ (0181-944 8080)
Embassy: Trafalgar Square, London WC2N 5DP (0171-930 4488)
British Embassy: 255 Hill St, Pretoria. Tel: (12) 433121; Fax: (12) 433 207 (from JulDec). 91 Parliament St, Cape Town. Tel: (21) 461 7220; Fax: (21) 461 0017. (JanJune). Consulates in Johannesburg, East London, Port Elizabeth and Durban
Visa required: No
Yellow fever certificate: Yes, if over 1 year of age and coming from an infected area
HIV test: There are restrictions on HIV-positive individuals

Recommended health precautions
Immunisations: Hep A; Typh; Pol; Tet. Consider also Rab; Hep B

Malaria prophylaxis: There is a risk in Transvaal (inc. Kruger National Park) and eastern Natal. Drug resistant *P. falciparum* common form. At the moment chloroquine and proguanil or mefloquine recommended (not for children under 15 kg, in first trimester of pregnancy or where history of epilepsy or psychiatric problems). Use nets/repellents

Low risk of TD in urban areas. If travelling rurally implement all food and water hygiene precautions. Note that SA has excellent medical facilities in major cities

---

SWAZILAND

+ 2 hours GMT
Capital: Mbabane
High Commission: 58 Pont Street, London SW1X 0AE (0171-581 4976)
British High Commission: Allister Miller Street, Mbabane. Tel: 42581; Fax: 42585
Visa required: No
Yellow fever certificate: Yes, all travellers arriving from infected areas
HIV test: No

Recommended health precautions
Immunisations: Hep A; Typh; Pol; Tet. Consider also Rab; Hep B

Malaria prophylaxis: There is a risk of malaria all year-round in low veld areas. Highly chloroquine-resistant *P. falciparum* common form. Mefloquine prophylaxis recommended (not for children under 15 kg, in the first trimester of pregnancy or where history of epilepsy or psychiatric problems), or chloroquine and proguanil. Use nets/repellents

High risk of TD; water supplies in towns usually safe, but bottled/sterilised water preferable. If travelling rurally implement strict food and water hygiene precautions and avoid bathing in fresh water (risk of Schis). Take precautions against tick bites, which may transmit a variety of diseases, and soil-borne parasites (wear shoes)

ZIMBABWE

+ 2 hours GMT
Capital: Harare
UK Tourist Office: Zimbabwe Tourist Office, Zimbabwe High Commission, 429 The Strand, London WC2R 0QE (0171-836 7755)
British Consulate: PO Box 4490, Stanley House, Jason Moyo Avenue, PO Box 4490, Harare. Tel: (4) 793781; Fax: (4) 728380
Visa required: No
Yellow fever certificate: Yes, all travellers arriving from an infected area
HIV test: No

Recommended health precautions
Immunisations: Hep A; Typh; Pol; Tet. Consider also Rab; Hep B. Men occa-

sionally recommended for long-term health workers

Malaria prophylaxis: Risk Nov–June, except in northern areas where it is a problem all year. Drug resistant *P. falciparum* common. Mefloquine prophylaxis recommended (not for children under 15 kg, in the first trimester of or psychiatric problems), or chloroquine and proguanil. Use nets/repellents

V. high risk of TD: implement all food and water hygiene precautions. High hookworm infestations in rural areas: wear shoes

18.2 THE AMERICAS

NORTH AMERICA

North America includes Canada and the United States. The main health problem, particularly in the USA, is the cost of treatment. It is essential to ensure you have adequate insurance cover.

CANADA

-3.5 to -8 hours GMT

Capital: Ottawa

UK Tourist Office: Tourism Canada, Canada House, 1 Cockspur St, Trafalgar Sq, London SW1Y 5BJ (0171-258 6346)

British High Commission: 80 Elgin St, Ottawa K1P 5KP Tel: 613237 1530; Fax: 613-237 7980. Consulates in Edmonton, Halifax, St John's, Montreal, Toronto, Vancouver, Winnipeg

Visa required: No

Yellow fever certificate: No

HIV test: No

Recommended health precautions

Immunisations: None recommended, though Hep B may be considered for workers in Inuit populations. Those working with wild animals may consider Rab. No untoward health risks unless you go looking for them

USA

-5 to -8 hours GMT

Capital: Washington DC

UK Tourist Office: US Travel and Tourism, PO Box 1EN, London W1A 1EN (0171-495 4466)

British Embassy: 3100 Massachusetts Ave, NW Washington DC 20008. Tel: Washington DC (202) 462 1340. There are consulates in Anchorage, Atlanta, Boston, Chicago, Cleveland, Dallas, Houston, Kansas City, Los Angeles, New Orleans, New York, Miami, Norfolk, Philadelphia, Portland, Puerto Rico, San Francisco and Seattle

Visa required: No

Yellow fever certificate: No

HIV test: There are possible restrictions on HIV-positive travellers; a waiver is required. Residence refused to HIV-positive individuals.

Recommended health precautions

Immunisations: None required or recommended, though anyone working with wild animals should consider Rab. Main risk to health is worry over medical bills: ensure at least £2m health cover, just in case you end up on a life support machine. There are some occasional health hazards: the bacterial Lyme disease, spread by ticks, is found in some states during spring and summer. Protect against bites. Protect also against mosquitoes in southern states: some carry encephalitis, though incidence rare

---

CENTRAL AMERICA

Central America includes Belize, Costa Rica, El Salvador, Guatemala, Honduras, Mexico, Nicaragua and Panama.

Note that the code for dialling the UK from these countries should be standardised to 0044- by mid-1995.

HEALTH RISKS THROUGHOUT THE REGION

Malaria: Widely scattered throughout the region, but the risk varies even within a country, see individual country listings. Note that the disease is shifting. It is important to consult a clinic or GP before travelling. The dominant form throughout the region is the (relatively) benign *P. vivax*, with a small amount of *P. falciparum*.

Yellow fever: Cases are rare, and immunisation is not routinely recommended unless travelling to Panama, though it may be suggested if your itinerary involves plenty of rural/jungle travel in certain countries. However Belize, El Salvador, Guatemala, Honduras, Mexico and Nicaragua require a yellow fever certificate if travelling from an infected area. (This usually applies only to travellers over 12 months old, but El Salvador and Mexico, over 6.) Note that immunisation is not normally recommended for children under 9 months. Costa Rica has no yellow fever requirements, but ongoing travel may be a problem if not immunised. The 'endemic' countries, which does **not** mean the disease is active, are:

Angola, Belize, Benin, Bolivia, Botswana, Brazil, Burkina Faso, Burundi, Cameroon, Central African Republic, Chad, Colombia, Congo, Costa Rica, Cote d'Ivoire, Ecuador, Equatorial Guinea, Ethiopia, French Guyana, Gabon, Gambia, Ghana, Guatemala, Guinea, Guinea-Bissau, Guyana, Honduras, Kenya, Liberia, Mali, Mauritania, Nicaragua, Niger, Nigeria, Panama, Peru, Rwanda, Sao Tome and Principe, Senegal, Sierra Leone, Somalia, Sudan, Suriname, Tanzania, Togo, Trinidad & Tobago, Uganda, Venezuela, Zaire, Zambia.

Other health risks: Dengue fever, spread by mosquitoes, with recent epidemics in Belize, El Salvador, Guatemala, Honduras, Mexico and Nicaragua. Filariasis (small worms, transmitted by mosquitoes), leishmaniasis (protozoan, sandflies), onchocerciasis (worms, blackflies), oropouche virus (gnats/midges) and Chagas' disease (trypanosomiasis, a protozoan, caused by assassin or cone nose bugs in hut walls) occur across the region, as does schistosomiasis (bilharzia, flukes from some fresh water snails). The risk of these diseases for most travellers is low, but as always it is best to avoid insect bites.

Note that there have been cholera epidemics among local populations in Mexico and Guatemala, and all the other Central American countries have reported cases. Good food and water hygiene essential. Rabies is endemic throughout the region. Hookworm, tapeworm, roundworm (*Ascaris*) and various flukes are common parasites: wear shoes, cook food and drink only sterilised water. Avoid dairy products unless pasteurised: risk of brucellosis. There is a moderate risk of hepatitis B and HIV, with sexual transmission the main route of infection for the latter, though unscreened blood must be avoided.

Note also that not all recommended immunisations may be required (though this is one region of the world where they probably will be). Check with your travel clinic or GP. Long-stay visitors should have their diphtheria and tuberculosis protection brought up to date.

BELIZE

-6 hours GMT
Capital: Belmopan
Belize High Commission: 10 Harcourt House, 19A Cavendish Square, London W1M 9AD (0171-499 9728)

British High Commission: PO Box 91, Embassy Sq. Belmopan. Tel: (8) 221 4617; Fax: 22761
Visa required: No
Yellow fever certificate: Yes, all travellers arriving from an infected area
HIV test: Yes, if seeking residence

Recommended health precautions

Immunisations: Hep A; Typh; Pol; Tet. Consider also Hep B; YF (may be needed for onward travel); Rab less important

Malaria prophylaxis: Mainly a threat in rural areas, but a great many visitors do travel to the rainforest and islands. Use chloroquine or proguanil. Use nets and repellents

Some risk of TD if you stray from resorts/hotels; best to implement usual food and drink precautions, and avoid dairy produce. Risk of DF, and The Liverpool School of Tropical Medicine has recently seen a number of cutaneous leishmaniasis cases: avoid sandfly bites

---

COSTA RICA

-7 hours GMT (-6 Jan–Mar)
Capital: San Jose
Embassy: 2nd Floor, 36 Upper Brooke St, London W1Y 1PE (0171-495 3985)
British Consulate: Apartado 815, Edificio Centro Colon, 11th Floor, San Jose 1007. Tel: 21 55 66; Fax: 33 99 38
Visa required: No
Yellow fever certificate: No
HIV test: Yes, for long stay visitors

Recommended health precautions

Immunisations: YF not a great risk, but a certificate may be required for ongoing travel. Hep A; Typh; Pol; Tet. Consider also Rab; low risk of Hep B

Malaria prophylaxis: All year risk in rural areas below 500 m. Chloroquine or proguanil effective. Use nets and repellents

Risk of TD utside main cities: implement all food and water hygiene precautions. Local produce, including dairy products, generally considered safe. DF on coast (increase in the number of cases noted in late 1993), Leish near jungle; avoid insect bites

---

EL SALVADOR

-6 hours GMT
Capital: San Salvador
Embassy: 1st Floor, 5 Great James Street, London WC1N 3DA (0171-430 2141)
British Embassy: PO Box 1591, The Inter Inversion Building, Paseo General Escalon, 4828 San Salvador. Tel: 240473; Fax: 23 5817
Visa required: No
Yellow fever certificate: Yes, travellers over 6 months old arriving from an infected area
HIV test: No

Recommended health precautions

Immunisations: Hep A; Typh; Pol; Tet.

YF may be required if travelling from El Salvador and, though not routinely recommended, also consider if travelling extensively in remote areas. Consider also Rab, which is very widespread, and perhaps Hep B

Malaria prophylaxis: A risk all year round. Chloroquine and proguanil, plus nets and repellent, recommended

V. high risk of TD: implement all food and water hygiene precautions. Other local diseases (see above) active, including DF.

GUATEMALA

-6 hours GMT
Capital: Guatemala City
Embassy: 13 Fawcett Street, London SW10 9HN (0171-351 3042)
British Embassy: Edificio Centro Financerio, 7th Floor, Tower 2, 7a Avenida 5–10, Zona 4, Guatemala City. Tel: (2) 321601; Fax: (2) 341904
Visa required: No, if arriving by air, yes if arriving overland (situation changing: contact Embassy)
Yellow fever certificate: Yes, all travellers over 1 year old arriving from an infected area
HIV test: No

Recommended health precautions
Immunisations: Hep A; Typh; Pol; Tet. YF may be required for ongoing travel and, though not routinely recommended, may be a good idea if extensively travelling outside urban areas. Consider also Rab; Hep B

Malaria prophylaxis: The disease is active in most of the country. Use chloroquine or proguanil, nets and repellents

V. high risk of TD: implement all food and water hygiene precautions. Avoid the usual insect suspects (there is patchy Onch); most regional diseases present

---

HONDURAS

-6 hours GMT
Capital: Tegucigalpa
Embassy: 115 Gloucester Place, London W1H 3PJ (0171-486 4880)
British Embassy: Apartado Postal 290, Edificio Palmira, 3 Piso, Colonia Palmira, Tegucigalpa. Tel: 325429/320612; Fax: 325480
Consulate: Apartado Postal 298, Terminales de Puerto Cortes, San Pedro Sula. Tel: 54 2600
Visa required: No
Yellow fever certificate: Yes, for all travellers over 1 year arriving from an infected area
HIV test: No

Recommended health precautions
Immunisations: Hep A; Typh; Pol; Tet.

YF may be required for onward travel. Consider also Rab; Hep B

Malaria prophylaxis: The disease is active in most of the country. Use chloroquine or proguanil, nets and repellents

V. high risk of TD: implement all food and water hygiene precautions. Other insect-borne diseases, particularly DF, occur

---

MEXICO

-6 to -8 hours GMT
Capital: Mexico City
UK Tourist Office: 3rd Floor, 6061 Trafalgar Square, London WC2N 5DS (0171-734 1058)
Embassy: 8 Halkin Street, London SW1X 7DW (0171-235 6393)
British Embassy: Rio Lerma 71, Colonia Cuauhtemoc, 06500 Mexico City. Tel: (5) 207 2089; Fax: (5) 207 7672. Consulates in Mexico City, Acapulco, Ciudad Juarez, Guadalajara, Merida, Monterrey and Tampico
Visa required: No
Yellow fever certificate: Yes, all travellers over 6 months old arriving from an infected area
HIV test: Yes, if seeking residence

Recommended health precautions
Immunisations: Hep A; Typh; Pol; Tet. Consider also Rab and possibly Hep B

Malaria prophylaxis: There is no malaria in Mexico City and the states north of it, and there is no need for prophylaxis in major coastal resorts. Rural areas of Oaxaca, Chiapas (high incidence of *P. falciparum*), Guerrero, Campeche, Quintana Roo, Sinaloa, Michoacan, Nayarit, Colima and Tabasco all have the disease. Use chloroquine or proguanil, nets and repellents

V. high risk of TD outside of the major resorts/hotels. Safety of food highly variablethroughout country: implement all food and water hygiene precautions

Note that Mexico City has a high altitude and plenty of pollution: this can be a debilitating combination, particularly for asthma sufferers

---

NICARAGUA

-6 hours GMT
Capital: Managua
Embassy: 8 Gloucester Road, London SW7 4PP (0171-584 4365)
British Consulate: Apartado A169, El Reparto 'Los Robles', Entrada Principal de la Carretera a Masaya, Cuarta Casa a Mano Derecha, PO Box A169, Managua. Tel: (2) 780014; Fax: (2) 784085
Visa required: No

Yellow fever certificate: Yes, all travellers over 1 year old arriving from an infected area
HIV test: No

Recommended health precautions
Immunisations: Hep A; Typh; Pol; Tet. YF may be required for ongoing travel. Consider also Rab; Hep B

Malaria prophylaxis: The disease is active in most of the country outside of major cities. Use chloroquine or proguanil, nets and repellents

V. high risk of TD: implement all food and water hygiene precautions. All the regional specialities active, particularly DF: avoid mosquito bites

---

PANAMA

-5 hours GMT
Capital: Panama City
Embassy: 119 Crawford Street, London W1H 1AF (0171-487 5633)
British Embassy: Apartado 889, 4th & 5th Floor, Torre Banco Sur, Calle 53 Este, Panama 1. Tel: 69 0866; Fax: 23 0730
Visa required: No
Yellow fever certificate: Yes, travellers over 1 year old arriving from an infected area
HIV test: Yes, if staying over 1 year

Recommended health precautions
Immunisations: Hep A; Typh; Pol; Tet. YF recommended if travelling outside Panama City (esp. Darien Gap), and it will be a requirement for onward travel. Consider also Rab; Hep B

Malaria prophylaxis: The disease is active in many rural areas, and chloroquine resistance is increasing. Use both chloroquine and proguanil, nets and repellents

There is a risk of TD, even though city water is heavily chlorinated. Local produce generally safe

---

SOUTH AMERICA (NORTH)

The northern, tropical, section of South America includes Bolivia, Brazil, Colombia, Ecuador, French Guyana, Paraguay, Peru, Suriname and Venezuela.

Note that the code for dialling the UK from these countries should be standardised at 0044- by mid-1995.

HEALTH RISKS THROUGHOUT THE REGION

Malaria: Exists throughout the year in many parts of tropical South America. The risk varies even within a country, see individual country listings. There is drug resistance, and the distribution pattern is shifting: it is important to consult a clinic or GP before travelling. Some countries specialise in the relatively benign *Plasmodium vivax*, but the amount of *P. falciparum* is increasing, and in some areas may be over 50 per cent of all cases. The WHO notes that drug resistance is also increasing, especially in the Amazon region.

Yellow fever: The disease is active across the region, though at a very low level, if at all, in Ecuador, French Guyana, Guyana, Paraguay and Suriname. The risk of catching this viral, mosquito-borne disease is higher in rural areas. French Guyana requires a certificate from all visitors. Venezuela does not require any yellow fever certificate, but Bolivia, Brazil, Ecuador, Guyana, Peru and Suriname require an immunisation from travellers coming from infected countries. (This usually applies to travellers over 12 months old, though there are exceptions). Note that children under 9 months should not be immunised. The 'endemic' countries, which does **not** mean the disease is active, are:

Angola, Belize, Benin, Bolivia, Botswana, Brazil, Burkina Faso, Burundi, Cameroon, Central African Republic, Chad, Colombia, Congo, Costa Rica, Cote d'Ivoire, Ecuador, Equatorial Guinea, Ethiopia, French Guyana, Gabon, Gambia, Ghana, Guatemala, Guinea, Guinea Bissau, Guyana, Honduras, Kenya, Liberia, Mali, Mauritania, Nicaragua, Niger, Nigeria, Panama, Peru, Rwanda, Sao Tome and Principe, Senegal, Sierra Leone, Somalia, Sudan, Suriname, Tanzania, Togo, Trinidad & Tobago, Uganda, Venezuela, Zaire and Zambia.

Most of these countries are recognised as endemic by South American countries (exceptions are Botswana, Zambia and Trinidad & Tobago; certification may be waived if arriving in South America from one of these countries: check current requirements. I would have an immunisation just in case the requirements changed en route). Oddly, Paraguay requires a certificate if you are leaving to travel **to** infected countries.

Other health risks: There has been a cholera epidemic across South America. Against WHO guidelines, some countries may insist on seeing proof of immunisation prior to entry. The immunisation is largely discredited, and travellers who practise reasonable food and water hygiene are not at risk. Nonetheless, it may be worth considering having a single cholera immunisation in order to get a certificate, particularly if travelling off the beaten track, where you are likely to encounter remote officialdom.

There have been recent epidemics of dengue fever, spread by mosquitoes, in Brazil, Colombia, Ecuador, French Guyana, Suriname, Venezuela and parts of

Bolivia, Paraguay and Peru. Avoid day-biting mosquitoes. Filariasis (thread-like worms, from mosquitoes) is a risk in Brazil, Suriname and parts of Venezuela; leishmaniasis (protozoa, sandflies) is active throughout the region. Protect against insect bites. Onchocerciasis (worms, blackflies) is also a risk, mainly in Brazil, Colombia, Ecuador and Venezuela, near fast flowing rivers in rural areas. Schistosomiasis (bilharzia) is present; avoid swimming/bathing in fresh water where the snails that harbour the flukes may lurk.

Rabies is endemic throughout most of the region (and may be carried by vampire bats). Hookworm, whipworm, tapeworm (including echinococcus), roundworm and various flukes (including paragonimiasis, the oriental lung fluke) are common parasites in rural populations. Wear shoes, cook food and drink only sterilised water if you want to avoid these parasites.

Avoid dairy products unless pasteurised: it carries a risk of brucellosis. Travellers' diarrhoea, caused by *Salmonella*, *Esherichia coli*, *Giardia*, *Entamoeba* or similar is the commonest illness visitors face.

Chagas' disease, spread by triatomid or kissing bugs, found in rural areas, where the bugs live in the walls of adobe-style huts. There is a moderate risk of hepatitis B and HIV, with sexual transmission the main route of infection, though unscreened blood must be avoided. However, the average traveller is under little or no threat (see Chapter 9).

Note also that not all recommended immunisations may be required. Check with your travel clinic or GP. Long-stay visitors should ensure their diphtheria and tuberculosis protection is brought up to date.

BOLIVIA

-4 hours GMT
Capital: La Paz
Embassy: 106 Eaton Square, London SW1W 9AD (0171-235 4248)
British Embassy: Casilla 694, Avenida Arce 27322754, La Paz, Bolivia. Tel: (2) 329401/2/3; Fax: (2) 391063
Visa required: Not for tourists
Yellow fever certificate: Yes, all travellers arriving from an infected area
HIV test: Yes, if staying more than 90 days.

Recommended health precautions
Immunisations: YF; Hep A; Typh; Pol; Tet. Consider Rab; Hep B (though rate in population low)

Malaria prophylaxis: The disease is only a threat in lowland (below 2500 m) rural areas, mainly in the east. La Paz and other cities clear. Some chloroquine resistance developing. The benign *P.vivax* form predominates. Chloroquine and/or proguanil usually recommended. If travelling to risk areas in the Amazon basin, mefloquine (not for children under 15 kg, in the first first trimester of pregnancy or if history of psychiatric problems or epilepsy) may be suggested. Use nets and repellents. There have been yellow fever cases in La Paz and the departments of Deni, Chuquisaca, Coclamba, Pando and Tansi

All water suspect, high risk of TD: implement all food and water hygiene precautions. Travellers flying into La Paz may experience altitude sickness

---

BRAZIL

-3 hours GMT (-2 in summer)
Capital: Brasilia
Embassy: 32 Green Street, London W1Y 4AT (0171-499 0877)
British Embassy: Caixa Postal 07-0586, Setor de Embaixadas Sul, Quadra 801, Conjunto K, 70 408. Tel: (61) 225 2710; Fax: (61) 225 1777
Visa required: No
Yellow fever certificate: Yes, any traveller over 6 months old arriving from infected area
HIV test: No

Recommended health precautions
Immunisations: YF; Hep A; Typh; Pol; Tet. Consider also Rab; Hep B. Men sometimes recommended, but the most recent outbreaks have been of type B, whereas the immunisation only protects against A and C

Malaria prophylaxis: *P. falciparum* accounts for over half of cases in many regions. The disease is also becoming multi-drug resistant, including to mefloquine. The risk is in Acre and Rondonia states, territories of Amapa and Roraima and in parts of Amazonas, Goias, Maranhao, Mato Grosso and Para States, all some way inland from the coast. Prophylaxis is mefloquine (not for children under 15 kg, in the first trimester of pregnancy or if history of psychiatric problems or epilepsy) with Chloroquine and proguanil backup. However, different regimes may be recommended to try and combat resistance: take up to date advice. Use nets and repellents. Yellow fever active west of Brasilia, esp. on Bolivia/Paraguay borders

Mains water unsafe. Risk of TD: implement all food and water hygiene precautions. Local produce, including dairy products, generally considered safe in cities, suspect elsewhere. DF on coast and Fil risk, both mainly in north, plus risk of all types of Leish almost nationwide. Chagas' disease, caused by kissing or assassin bugs, common in rural areas. The cities of Brazil have the highest rate of HIV infection in the region. Schis risk in fresh water lakes, rivers, etc., again esp. in north. Do not swim/bathe in unchlorinated water

---

COLOMBIA

-5 hours GMT
Capital: Bogota
Embassy: 3 Hans Crescent, London SW1X OLR (0171-589 9177).
British Embassy: Apdo Aereo 4508. Toree Propaganda Sancho, Calle 98, No 903, Piso 4, Bogota. Tel: (1) 218 5111 Fax: (1) 218 2460. Consulates in Barranquilla, Cali and Medellin
Visa required: No
Yellow fever certificate: No (but may be needed if travelling onwards)
HIV test: Yes if seeking residence

Recommended health precautions
Immunisations: Hep A; Typh; Pol; Tet. YF if travelling to rural areas, and may be required for onward travel. Consider also Rab; Hep B

Malaria prophylaxis: Year-round risk in rural areas below 800 m. *P. falciparum* responsible for high percentage of cases, with drug resistance growing (to both chloroquine and Fansidar, the latter used for treatment). Use mefloquine (see Brazil), which is now the preferred drug, or chloroquine or proguanil. Use nets and repellents

Public water supplies outside of Bogota may be contaminated, therefore high risk of TD: implement all food and water hygiene precautions. Regional specialities (DF, Chagas' disease, etc.) present in full force

---

ECUADOR

-5 hours GMT
Capital: Quito
Embassy: Flat 3B, 3 Hans Crescent, London SW1X OLS (0171-584 1367)
British Embassy: Casilla 314, Calle Gonzalez Suarez III, Quito. Tel: (2) 560 670; Fax: (2) 560 730
Visa required: No
Yellow fever certificate: Yes, all travellers over 1 year old arriving from an infected area
HIV test: Possibly for long-term visitors; check with Embassy

Recommended health precautions
Immunisations: YF; Hep A; Typh; Pol; Tet. Consider also Rab; Hep B; Dip

Malaria prophylaxis: Risk of mainly benign forms in provinces along eastern border and Pacific coast. Not in Quito, central highlands or Galapagos. *P. falciparum* is present, as is some chloroquine resistance. Use mefloquine (see Brazil) or chloroquine and proguanil; the latter is still the first choice of many health professionals. Use nets and repellents

Don't trust the water, there is a high risk of TD: implement all food and water hygiene precautions. Some risk of DF, though mainly outside standard tourist routes. There is Onch in the NE. Note that flying straight into Quito (3000 m) may cause altitude sickness. There have been cases of Dip in Quito (March 1994): long-term workers should boost their protection

---

FRENCH GUYANA (OR FRENCH GUIANA)

-3 hours GMT
Capital: Cayenne
Embassy: Through French Consulate General, PO Box 57, 6A Cromwell Road, London SW7 2JA (0171-581 5292)
British Embassy: No
Visa required: No
Yellow fever certificate: Yes, all travellers over 1 year old from all countries
HIV test: No

Recommended health precautions
Immunisations: YF; Hep A; Typh; Pol; Tet. Consider also Rab; Hep B

Malaria prophylaxis: The disease is a risk in all areas, with *P. falciparum* dominant. Chloroquine resistance reported. Use mefloquine (not in children under 15 kg, during the first trimester of pregnancy or if history of epilepsy or psychotic episodes) or chloroquine and proguanil. Use nets and repellents

Heavily chlorinated water in Cayenne should kill most things, but in rural areas and away from good hotels there is a risk of TD: implement all food and water hygiene precautions. Local produce, including dairy products, generally considered safe to eat, esp. in Cayenne. HIV risk with medical or dental procedures and unsafe sex. Leish near jungle; avoid sandfly bites. Risk of DF on coast

---

GUYANA

-3 hours GMT
Capital: Georgetown
High Commission: 3 Palace Court, Bayswater Road, London W2 4LP (0171-229 7684)
British High Commission: PO Box 10849, 44 Main Street, Georgetown, Guyana. Tel: (2) 65881/2/3/4; Fax: (2) 53555
Visa required: No (subject to change: check)
Yellow fever certificate: Yes, all travellers arriving from an infected area (check with High Commission)
HIV test: No

Recommended health precautions
Immunisations: YF (may also be required for onward travel); Hep A;

Typh; Pol; Tet. Consider also Rab; Hep B

Malaria prophylaxis: Year-round risk throughout the country (lower risk in Georgetown), with chloroquine resistant *P. falciparum*. Current recommendations are to use mefloquine (see Brazil) or chloroquine and proguanil if mefloquine not suitable. Use nets and repellents

Mains water chlorinated, but outside of best hotels there is a risk of TD: implement all food and water hygiene precautions. Local fish and meat, but not dairy products, generally considered safe. Fil common; avoid day-biting mosquitoes as well as dawn and dusk ones. DF, Schis, etc. also present

---

PARAGUAY

-4 hours GMT
Capital: Asuncion
Embassy: Braemar Lodge, Cornwall Gardens, London SW7 4AQ (0171-937 1253)
British Embassy: Casilla 404, Calle Presidente Franco 706, Asuncion. Tel: (21) 444-72; Fax: (21) 446 385
Visa required: No
Yellow fever certificate: Yes, but curiously only to get out if going to endemic area
HIV test: No

Recommended health precautions
Immunisations: Hep A; Typh; Pol; Tet. Consider also Rab; low risk of Hep B. Note you will need a YF certificate to leave Paraguay and go to most other countries in the region

Malaria prophylaxis: Risk Oct–May in some rural areas. WHO notes that benign *P. vivax* form predominates, chloroquine or proguanil effective. Use nets and repellents

Public water supply chlorinated. However, there is still a risk of TD, particularly away from large cities: implement all food and water hygiene precautions. Other risks include Leish and DF: avoid bites

---

PERU

-5 hours GMT
Capital: Lima
Embassy: 52 Sloane Street, London SW1X 9SP (0171-235 1917)
British Embassy: Casilla 854, Edificio El Pacifico Washington (Piso 12), Plaza Washington, Avenida Arequipa, Lima 100. Tel: (14) 334 738; Fax: (14) 334 735
Visa required: No

Yellow fever certificate: Yes, for anyone older than 6 months arriving from an infected area
HIV test: No

Recommended health precautions
Immunisations: YF; Hep A; Typh; Pol; Tet. Consider also Rab; Hep B for health workers, etc.

Malaria prophylaxis: The disease is not a problem for much of the tourist route (e.g. Lima, Cuzco, Machu Picchu, Lake Titicaca), but is in other rural areas below 1500 m. The benign form dominates, though WHO reports *P. falciparum* and drug resistance found near Brazilian border. Chloroquine and proguanil recommended, but mefloquine if travelling near border (very likely to become preferred drug in future: check before departure). Use nets and repellents

Although mains water chlorinated in cities, there is high risk of TD everywhere: implement all food and water hygiene precautions. Most other regional diseases (e.g. Leish, DF) only occur at low altitudes. Note that many of the tourist sites are at high elevations: altitude sickness a distinct possibility. Note also parts of the country still dangerous, thanks to the activities of the Shining Path

---

SURINAME

-3 hours GMT
Capital: Paramaribo
Embassy: Contact The Hague (70365 08 44)
British **Consulate:** PO Box 1300, c/o VSH Buildings Van't Hogerhuysstraat, Paramaribo. Tel: 72870; Fax: 75515
Visa required: No
Yellow fever certificate: Yes, all travellers arriving from an infected area
HIV test: No

Recommended health precautions
Immunisations: YF; Hep A; Typh; Pol; Tet. Consider also Rab; Hep B if extended stay

Malaria prophylaxis: Year-round risk everywhere except capital. *P. falciparum* dominates, chloroquine resistance reported by WHO. Mefloquine (see Brazil) increasingly first choice, though chloroquine and proguanil may be suggested if mefloquine not suitable. Get up-to-date advice. Use nets and repellents

Chlorinated mains water in Paramaribo, elsewhere quality suspect. High risk of TD: implement all food and water hygiene precautions. Avoid local dairy products (usually unpasteurised). Various insect borne diseases (e.g. Fil, Leish, DF) particularly in rural areas. Schis present: avoid swimming/bathing in fresh water unless chlorinated

---

VENEZUELA

-4 hours GMT
Capital: Caracas
Embassy: 1 Cromwell Road, London SW7 2HW (0171-584 4206)
Consulate: 0171-387 6727
British Embassy: Apartado 1246, Piso 3, Edificio Torre Las Mercedes, Avenida la Estancia, Chuao, Caracas 1060. Tel: (2) 751 1022; Fax: (2) 923 292
Visa required: No, but tourist card needed (this will be given to you on the aeroplane or ship)
Yellow fever certificate: No
HIV test: No

Recommended health precautions
Immunisations: Hep A; Typh; Pol; Tet. YF advised if travelling outside cities. Consider also Rab; Hep B if extended stay

Malaria prophylaxis: Disease is active in rural areas, mainly in the south and in the border states. *P. falciparum* present, and, according to the WHO, is 'highly chloroquine resistant'. Chloroquine and proguanil (Paludrine) combination still recommended, though mefloquine (see Brazil), if suitable, may be suggested if itinerary includes Amazon basin. (Mefloquine is likely to become the first choice drug.) Use nets and repellents

Mains water in cities chlorinated, but not always trustworthy. High risk rurally of TD: implement all food and water hygiene precautions. Local produce, including dairy products, generally considered safe in resorts/tourist areas. Usual battery of insect borne diseases, plus a few new viral ones: avoid mosquito (there are over 6000 DF cases per annum) and sandfly bites, particularly in rural areas. Schis present, avoid swimming/bathing in suspect fresh water

---

SOUTH AMERICA (SOUTH)

The southern, temperate, section of South America includes Argentina, Chile, the Falkland Islands and Uruguay. Note that the code for dialling the UK from these countries should be standardised at 0044- by mid-1995.

HEALTH RISKS THROUGHOUT THE REGION
Malaria: A malaria risk only exists in northern Argentina, the other countries are malaria free.

Yellow fever: There is risk for visitors to the northeast of Argentina only, the other countries are free of the disease. There are no immunisation requirements by any of the countries.

Other health risks: There has been a cholera epidemic across South America. Argentina and Chile have both reported cases. Against WHO guidelines, some countries may insist on seeing proof of immunisation prior to entry if coming from an 'infected' region. The immunisation is largely discredited, and travellers who practise reasonable food and water hygiene are not at risk. Nonetheless, it may be worth considering having a single cholera immunisation in order to get a certificate, particularly if travelling off the beaten track, where you are likely to encounter remote officialdom.

There is a very low risk of dengue fever, spread by day-biting mosquitoes, though there are pockets of leishmaniasis (sandflies). Echinococcosis (hydatid disease, from dog faeces) common in sheep- and cattle-rearing areas. Chagas' disease is common in many rural areas; it is caused by the bite of the assassin or kissing bug which lives in the walls of adobe style huts. There is a low rabies risk. Hookworm, various tapeworms, roundworms (*Ascaris*), trichinosis and various flukes are present in rural populations. Wear shoes, cook food and drink only sterilised water if you want to avoid these parasites. Travellers' diarrhoea, caused by organisms such as *Giardia*, *Esherichia coli* and *Entamoeba* is the commonest affliction among visitors.

Avoid dairy products unless pasteurised: they carry a risk of brucellosis. Generally the HIV and hepatitis B rate is low; precautions against unsterile medical and dental practices should be observed.

Note also that not all recommended immunisations may be required. Check with your travel clinic or GP. Long-stay visitors should consider having their diphtheria and tuberculosis protection brought up to date.

ARGENTINA

-3 hours GMT
Capital: Buenos Aires
Embassy: 53 Hans Place, London SW1X 0LA (0171-584 6494)
British Embassy: Dr Luis Agote 2412/52, Casilla 2050, 1425 Buenos Aires. Tel: (1) 803 7070; Fax: (1) 803 1731
Visa required: No
Yellow fever certificate: No
HIV test: No

Recommended health precautions
Immunisations: Depends on whether travelling beyond Buenos Aires. Consider Hep A; Typh; Pol; Tet. Low risk of Hep B; Rab. YF may be suggested if visiting the NE of the country

Malaria prophylaxis: Only a risk at low elevations in the NW, mainly Oct–May, in the *P. vivax* form. Chloroquine or proguanil recommended. Use nets and repellents

Water in capital considered safe, suspect beyond, so risk of TD. Much local produce safe, but brucellosis does occur: avoid unpasteurised milk. Leish in north, Chagas' disease in rural areas, again mainly in the north. Ech is a risk. Good hygiene usually prevents contamination.

CHILE

-4 hours GMT (-3 Oct–Mar)
Capital: Santiago
Embassy: 12 Devonshire Street, London W1N 2DS (0171-580 6392)
British Embassy: Casilla 72-D or casilla 16552, Concepcion 177, Santiago. Tel: (2) 223 9166; Fax: (2) 223 1917. Consulates in Arica, Concepcion, Punta Arenas, Valparaiso
Visa required: No
Yellow fever certificate: No
HIV test: No

Recommended health precautions
Immunisations: Hep A; Typh (very active in Chile); Pol; Tet. Low risk of Rab; Hep B

Malaria prophylaxis: No malaria

High risk of TD: implement all food and water hygiene precautions. Water quality, even in Santiago, cannot be relied upon. Observe all food/water hygiene precautions, particularly outside best hotels. Chagas' disease in rural areas, but most other insect problems of the continent absent, although watch for is hookworm and food-borne parasites (e.g. tapeworms) in rural areas. Note that in 1993 there was a 20% increase in the number of cases of Men type B in Santiago, the one the immunisation does not protect against

---

FALKLAND ISLANDS

-3 hours GMT (-4 May–Aug)
Capital: Port Stanley
UK Tourist Board: Falkland Islands Tourist Board: 14 Broadway, London SW1H 0BH (0171-222 2542)
Visa required: No, Crown Colony
Yellow fever certificate: No
HIV test: No

Recommended health precautions
Immunisations: None advised

Malaria prophylaxis: None on islands

Water supplies and food generally safe

URUGUAY

-3 hours GMT
Capital: Montevideo
Embassy: 140 Brompton Road, London SW3 1HY (0171-584 8192).
British Embassy: Marco Bruto 1073, Montevideo 11300. Tel: (2) 623630/ 623650; Fax: (2) 627815
Visa required: No
Yellow fever certificate: No
HIV test: No

Recommended health precautions
Immunisations: Hep A; Typh; Pol (low risk); Tet. Very low risk of Hep B or Rab, though the latter is present

Malaria prophylaxis: No

Public water supplies generally good, though it is worth implementing food and water hygiene precautions away from towns and cities. There is no reported Chol. Local produce, including dairy products, generally considered safe. Chagas' disease in rural areas

---

THE CARIBBEAN

This includes many islands, not all of which (e.g. Bermuda) are strictly within the Caribbean, but which are grouped together for convenience:

ABCs (Aruba, Bonaire, Curacao: part of Netherlands Antilles), Anguilla, Antigua & Barbuda, Bahamas, Barbados, Bermuda, Cayman Islands, Cuba, Dominica, Dominican Republic, Grenada, Guadeloupe, Haiti, Jamaica, Martinique, Montserrat, Netherlands (Dutch) Antilles, Puerto Rico (a US Commonwealth), Saint Lucia, St Vincent and theGrenadines, St Kitts & Nevis, Trinidad & Tobago, Turks & Caicos, British Virgin Islands, US Virgin Islands.

Note that from mid-1995 the dialling code to the UK from all islands should be 0044-.

HEALTH RISKS THROUGHOUT THE REGION

Malaria: A risk in the Dominican Republic and Haiti. All other islands are clear.

Yellow fever: There is a small risk in rural areas of Trinidad & Tobago. This will not affect most tourists. However, you may be required to produce a certificate if travelling on from Trinidad & Tobago: check your itinerary. Some Caribbean islands also insist on a certificate if you are coming from an endemic yellow fever country. At the time of writing this list was quite short, but check current status. If travelling from:

Angola, Bolivia, Brazil, Cameroon, Colombia, Ecuador, Gambia, Guinea, Kenya, Mali, Nigeria, Peru, Sudan or Zaire

to:

Antigua & Barbuda, Bahamas, Barbados, Dominica, Grenada, Guadeloupe, Haiti, Jamaica, Martinique, Montserrat, Netherlands (Dutch) Antilles (including ABC), Saint Lucia, St Vincent and the Grenadines, St Kitts & Nevis, Trinidad & Tobago

you will need a yellow fever certificate. Children under 9 months should not be immunised. Most countries in the world ask for immunisation over 12 months, the Netherlands Antilles over 6 months, but some countries simply stress all travellers must be immunised. If you are travelling with a young child, check carefully, as individual countries liable to change their policy.

Other health risks: Dengue fever is present on most islands. It is a viral disease spread by mosquitoes, and the level of infection is low. The Cayman islands appear to be free of it. There is some risk of leishmaniasis, schistosomiasis and filariasis on some islands. Chagas' disease may be a risk in some rural areas of Antigua, Aruba, Curacao, Guadeloupe, Jamaica and Martinique, but only if staying in relatively primitive accommodation.

There is a risk of HIV, particularly in Haiti under certain circumstances, though the average traveller is not under threat (see Chapter 13). (Note, many of the countries in the region have excellent medical facilities, including screening blood for HIV.) Rabies is only known on a handful of islands: Dominican Republic, Grenada, Haiti, Puerto Rico and Trinidad & Tobago. The risk is low. There is a risk of typhoid in some rural areas, particularly Haiti and the Dominican Republic. Given the usual pattern of tourism in the region, which increasingly involves resort-style complexes, most tourists are unlikely to be at risk from the majority of diseases present in the area. However, the nature of Caribbean holidays brings its own risks; watch for marine hazards, from drowning to jellyfish, and for ciguatera, food poisoning caused by toxins in certain reef fish.

Discuss your needs with a travel clinic or GP: it is possible you will not require any immunisations, particularly if staying in one resort hotel. (There is an argument for having at least your polio and tetanus brought up to date.) However, long-term workers in more remote ares should consider having their TB checked, and polio and diphtheria brought up to date.

ANGUILLA

-4 hours GMT
Capital: The Valley
UK Tourist Office: 3 Epirus Road, London SW6 7UJ (0171-937 7725)
Visa required: No
Yellow fever certificate: No
HIV test: No

Recommended health precautions
Immunisations: Pol and Tet up to date; very low risk of Hep A and Typh

There is some chance of TD outside major resorts/hotels. If in rural areas take food and water hygiene precautions

---

ANTIGUA & BARBUDA

-4 hours GMT
Capital: St John's
High Commission: 15 Thayer Street, London W1M 5LD (0171-486 7073)
Office of British Government Representative: PO Box 483, 11 Old Parham Road, St John's Antigua. Tel: 462 0008/9; Fax: 462 2806
Visa required: No
Yellow fever certificate: Yes, travellers over 1 year old coming from infected area
HIV test: Sometimes, if suspected of being HIV positive

Recommended health precautions
Immunisations: Consider Pol; Tet. V. low risk of Hep A; Typh

There is a low risk of TD in tourist resorts

Schis present: avoid swimming or bathing in rivers, streams, etc. Use chlorinated pools

---

ARUBA, BONAIRE, CURACAO

Although Aruba is now politically separate, these three islands still form a distinct group
-4 hours GMT
Capital: Oranjestad (Aruba), Kralendijk (Bonaire), Willemstad (Curacao)
Embassy: For Aruba contact the Aruba Tourism Authority, The Hague (70-356 6220). For Bonaire and Curacao contact The Office for Netherland Antilles, The Hague (70-351 2811)
British Embassy: N/a
Visa required: No (up to 14 days for B & C)
Yellow fever certificate: Yes, for travellers over 6 months of age coming from an infected area
HIV test: No

Recommended health precautions
Immunisations: Pol; Tet. Occasionally Hep A; Typh, but risks to tourists small

Risk of TD low

Some DF: avoid bites

BAHAMAS

-5 hours GMT (-4 in summer)
Capital: Nassau
UK Tourist Office: 10 Chesterfield Street, London W1X 8AH (0171-629 5238). High Commission at same address. Tel 0171-408 4488
British High Commission: PO Box N7516, 3rd Floor, BITCO Building, East Street, Nassau. Tel: 325 7471/2/3; Fax: 323 3871
Visa required: No
Yellow fever certificate: Yes if over 1 year and travelling from an infected area
HIV test: No

Recommended health precautions
Immunisations: Pol; Tet. Consider Typh; Hep A (low risk)

Slight risk of TD outside major resorts and hotels. If in rural areas implement usual food and water hygiene

---

BARBADOS

-4 hours GMT
Capital: Bridgetown
UK Tourist Office: 263 Tottenham Court Road, London W1P 9AA (0171-636 9448)
High Commission: 1 Great Russell Street, London WC1B 3JY (0171-631 4975)
British High Commission: PO Box 676, Lower Collymore Rock, St Michael, Barbados. Tel: 436 6694; Fax: 436 5398
Visa required: No
Yellow fever certificate: Yes, if over 1 year and travelling from an infected area
HIV test: No

Recommended health precautions
Immunisations: Pol; Tet. Sometimes Typh; Hep A but risks low (two cases of Hep A in 1993, no Typh) Hep B for long-stay

Water, food and drink generally very safe unless travelling to remote rural areas

---

CAYMAN ISLANDS

Grand Cayman, Little Cayman and Cayman Brac
-5 hours GMT
Capital: George Town
UK Tourism and Government Office: 100 Brompton Road, Knightsbridge, London SW3 1EX (0171-581 9960/ 0171-581 9418)
Visa required: No
Yellow fever certificate: No
HIV test: Yes, HIV-free certificate required if applying to work

Recommended health precautions
Immunisations: Possibly Pol; Tet. Maybe even Typh; Hep A, but risks to tourists low. There have been some cases of dengue fever, however, so avoid insect bites

---

CUBA

-4 hours GMT (-5 Oct–Mar)
Capital: Havana
Embassy: 167 High Holborn, London WC1V 6PA (0171-240 2488)
Consulate: 15 Grape Street, WC2 8DR (0171-240 2488)
British Embassy: Carcel No 101103, Edificio Bolivar e Morro y Prado, Apdo Havana. Tel: (7) 623 071
Visa required: Yes
Yellow fever certificate: No
HIV test: Not tourists, sometimes for others

Recommended health precautions
Immunisations: Pol; Tet; Typh; Hep A. Longstay workers may consider Hep B; Rab

There is a risk of TD; water is chlorinated, but quality unreliable: observe all food and drink precautions

Some risk of DF: avoid mosquito bites

DOMINICA

-4 hours GMT
Capital: Roseau
UK Tourist Office: 120 Wilton Rd, London SW1V 1JZ (0171-233 8382)
High Commission: 1 Collingham Gardens, Earls Court, London SW5 0HW (0171-370 5194/5)
British High Commission: C/o PO Box 676, Lower Collymore Rock, St Michael, Barbados. Tel: 436 6694; Fax: 436 7916
Visa required: No
Yellow fever certificate: Yes, travellers over 1 year old arriving from an infected area
HIV test: No

Recommended health precautions
Immunisations: Pol; Tet. Possibly Typh; Hep A if away from resorts

Tap water chlorinated and usually reliable, but may be some food/drink risks in rural areas: observe hygiene precautions

DF risk: avoid bites. Some Schis: do not swim or bathe in lakes, streams, etc.

DOMINICAN REPUBLIC

-4 hours GMT

Capital: Santo Domingo

Honorary Consulate: 6 Queens Mansions, Brook Green, London W6 7EB (0171-602 1885)

British Consulate: St George's School, Avenida Abraham Lincoln, 552, Santo Domingo. Tel: 540 3132; Fax: 562 5015

Visa required: No

Yellow fever certificate: No

HIV test: No

Recommended health precautions

Immunisations: Pol; Typh strongly advised, esp. if travelling away from the 'packaged' enclaves. Also Tet; Hep A. Consider Hep B

Malaria prophylaxis: There is a malaria risk in some urban and rural areas, the nasty *P. falciparum* form. Chloroquine or proguanil recommended. Use nets and repellents

Low risk of TD in major hotels and resorts, but there is a risk away from these: observe usual food and drink hygiene precautions

Some risk of DF, Schis

GRENADA

-4 hours GMT

Capital: St George's

UK Tourist Office and High Commission: 1 Collingham Gardens, Earls Court, London SW5 0HW (0171-370 5164/5; 0171-373 7800/9)

British High Commission: 14 Church Street, St George's. Tel: 440 3222 or 3536; Fax: 440 4939

Visa required: No

Yellow fever certificate: Yes, all travellers over 1 year old coming from an infected area

HIV test: No

Recommended health precautions

Immunisations: Pol; Tet. Consider Typh; Hep A; Rab

Public water supplies chlorinated, but still some risk of TD, especially if travelling in rural areas

Some Schis, Rab present

GUADELOUPE

-4 hours GMT
Capital: Basse-terre
Embassy: Through French Embassy, 58 Knightsbridge, SW1X 7JT (0171-235 8080)
Visa required: No
Yellow fever certificate: Yes, all travellers over 1 year old if arriving from an infected area
HIV test: No

Recommended health precautions
Immunisations: Pol; Tet; Typh. Low risk of Hep A; Hep B for at-risk groups

Low risk of TD in hotels/resorts; care needed in rural areas

Some DF, Schis, Leish, but risk to tourists low

HAITI

-5 hours GMT
Capital: Port-au-Prince
Embassy: Contact Brussels (2 649 7381; Fax: 2 640 6080)
British Consulate: PO Box 1302, Hotel Montana, Port-au-Prince. Tel: 73969; Fax: 74048
Visa required: No
Yellow fever certificate: Yes, all travellers arriving from an infected area
HIV test: No

Recommended health precautions
Immunisations: Pol; Typh;. Tet; Hep A. Consider Rab; Hep B if extended stay

Malaria prophylaxis: There is a risk below 1000 m in rural and suburban areas all year round. *P. falciparum* the culprit; chloroquine or proguanil the recommended drugs. Use nets and repellents.

V. high risk of TD, implement the full battery of food and drink hygiene precautions

Risk of DF, Fil: avoid insect bites

Note, at the time of writing the situation in Haiti is unstable: check with Foreign office, 0171-270 4129

JAMAICA

-5 hours GMT
Capital: Kingston
UK Tourist Board and High Commission: 12 Prince Consort Road, SW7 2BZ (0171-823 9911)
British High Commission: PO Box 575, Trafalgar Road, Kingston 10. Tel: 926 9050; Fax: 929 7868
Visa required: No
Yellow fever certificate: Yes, if over 1 year old travelling from an infected area
HIV test: No

Recommended health precautions
Immunisations: Pol; Tet. Occasionally Typh; Hep A, but risk to most visitors low

Mains water chlorinated, but bottled preferable. Low risk of TD esp. in resorts/hotels

---

MARTINIQUE

The island is actually a department of France, so all dealings through French Embassies etc.
-4 hours GMT
Capital: Fort-de-France
Visa required: No
Yellow fever certificate: Yes, travellers over 1 year old arriving from an infected area
HIV test: No

Recommended health precautions
Immunisations: Pol; Tet. Occasionally Typh; Hep A, but risk to most visitors low

Mains water chlorinated, but bottled water preferable (essential outside main towns). Some risk of TD in rural areas

Some DF, Leish, Schis present, but again risks to tourists low. Avoid insect bites and swimming in fresh water lakes and streams, just to be certain

---

MONTSERRAT

-4 hours GMT
Capital: Plymouth
High Commission: N/a. Contact British Dependent Territories, Room 203, Clive House, 70 Petty France, London SW1H 9HD (0171-271 8616)
Visa required: No
Yellow fever certificate: No
HIV test: Yes, for residence/work permits

Recommended health precautions
Immunisations: Pol; Tet. Occasionally Typh; Hep A, but risk to most visitors low

Schis (low risk) and DF present: avoid mosquito bites

NETHERLANDS ANTILLES

This includes: Bonaire, Curacao (see above), Saba, St Eustatius and Saint Maarten (part of the island that also contains St Martin
-4 hours GMT
Capital: Willemstad (Curacao)
Embassy: see ABCs
Visa required: No
Yellow fever certificate: Yes, if travel-

ling from an infected area (usually any visitor over 6 months old)
HIV test: No

Recommended health precautions
Immunisations: Pol; Tet. Occasionally Typh; Hep A, but risk to most visitors low.

Low risk of TD, local produce generally safe, potable water in main centres on all the islands

Avoid insect bites for the usual reasons

PUERTO RICO

The island is a US Commonwealth, represented through US embassies
-4 hours GMT
Capital: San Juan
British Consulate: Suite 5E, Taft Street, Santurce 00911. Tel: 728 6715
Visa required: No
Yellow fever certificate: No
HIV test: No

Recommended health precautions
Immunisations: Pol; Tet. Occasionally Typh; Hep A, but risk to most visitors low. Long-term visitors sometimes recommended Hep B; Rab

Water safe in main towns, but bottled may be preferable, and certainly is in rural areas. Most food generally safe

Some Schis present: avoid swimming or bathing in fresh water lakes, rivers

---

ST BARTHELEMY

See entry for Martinique

ST KITTS AND NEVIS

-4 hours GMT
Capital: Basseterre
High Commission for Eastern Caribbean States: 10 Kensington Court, London W8 5BL (0171-937 9522)
British High Commission: Through Antigua
Visa required: No
Yellow fever certificate: Yes, travellers over 1 year old coming from an infected area
HIV test: No

Recommended health precautions
Immunisations: Pol; Tet. Occasionally Typh; Hep A, but risk to most visitors low

Mains water chlorinated, but bottled may be preferable. Low risk of TD in main resorts/hotels, usual food and drink precautions best observed elsewhere

Some DF risk: avoid insect bites

ST LUCIA

-4 hours GMT
Capital: Castries
UK Tourist Office: High Commission for Eastern Caribbean States: 10 Kensington Court, London W8 5DL (0171-937 9522)
British High Commission: PO Box 227, Columbus Square, Castries. Tel: 22484; Fax: 31543
Visa required: No
Yellow fever certificate: Yes, travellers over 1 year old arriving from an infected area
HIV test: No

Recommended health precautions
Immunisations: Pol; Tet. Occasionally Typh; Hep A, but risk to most visitors low

Mains water chlorinated, but bottled may be preferable. Low risk of TD, most local produce generally safe. Take care away from resorts/hotels: reports of parasites caught from undercooked food

---

ST MARTIN

See entry for Martinique or Netherland Antilles (it is part of the same island as Saint Maarten)

ST VINCENT & THE GRENADINES

Includes Bequia, Mustique, Canouan, Mayreau, Tabago Cays, Union, Petit St Vincent
-4 hours GMT
Capital: Kingstown
UK Tourist Board and High Commission for Eastern Caribbean States: 10 Kensington Court, London W8 5DL (0171-937 9522)
British High Commission: PO Box 132, Granby Street, Kingstown, St Vincent. Tel: (45) 71701/2; Fax: (45) 62750
Visa required: No
Yellow fever certificate: Yes, for travellers over 1 year old entering from an infected area
HIV test: No

Recommended health precautions
Immunisations: Pol; Tet. Occasionally

Typh; Hep A, but risk to most visitors low

Mains water chlorinated, but bottled may be preferable. Low risk of TD; local produce generally considered safe

Some DF, Fil: avoid bites

TRINIDAD & TOBAGO

-4 hours GMT
Capital: Port of Spain
UK Tourist Office: 8a Hammersmith Broadway, London W6 7AL (0181-741 4466)
High Commission: 42 Belgrave Square, SW1X 8NT (0171-245 9351)
British High Commission: PO Box 778, 3rd & 4th Floors, Furness House, 90 Independence Square, Port of spain. Tel: 625 2861/2/3/4/5; Fax: 623 0621
Visa required: No
Yellow fever certificate: Yes, if over 1 year coming from an infected area
HIV test: Yes, if applying to stay over 12 months

Recommended health precautions
Immunisations: Pol; Tet. Occasionally Typh; Hep A, but risk to most visitors low. YF in jungle areas of Trinidad, but not a threat to most tourists. Consider immunisation if going into jungle. Certificate may be needed for onward travel: check itinerary. There is Rab, but again risk not high for most visitors

Malaria prophylaxis: The disease is present in SW of island, but no risk in main towns and resorts, little risk to tourists. Travellers to malarious area should take chloroquine or proguanil, and use nets and repellents

Low risk of TD in resorts/hotels. Local produce generally safe, but hygiene precautions should be implemented away from main towns/resorts

DF present: avoid mosquito bites

TURKS & CAICOS

-5 hours GMT
Capital: Cockburn Town
Information Office: 47 Chase Side, Enfield EN2 6NB (0181-364 5188)
Visa required: No
Yellow fever certificate: Yes, if travelling from an infected area
HIV test: No

Recommended health precautions
Immunisations: Pol; Tet. Occasionally Typh; Hep A, but risk to most visitors low

Some risk of TD: local water supplies suspect. Implement all food and water hygiene precautions outside main resorts/hotels

---

VIRGIN ISLANDS (BRITISH)

Includes Jost van Dyke, Tortola, Beef Island, Peter Island, Norman Island, Virgin Gorda and Anegada
-4 hours GMT
Capital: Road Town, Tortola
UK Tourist Board: 110 St Martin's Lane, London WC2N 4DY (0171-240 4259)
Visa required: No
Yellow fever certificate: No
HIV test: Immigrants/long stay workers may be asked for negative test result

Recommended health precautions
Immunisations: Pol; Tet. Occasionally Typh; Hep A, but risk to most visitors low

Low risk of TD

VIRGIN ISLANDS (US)

Includes St Thomas, St Croix, St John
-4 hours GMT
Capital: Charlotte Amalie, St Thomas
Embassy: All handled through US Embassy (0171-499 9000)
Visa required: No
Yellow fever certificate: No
HIV test: No

Recommended health precautions
Immunisations: Usually none, but consider Pol; Tet

Risk of TD low, though food and drink precautions advised outside of main towns

Some Schis present: avoid swimming/ bathing in fresh water streams, etc. Some risk of DF: avoid mosquito bites

---

18.3 EAST ASIA

This region includes: China, Hong Kong, Japan, North Korea, South Korea, Macau, Mongolia, Taiwan

Note that as of mid-1995 the dialling code to ring the UK from any of these countries should be 0044-, though the time of adoption of this code varies.

HEALTH RISKS THROUGHOUT THE REGION

Malaria: There is a malaria risk in parts of China (mainly *Plasmodium vivax*, with *P.*

falciparum also present), but not on the usual tourist routes.

Yellow fever: There is no yellow fever in East Asia, though the mosquitoes that carry it are found in the region. Immunisation is not required, but some countries may want a certificate if travelling from a country on the WHO list of yellow fever countries, or countries they consider to be an infected area.

The 'endemic' countries, which does **not** mean the disease is active, are:

Angola, Belize, Benin, Bolivia, Botswana, Brazil, Burkina Faso, Burundi, Cameroon, Central African Republic, Chad, Colombia, Congo, Costa Rica, Cote d'Ivoire, Ecuador, Equatorial Guinea, Ethiopia, French Guyana, Gabon, Gambia, Ghana, Guatemala, Guinea, Guinea Bissau, Guyana, Honduras, Kenya, Liberia, Mali, Mauritania, Nicaragua, Niger, Nigeria, Panama, Peru, Rwanda, Sao Tome and Principe, Senegal, Sierra Leone, Somalia, Sudan, Suriname, Tanzania, Togo, Trinidad & Tobago, Uganda, Venezuela, Zaire and Zambia. Not all of these may be recognised as countries requiring certification by your destination: check your itinerary carefully. Note, children under 9 months should not be immunised.

Other health risks: Dengue fever, an urban viral disease spread by day-biting mosquitoes, common in China; and Japanese encephalitis, again spread by mosquitoes, but this time in rural areas. Schistosomiasis (bilharzia), a fluke disease caught from fresh water snails, is also endemic. Avoid bathing or swimming in fresh water lakes, ponds and streams. Leishmaniasis (protozoa, from sandflies) and filariasis (worms, from mosquitoes) various tick-borne (Lyme disease, Congo-Crimean haemorrhagic fever) and mite-borne (scrub typhus) diseases need to be protected against in many rural areas. Insects are best repelled by appropriate clothing (i.e. long sleeves if mosquitoes, long trousers for ticks) and repellents such as DEET.

There are a whole variety of other worm infections across the region, including paragonimiasis, the oriental lung fluke (from raw crustacea, such as crayfish), and flukes spread by eating watercress, water chestnuts and other aquatic plants on which snails have deposited little infective stages, causing fascioliasis (liver fluke) or worse, fasciolopsiasis, the Giant Intestinal Fluke, which is due to sewage-contaminated plants. Watch also for parasites caught from raw fish and under-cooked meat. Shoes prevent soild-welling parasites such as hookworm and strongyloides, which tend to penetrate skin.

In some areas there is a risk of typhoid and hepatitis A: immunisations for these should be considered. There is active cholera (especially in parts of China), and in some cases travellers may be asked for proof of immunisation if coming from, or in some cases, going to a cholera area. Although the WHO no longer recommends the immunisation, it may be worth having a single shot to obtain an official-looking piece of paper. The best way to avoid cholera is good food and water hygiene.

Rabies is another endemic disease, though there is no risk in Japan and Taiwan. Consider immunisation, but remember, post-exposure treatment also essential.

Travellers might wish to avoid unscreened blood products and carry their own supply of syringes, as there is a risk of hepatitis B and (low risk) of HIV.

As always the most likely complaint the traveller will have to endure is the so-called travellers' diarrhoea. This may be caused by a variety of agents, from bacteria such as *Esherichia coli* and *Salmonella*, to protozoa such as *Entamoeba* and *Giardia*. Good food and drink hygiene is essential where water and food quality are suspect: wash hands, make sure all meat is cooked, drink bottled water, peel fruit, etc. Avoid unpasteurised dairy products, as there is a risk of brucellosis.

The usual precautions can be switched off in certain locations: sushi in Tokyo, for example, and street restaurants in Hong Kong and Macau are usually fine as long as you choose carefully (eating shellfish from the waters around Hong Kong in particular is not advisable).

Immunisations for the region include tetanus, typhoid, hepatitis A, polio, plus rabies, hepatitis B (for health workers etc.) and Japanese encephalitis. Long-stay workers may have to make sure their diphtheria and tuberculosis are up to date.

Note that just because a disease is present in a country, it does not follow that a tourist/traveller will be exposed to it. Nor will they necessarily need all the advised immunisations (e.g. if travelling just to Hong Kong, Seoul or Beijing, or staying in western-style resorts, typhoid is not always considered necessary). Seek advice from your GP or travel clinic.

CHINA

+8 hours GMT (+ 9 in summer)
Capital: Beijing
Embassy: 49–51 Portland Place, London W1N 3AH (0171-636 9375). Consular sections: 31 Portland Place (0171-636 1430)
Tourist Office: 4 Glentworth Street, London NW1 5PG (0171-935 9787)
British Embassy: 11 Guang Hua Lu, Jian Guo Men Wai, Beijing. Tel: (1) 532 1961/5; Fax: (1) 532 1939
Visa required: Yes
Yellow fever certificate: Yes, all travellers arriving from infected areas

HIV test: Yes, if staying 12 months or more

Recommended health precautions

Immunisations: Pol; Typh; Tet; Hep A. Hep B if extended stay. (Note Hep E also present, but no immunisation available; it is a risk for pregnant women in particular.) Consider Rab. JE is worth considering, common in rural and suburban areas, esp. May–Oct (2000 cases per annum)

Malaria prophylaxis: Risk of the disease in many, but not all, rural areas, with very little threat around the usual tourist sights/itineraries. However, there is drug resistant *Plasmodium falciparum* in the south, near border areas. For the northern areas, chloroquine and proguanil or mefloquine (not for children under 15 kg, during the first trimester of pregnancy or if history of epilepsy, psychiatric problems) for the Hainan and Yunan provinces. For anywhere close to Laos/Cambodia, mefloquine usually first choice, with doxycycline (see entry for Cambodia under South East Asia) as an alternative. Nets/repellents should also be deployed. It must be stressed that the majority of visitors will not need a prophylactic drug regime

The main hotels and restaurants treat their water and have reasonable food hygiene. Away from these, particularly if in remote rural areas, implement usual precautions and watch for parasitic infections

Both forms of Leish, Fil and Lyme disease also reported from more remote areas: avoid all insect bites just to be certain. DF more of a threat: avoid day-biting mosquitoes, even in urban areas. Schis is estimated to infect 1 million residents at any one time.

HONG KONG

Hong Kong is a British Crown Colony until 1997, when it and the New Territories revert to China

+8 hours GMT

HK Tourism: 125 Pall Mall, London SW1Y 5EA (0171-930 4775).

Government Office: 6 Grafton Street, London W1X 3LB (0171-499 9821)

Visa required: No

Yellow fever certificate: No

HIV test: No

Recommended health precautions

Immunisations: If travelling through en route to, say, Australia, then think about immunisations very carefully. The advised list is the full Tet; Typh; Pol; Hep A. Sometimes JE; Hep B for extended stay, though this is probably overcautious *unless* venturing well away from the urban centre. Discuss you itinerary with a travel clinic or GP. If you intend to eat a lot of seafood, however, Hep A is advisable

Malaria prophylaxis: none required

There is good drinking water, dairy products etc., and a low risk of stomach troubles

Some DF risk: avoid mosquito bites. There have been some cases of JE, but the risk to the average tourists is very low

---

JAPAN

+9 hours GMT
Capital: Tokyo
Embassy: 101–104 Piccadilly, London W1V 9FN (0171-465 6500)
Tourist Office: 167 Regent Street, W1R 7FD (0171-734 9638)
British Embassy: No 1 Ichibancho, Chiyodaku, Tokyo 102. Tel: (3) 3265 5511; Fax: (3) 5275 3164. Consulates also in Osaka, Hiroshima, Fukoaka and Nagoya
Visa required: No
Yellow fever certificate: No
HIV test: HIV-positive foreigners are sometimes refused entry

Recommended health precautions
Immunisations: Sometimes JE if travelling rurally May–Oct (but risk low). Sometimes Typh and Pol, but usually nothing for major cities/tourist routes. Long-stay workers should consider Hep B

Malaria prophylaxis: none required

Food and water safe, though there is always a small risk of parasites and toxins from raw fish and undercooked shellfish and crayfish

---

NORTH KOREA
(Democratic People's Republic)

+9 hours GMT
Capital: Pyongyang
Embassy: There is no diplomatic mission
Visa required: Yes. Advice from Regent Holidays, 15 John Street, Bristol BS1 2HR (01272-211711)
Yellow fever certificate: No
HIV test: No

Recommended health precautions
Immunisations: Tet; Typh; Pol. Hep A. Consider JE; Hep B; Rab.

Malaria prophylaxis: none needed

Take all food/water hygiene precautions, and avoid dairy products

Cholera is active. There is a risk of DF: avoid mosquito bites

---

KOREA

(Republic of Korea)

+ hours GMT

Capital: Seoul

Embassy: 4 Palace Gate, London W8 5NF (0171 581 0247). Visas: 0171-581 3330/9

Tourist Office: 20 George Street, London W1R 9RD (0171-409 2100)

British Embassy: 4 Chung-dong, Chung-ku, Seoul 100. Tel: (2) 735 7341; Fax: (2) 733 8368

Visa required: No, not for up to 2 months

Yellow fever certificate: No

HIV test: Yes, if staying over 90 days

Recommended health precautions

Immunisations: Pol; Tet; Typ;. Hep A. Consider Rab; Hep B if extended stay. Immunisation profile will depend on where you visit. Rural travellers should consider JE

Malaria prophylaxis: none needed. There is, however, some (low) risk of DF and Fil, so avoid mosquito bites

Good hotels and restaurants serve safe food and water. Elsewhere observe the usual food and water hygiene, including sticking to bottled water (mains water normally chlorinated in larger towns/cities).

MACAU

Portuguese enclave reverting to China in 1999

+8 hours GMT

UK Tourist Board: 6 Sherlock Mews, Paddington Street, London W1M 3RH (0171-224 3390)

Visa required: No

Yellow fever certificate: No

HIV test: No

Recommended health precautions

Immunisations: Tet; Pol; Typh; Hep A; Hep B if staying long-term; and JE all recommended. In fact Macau is much like Hong Kong, with low risks, except possibly for Hep A if you have a fondness for raw oysters. Consult with your local travel clinic or GP

Malaria prophylaxis: none required

Excellent local food safe in the majority of places, exercise caution in some of the more rustic locations

---

MONGOLIA

+8/9 hours GMT

Capital: Ulan Bator

Embassy: 7 Kensington Court, London W8 5DL (0171937 0150)

British Embassy: PO Box 703, 30 Enkh Taivny Gudamzh, Ulan Bator. Tel: 510330; Fax: 445 143

Visa required: Yes
Yellow fever certificate: No
HIV test: Yes, on arrival for some categories. May be waived; check with embassy

Recommended health precautions
Immunisations: Pol; Tet; Typh; Hep A. Consider Rab; Hep B if extended stay

Malaria prophylaxis: none needed

All water should be judged unreliable. Food and water hygiene precautions essential, to prevent both illness and parasitic diseases. Avoid all dairy products TRAVAX reported an outbreak of meningitis in early 1994 (over 1000 cases), the B strain, for which immunisation ineffective

---

TAIWAN

(aka The Republic of China)

+8 hours GMT
Capital: Taipei
UK Representative: 50 Grosvenor Gardens, London SW1 0EB (0171-396 9152, visas 0171-396 9143)
Visa required: Yes
Yellow fever certificate: Yes, all travellers arriving from an infected area
HIV test: Yes, if staying more than 3 months

Recommended health precautions
Immunisations: Pol; Typh; Tet; Hep A. Consider Hep B; Rab if extended stay; JE if travelling rurally

Malaria prophylaxis: none needed, but risk of DF: avoid daytime-biting mosquitoes

Outside of best hotels/restaurants observe all food/water hygiene precautions, especially as there is a high incidence of parasites from undercooked or raw fish, meat and water vegetables (e.g. watercress and waterchestnuts)

18.4 INDIAN SUBCONTINENT

This region includes: Afghanistan, Bangladesh, Bhutan, India, Maldives, Nepal, Pakistan and Sri Lanka.

Note that as of mid-1995 the dialling code to ring the UK from any of these countries should be 0044-, though the time of adoption of this code varies.

HEALTH RISKS THROUGHOUT THE REGION

Malaria: There is a malaria risk throughout the region, with the exception of the Maldives, where there is none at all. There is both *Plasmodium vivax* and the more malevolent *P. falciparum*. See individual countries for risk areas.

Yellow fever: There is no yellow fever in the Indian subcontinent. Immunisation is not required if travelling from the UK, but some countries may want a certificate if travelling from a country on the WHO list of yellow fever countries, or countries they consider to be an infected area.

The infected countries, which does **not** mean the disease is active, are:

Angola, Belize, Benin, Bolivia, Botswana, Brazil, Burkina Faso, Burundi, Cameroon, Central African Republic, Chad, Colombia, Congo, Costa Rica, Cote d'Ivoire, Ecuador, Equatorial Guinea, Ethiopia, French Guyana, Gabon, Gambia, Ghana, Guatemala, Guinea, Guinea Bissau, Guyana, Honduras, Kenya, Liberia, Mali, Mauritania, Nicaragua, Niger, Nigeria, Panama, Peru, Rwanda, Sao Tome and Principe, Senegal, Sierra Leone, Somalia, Sudan, Suriname, Tanzania, Togo, Trinidad & Tobago, Uganda, Venezuela, Zaire and Zambia. Not all of these may be recognised as countries requiring certification by your destination: check your itinerary carefully.

Other health risks: Dengue fever, an urban viral disease spread by day-biting mosquitoes, common in Bangladesh, India, Maldives and Sri Lanka, though risks to foreign tourists are small. Japanese encephalitis, again spread by mosquitoes, is active in rural parts (usually during the rainy season) of Bangladesh, India, Nepal and Sri Lanka. Leishmaniasis (sandflies) and filariasis (mosquitoes) also present.

There has been an outbreak of a serious strain of cholera in the region, and reports of officials asking for certificates of immunisation. Cholera is not a disease of tourism, and the immunisation is not particularly effective. However, it might be worth having one jab just to get an official-looking piece of paper before travelling (see Chapter 3). The best way to avoid cholera is good food and water hygiene.

Rabies is highly active across the subcontinent, with the highest risk in India and Pakistan. Consider immunisation, but remember, post-exposure treatment also essential.

HIV is not the risk it is in some parts of the world, though its incidence seems to be increasing. Although the average traveller is not at risk (see Chapter 13) avoid medical and dental procedures and carry your own supply of syringes and needles: even without HIV, there is still a risk of hepatitis B.

As always the most likely complaint the traveller will have to endure is the so-called travellers' diarrhoea. This may be caused by a variety of agents, from bacteria such as *Esherichia coli* and *Salmonella*, to protozoa such as *Entamoeba* and *Giardia*. Good food and drink hygiene is essential where water and food quality are suspect: wash hands, make sure all is meat cooked, drink bottled water, peel fruit, etc. Avoid unpasteurised dairy products, as there is a risk of brucellosis, etc.

Immunisations for the region include tetanus, typhoid, hepatitis A, polio, plus rabies, meningitis, hepatitis B (for health workers etc.), Japanese encephalitis. Long-stay workers should ensure their diphtheria and tuberculosis are up to date.

Note that just because a disease is present in a country, it does not follow that a tourist/traveller will be exposed to it. Nor will they necessarily need all the advised immunisations, though in this part of the world it is likely they will. Seek advice from your GP or travel clinic.

AFGHANISTAN

+4.5 hours GMT
Capital: Kabul
Embassy: 31 Prince's Gate, London SW7 1QQ (0171-589 8891)
British Embassy: Karte Parwan, Kabul. Tel: (93) 30511
Visa required: Yes
Yellow fever certificate: Yes, all travellers arriving from an infected area
HIV test: No

Recommended health precautions
Immunisations: Pol; Tet; Typh; Hep A. Consider Rab; Hep B if extended stay

Malaria prophylaxis: There is a risk of malaria in all areas below 2000 feet, mainly May–Nov. WHO warns of some drug-resistant *P. falciparum* in the east. For most of the country chloroquine and proguanil is recommended. If on the Pakistan border, mefloquine (not for children under 15 kg, during the first trimester of pregnancy or if history of epilepsy or psychiatric problems)

Treat all water as potentially contaminated, observe strict food/drink hygiene: v. high risk of TD

Risk of cutaneous leishmaniasis (avoid sandfly bites) and Hep E (sewage contaminated water, serious threat to pregnant women) and Rab. Trachoma (flies, close contact) common in population. Avoid tick bites: a variety of viral diseases carried

BANGLADESH

+6 hours GMT
Capital: Dhaka
High Commission: 28 Queen's Gate, London SW7 5JA (0171-584 0081/4). Also Birmingham and Manchester
British High Commission: PO Box 6079, United Nations Road, Baridhara, Dhaka 12. Tel: (2) 882 705; Fax: (2) 883 437
Visa required: Yes
Yellow fever certificate: Yes, all travellers from or through a country with an infected area (and Bangladesh takes a very broad view of which countries are infected: check)
HIV test: No

Recommended health precautions
Immunisations: Pol; Tet; Typh; Hep A. Consider Rab; Hep B; Men; JE (if travelling rurally)

Malaria prophylaxis: There is a malaria risk everywhere except Dhaka. Much *P. falciparum* and chloroquine/Fansidar resistance. Use mefloquine (see Afghanistan), particularly in forested areas, or chloroquine and proguanil, along with nets and repellents

There is a very high risk of intestinal/ stomach disturbances from food and water, so implement all food and water precautions

JE active mainly in rural areas, May–Oct, but risk to travellers low unless spending long periods of time in agricultural communities. DF, visceral leishmaniasis (increasing) and Fil (common) all present, so protect against mosquito/sandfly bites

---

BHUTAN

+6 hours GMT
Capital: Thimphu
Bhutan Tourism Corporation: PO Box 159, Thimphu, Bhutan. Tel: 22647
Visa required: Yes, in writing to above or through tour operators. Expensive and limited. Note: can only enter via India, need documentation for that country as well
Yellow fever certificate: Yes, all travellers arriving from an infected area
HIV test: No

Recommended health precautions
Immunisations: Pol; Tet; Typh; Hep A. Consider Rab; Hep B; and possibly Men if long stay/aid worker. JE may also be recommended if travelling in the southern border regions

Malaria prophylaxis: Risk in the southern part of the country at low elevations, with *P. falciparum* and drug resistance. Tourists do not necessarily go into areas with malaria, so prophylaxis may not be needed. If it is, chloroquine and proguanil or, increasingly, mefloquine recommended (see

Afghanistan). Use nets and repellents

Hep E and Chol present, both waterborne. Treat all water as potentially contaminated: institute usual food and drink hygiene precautions

Note there is also a risk of altitude sickness, as the country rises to 22,000 feet

---

INDIA

+5.5 hours GMT
Capital: New Delhi
High Commission: India House, Aldwych, London WC2B 4NA (0171-836 8484)
Tourist Office: 7 Cork Street, London W1X 1PB (0171-437 3677)
British Embassy/High Commission: Shanti Path, Chanakyapuri, New Delhi 211 100. Tel: (11) 601 371; Fax: (11) 687 2882 (Embassy). Tel: (11) 601 371; Fax: (11) 609 940 (High Commission)
Visa required: Yes
Yellow fever certificate: Yes, all travellers over 6 months old arriving with 6 days of travelling through an infected area
HIV test: Yes, for students and long-stay workers, with some exemptions

Recommended health precautions
Immunisations: Pol (several cases of people visiting relatives catching it); Tet;. Typh; Hep A. Consider Rab; Hep B; Men (Hib for children under 5); JE if travelling rurally

Malaria prophylaxis: There is no malaria in Himachal Pradesh, Jammu and Kashmir and Sikkim. In the east there is risk from *P. falciparum*, less so elsewhere. Travellers usually recommended chloroquine and proguanil or mefloquine (see Afghanistan). Use nets and repellents. Reports of *P. falciparum* in Calcutta and Rajasthan

As the nickname Delhi belly suggests, there is a high risk of TD, and all precautions should be taken. Chol, Hep E, DF, Fil, Leish (east), JE and rabies all need protecting against. Trachoma and *Dracunulus* (guinea worm) found, plus other parasites, esp. in rural areas: take protective measures (e.g. wear shoes) TRAVAX reports 30% of prostitutes in Bombay are HIV positive

---

THE MALDIVES

+5 hours GMT
Capital: Male
UK Tourist Office: C/o Maldive Travel, 3 Esher House, 11 Edith Terrace, London SW10 0TH (0171-352 2246)
Visa required: Yes
Yellow fever certificate: Yes, all travellers arriving from an infected area

HIV test: No

Recommended health precautions
Immunisations: Pol; Tet; Typh; Hep A. Consider Rab; Hep B if extended stay. However, this whole battery may be unnecessary for a resort holiday. Consult your travel clinic or GP

Malaria prophylaxis: None required, though some risk of DF and Fil, so avoid mosquito bites

Food and water in hotels and restaurants usually safe; take care elsewhere

---

NEPAL

+5.75 hours GMT
Capital: Kathmandu
Embassy: 12a Kensington Palace Gardens, London W8 4QU (0171-229 1594)
British Embassy: PO Box 106, Lainchaur, Kathmandu. Tel: (1) 410583; Fax: (1) 411789
Visa required: Yes
Yellow fever certificate: Yes, all travellers arriving from an infected area
HIV test: No

Recommended health precautions
Immunisations: Pol; Tet; Typh; Hep A. Consider Rab; Hep B (widespread); possibly Men and JE

Malaria prophylaxis: Risk below 1500m. Kathmandu free. Some drug resistance, some *P. falciparum*. Chloroquine and proguanil or mefloquine (see Afghanistan) recommended. Use nets and repellents. Neither malaria nor Japanese encephalitis will be a problem on the usual trekking holidays

Best hotels have good water, reliable food, but take care elsewhere, esp. in rural areas. Civex Clinic (228531, Fax: 977-224675) good source of local advice

Although there is some DF, Leish and Fil present, mainly in low areas, the biggest threat to most travellers to the region is altitude sickness

---

PAKISTAN

+5 hours GMT
Capital: Islamabad
High Commission: 36 Lowndes Square, London SW1X 9JN (0171-235 2044)
British Embassy: PO Box 1048, Diplomatic Enclave, Ramna 5, Islamabad. Tel: (51) 826161; Fax: (51) 821 193
Visa required: Yes
Yellow fever certificate: Yes, if older than 6 months arriving from an infected area. (Note, mother must have been immunised before birth of child)
HIV test: Yes if staying more than 12 months

Recommended health precautions
Immunisations: Pol; Tet; Typh; Hep A. Consider Hep B; Rab (widespread); JE (low risk) if extended stay

Malaria prophylaxis: Required esp. in Punjab but throughout the country. Risk areas all below 2000m. Chloroquine and proguanil or, particularly for Punjab, mefloquine (see Afghanistan) recommended. Use nets and repellents

Water-borne diseases (e.g. Chol, Hep A, Typh) active: observe all food/drink hygiene precautions

Some risk of Leish: protect against sandfly bites (sandfly fever also a risk). Tick-borne diseases also present. Watch for food and soilborne parasites: watch what you eat and drink, and wear shoes

---

SRI LANKA

+ 5.5 hours GMT
Capital: Colombo
High Commission: 13 Hyde Park Gardens, London W2 2LU (0171-262 1841)
Tourist information: 0171262 5009
British Embassy: PO Box 1433, 190 Galle Rd, Kollupitiya, Colombo 3. Tel: (1) 437336; Fax: (1) 437334
Visa required: Yes
Yellow fever certificate: Yes, all travellers over 1 year old coming from an infected area
HIV test: HIV-positive foreign nationals may be refused entry

Recommended health precautions
Immunisations: Pol; Tet; Typh; Hep A. Consider Hep B; Rab. JE advised for rural travellers staying over 1 month

Malaria prophylaxis: no risk in capital. Elsewhere there are chloroquine resistant strains, most imp. *P. falciparum* (though *P. vivax* dominates). Use chloroquine and proguanil or, increasingly, mefloquine (see Afghanistan)

Best hotels have reliable water and food, otherwise instigate all food and drink hygiene precautions

DF (inc. haemorrhagic form) and filariasis present on SW coast: protect against mosquito bites at all times. Keep shoes on: there are soil-borne parasites

18.5 SOUTHEAST ASIA

This region includes the countries of Brunei, Cambodia, Indonesia, Laos (Lao People's Democratic Republic), Malaysia, Myanmar (Burma), Philippines, Singapore, Thailand and Vietnam.

Note that by mid1995 the dialling code for the UK from any of these countries should be standardised at 0044-.

HEALTH RISKS THROUGHOUT THE REGION

Malaria: Occurs in pockets throughout the region. It is a serious disease, but the risk of most travellers catching it is low compared with Africa. Nevertheless, there are areas where the lethal *P. falciparum* is the dominant form, and areas of drug resistance, so prophylaxis is essential where advised. The risk is mainly in rural areas and there is no risk in Brunei or Singapore.

Yellow fever: There is no yellow fever in South East Asia, though the mosquitoes that carry it are found in the region. Immunisation is not required, but some countries may want a certificate if travelling from a country on the WHO list of yellow fever countries.

The endemic countries, which does **not** mean the disease is active, are:

Angola, Belize, Benin, Bolivia, Botswana, Brazil, Burkina Faso, Burundi, Cameroon, Central African Republic, Chad, Colombia, Congo, Costa Rica, Cote d'Ivoire, Ecuador, Equatorial Guinea, Ethiopia, French Guyana, Gabon, Gambia, Ghana, Guatemala, Guinea, Guinea Bissau, Guyana, Honduras, Kenya, Liberia, Mali, Mauritania, Nicaragua, Niger, Nigeria, Panama, Peru, Rwanda, Sao Tome and Principe, Senegal, Sierra Leone, Somalia, Sudan, Suriname, Tanzania, Togo, Trinidad & Tobago, Uganda, Venezuela, Zaire and Zambia. Not all of these may be recognised as countries requiring certification by your destination: check your itinerary carefully. Children under 9 months should not be immunised.

Other health risks: Dengue fever, an urban viral disease spread by day-biting mosquitoes, is a risk throughout the region. There have been epidemics in Cambodia, Indonesia, Laos, Malaysia, Myanmar (Burma), Philippines, Singapore, Thailand and Vietnam. Avoiding being bitten is the only way to prevent the disease, though the risk to most travellers is low except during an epidemic.

Japanese encephalitis is another mosquito speciality, a viral disease associated mainly with rural areas, especially during the rainy season and where there are paddy fields. There is an immunisation, but whether you have it depends on your itinerary. If you are travelling to the rural areas of Cambodia, Indonesia, Laos, Malaysia, Myanmar, Philippines, Thailand or Vietnam then there is a risk of Japanese encephalitis. Filariasis, caused by parasitic roundworms, is also spread by several different types of mosquitoes. Avoid bites: use DEET or other similar repellents, and nets and appropriate clothing.

There is a variety of other worm infections across the region, including paragonimiasis, the Oriental lung fluke (from raw crustacea, such as crayfish), and flukes spread by eating watercress, water chestnuts and other aquatic plants on which snails have deposited little infective stages, causing fascioliasis (liver fluke) or worse, fasciolopsiasis, the Giant Intestinal Fluke, which is due to sewage-contaminated plants. Watch also for parasites caught from raw fish, undercooked meat.

There is a risk of typhoid and hepatitis A: immunisations for these should be considered. There is cholera in the area, and in some cases travellers may be asked for proof of immunisation if coming from, or in some cases, going to a cholera area. Although the WHO no longer recommends the immunisation, it may be worth some travellers having a single shot to obtain an official-looking piece of paper. The best way to avoid cholera is good food and water hygiene.

Rabies is another endemic disease. Thailand presents the highest risk, with a high percentage of animals infected, and an alarming number of visitors bitten or licked. Consider immunisation, but remember, post-exposure treatment also essential.

Thailand also has a high incidence of HIV, with reports of an average of 25% of all prostitutes HIV positive. However, HIV is not a threat to travellers except under exceptional circumstances, and risks can be minimised by following the guidelines in Chapter 13.

As always the most likely complaint the traveller will have to endure is the so-called travellers' diarrhoea. This may be caused by a variety of agents, from bacteria such as *Esherichia coli* and *Salmonella*, to protozoa such as *Entamoeba* and *Giardia*. Good food and drink hygiene is essential where water and food quality are suspect: wash hands, make sure all meat is cooked, drink bottled water, peel fruit, etc. Avoid unpasteurised dairy products, as there is a risk of brucellosis. Having said that, some of the best food in the world comes from this region, much of it sold on the street, and it would be a shame to let total food paranoia spoil that: just make sure it is hot, cooked and fresh.

South East Asia is also full of wonderful beaches and inviting waters, but there is a risk of various poisonous fish (e.g. scorpion and stone fish), jelly-fish, stingrays, etc. Take care: swim where there are other people.

Immunisations for the region include tetanus, typhoid, hepatitis A, polio, plus rabies, hepatitis B (for health workers, etc.), Japanese encephalitis. Long-stay workers should ensure their diphtheria and tuberculosis are up to date.

Note that just because a disease is present in a country, it does not follow that a tourist/traveller will be exposed to it. Nor will they necessarily need all the advised immunisations (e.g. if travelling just to Singapore and Bangkok or staying in western-style resorts). Typhoid is not always considered necessary. Seek advice from your GP or travel clinic.

BRUNEI

Brunei Darussalam is an Islamic monarchy, part of the island of Borneo
+8 hours GMT
Capital: Bandar Seri Begawan
High Commission: 19 Belgrave Square, London SW1X 8PG (0171-581 0521)
British High Commission: PO Box 2197, 3rd Floor, Hong Kong Bank Chambers, Jalan Pemancha. Tel: (2) 22223; Fax: (2) 26002
Visa required: No
Yellow fever certificate required: Yes, if over 12 months old and have passed through a yellow fever area in the last 6 days
HIV test: Yes, if working/residence, although it may be waived. Check with High Commission

Recommended health precautions
Immunisations: Pol; Tet; Typh; Hep A. If staying long term Hep B; occasionally Rab. (Note that if staying just in the capital, this battery is unlikely to be needed.) If travelling rurally, JE

Malaria prophylaxis: There is no risk of malaria, but the mosquitoes which bite during the day may transmit dengue fever: avoid being bitten

Food and drink in hotels and restaurants of capital reliable; outside observe food and drink precautions

---

CAMBODIA (KAMPUCHEA)

+7 hours GMT
Capital: Phnom Penh
British Mission to Cambodia: Cambodiana Hotel, 29 ST 75, Phnom Pehn. Tel: (23) 27124; Fax (23) 27125
Visa required: Yes (usually booked through tour operators, in UK, Hong Kong or Bangkok)

Yellow fever certificate required: Yes, all travellers over 1 year old arriving from an infected area
HIV test: Usually no, but has been known

Recommended health precautions
Immunisations: Pol; Tet; Typh; Hep A. If extended stay, Hep B (15% carrier rate in population), possibly Rab. If travelling rurally, JE (increasing problem)

Malaria prophylaxis: There is a risk of malaria in all rural areas, and on the border with Thailand the mosquitoes are resistant to a whole cocktail of drugs. *P. falciparum* is the dominant form. Specialist advice is needed. Mefloquine (not for children under 15 kg, in the first trimester of pregnancy or if history of epilepsy or psychiatric disorders) may be taken, but often doxycycline is recommended for the border area, as WHO reports mefloquine is becoming redundant, especially in the west. Doxycycline has its own problems: it cannot be used in pregnancy or during breast-feeding (it can discolour/deform the baby's teeth), by children under 12 and has side effects including skin photosensitivity. It also reduces the efficacy of the contraceptive pill somewhat, so women should use additional methods.

V. high risk of TD

DF and JE also present, along with Schis in fresh water. Several soil- and food-borne parasites, and to top it all, the political situation is highly unstable. Consult foreign office before travel.

INDONESIA

+7 to +9 hours GMT
Capital: Jakarta
Embassy: 38 Grosvenor Square, London W1X 9AD (0171-499 7661)
Tourist Board: 34 Hanover Street, W1R 9HH (0171-493 0030)
British Embassy: Jalan MH Thamrin 75, Jakarta 10310. Tel: (21) 330904; Fax: (21) 321824
Visa required: No
Yellow fever certificate required: Yes, all travellers arriving from an infected area
HIV test: No, but HIV-positive individuals visas not extended

Recommended health precautions
Immunisations: Pol; Tet; Typh; Hep A. If staying long term Hep B and perhaps Rab. If travelling rurally, JE (low risk). Note that cholera certificates have occasionally been ask for: check current regulations. Note also that Indonesia is a large, varied country: travelling to Bali and staying at the Four Seasons Hotel, you are unlikely to need the kind of protection if trekking in Java or Sumatra

Malaria prophylaxis: Equally the malaria risk varies: it is minimal in resort areas of Bali (though at the time of writing unofficial reports suggested a slightly increased risk: avoid bites), Lombok, Jakarta and Java resorts. It is high in Irian Jaya, the Indonesian part of New Guinea, and in Sumatra and other islands. Drug resistance reported, and mefloquine (see Cambodia) with chloroquine and proguanil alternative recommended. Use nets and repellents

Food and drink safe in resort areas such as those in Bali, but high risk of TD outside these: observe food and drink hygiene precautions

DF risk (and its more lethal cousin, dengue haemorrhagic fever) are present in urban areas: protect against bites. Schis, JE (mosquitoes, particularly during monsoon), Fil (more mosquitoes), Rab and soil parasites a risk.

LAOS

Lao People's Democratic Republic

+7 hours GMT
Capital: Vientiane
High Commission: Contact Paris (1 45 53 02 98)
British High Commission: Contact embassy in Thailand
Visa required: Yes, usually through tour operators in Bangkok
Yellow fever certificate required: Yes, all travellers coming from an infected area
HIV test: No

Recommended health precautions
Immunisations: Pol; Tet; Typh; Hep A. If staying long term Hep B and possibly Rab. If travelling rurally, JE. Laos has been known to insist on cholera immunisation for entry, even though WHO no longer deem it necessary. It may be worth having a single dose in order to get a certificate

Malaria prophylaxis: There is a malaria risk outside the capital, with multidrug resistance present near the Thai border. Seek specialist advice, but normally mefloquine or doxycycline (see Cambodia) suggested. Use nets and repellents

High risk of TD and food, soil and waterborne parasites. Observe all hygiene precautions rigidly, and watch watercress and water chestnuts

Rural risk of JE except at altitude, and of DF (epidemic summer 1994) with Fil completing the mosquitoborne trio. Schis present

---

MALAYSIA

+8 hours GMT
Capital: Kuala Lumpur
UK Tourist office: 57 Trafalgar Square, London WC2N 5DU (0171-930 7932)
High Commission: 45 Belgrave Square, SW1X 8QT (0171-235 8033)
British High Commission: 185 Jalan Semantang Ampang, 50450 Kuala Lumpur. Tel: (3) 248 2122; Fax: (3) 248 0880
Visa required: No, visitors pass issued on entry
Yellow fever certificate required: Yes, all travellers over 12 months old coming from infected area
HIV test: No

Recommended health precautions
Immunisations: Pol; Tet; Typh; Hep A. If staying long term Hep B and perhaps Rab (low risk). If travelling rurally, possibly JE. (Number of cases rising in Sabah.) In some cases a cholera certificate may be required if travelling on to a Chol infected country

Malaria prophylaxis: There is a malaria risk, highest in Sabah, and inland in peninsular Malaysia, below 1700 feet in rural areas. The WHO consider the coastal resorts to be generally clear. Chloroquine resistance reported, and diminishing proguanil effectiveness. Mefloquine likely to be recommended (not for children under 15 kg, in the first trimester of pregnancy or if history of epilepsy or psychiatric problems). Use nets/repellents

Food and water in better resorts generally safe, though it may be advisable to stick with bottled water. Take care away from usual tourist routes: various parasites can be picked up from undercooked fish and meat

Rural travellers have a chance, albeit a slim one, of coming across JE and DF (outbreak in Sabah, 93/94), particularly during monsoon season, and Fil: avoid mosquito bites. There is also Schis and leptospirosis (rural areas), though these are easily avoided by not swimming or bathing in fresh water

---

MYANMAR (BURMA)

+6.5 hours GMT
Capital: Rangoon (Yangan)
Embassy: 19a Charles Street, Berkeley Square, London W1X 8ER (0171-499 8841)
British Embassy: PO Box 638, 80 Strand Road, Yangon, Rangoon. Tel: (1) 81700; Fax: (1) 89566
Visa required: Yes
Yellow fever certificate: Yes, for all travellers coming from an infected area
HIV test: No

Recommended health precautions
Immunisations: Pol; Tet; Typh; Hep A. Hep B (and possibly Rab) if extended

stay. JE should also be considered, particularly during and just after the rainy season (May-Oct)

Malaria prophylaxis: The main risk is below 1500 feet; all year in the Karen state, seasonal (mainly April–Dec) elsewhere, though Rangoon is clear, as are other large city centres. Drug resistance common: take specialist advice. Mefloquine or doxycycline (see Cambodia) are usually recommended. Nets and repellents equally essential

V. high risk of TD: water supplies all unreliable. Take strict food/water hygiene precautions (esp. if pregnant: Hep E is common), avoid dairy products (risk of brucellosis, etc.)

Also take precautions against Fil, DF (mainly rainy season) and various soil/food worm parasites

---

PHILIPPINES

+8 hours GMT
Capital: Manila
Embassy: 9A Palace Green Road, London W8 4QE (0171-937 1600)
Tourist Office: 17 Albermarle Street, London W1X 7HA (0171-499 5443)
British Embassy: 15–17th Floors, LV Locsin Building, 6752 Ayala Avenue, Makati, Metro Manila. Tel: (2) 816 7116; Fax: (2) 819 7206
Visa required: No, not for tourism
Yellow fever certificate: Yes, all travellers older than 12 months coming from infected area (having left within last 6 days)
HIV test: Yes, for residence

Recommended health precautions
Immunisations: Pol; Tet; Typh; Hep A. Consider Rab; Hep B if extended stay; JE if travelling rurally, particularly during rainy season (Jul–Oct), though only 174 cases in total 1986–1990

Malaria prophylaxis: Risk below 1500 m, away from urban areas, but *P. falciparum* common, and WHO report it is highly chloroquine resistant. If travelling off the beaten track, take mefloquine (not children under 15 kg, during first trimester of pregnancy or if history of epilepsy or psychiatric problems) or chloroquine and proguanil. Note that in some guidelines chloroquine and proguanil are the first choice: discuss with your clinic. Use nets and repellents

Food and water hygiene precautions are needed outside better hotels and restaurants. Stick to bottled water. High incidence of various parasites in rural populations: cook all meat and fish thoroughly. Wear shoes to avoid soilborne worms

Some risk of DF during the rainy season; Fil also present: avoid mosquito bites. Do not swim or bathe in fresh water lakes or streams. Schis endemic

---

SINGAPORE

+8 hours GMT
Capital: Singapore
UK Tourist Office: 1st Floor, Carrington House, 126130 Regent Street, London W1R 5FE (0171-437 0033)
High Commission: 9 Wilton Crescent, London SW1X 8SA (0171-235 8315)
British High Commission: Tanglin Road, Singapore 1024. Tel: 473 9333; Fax: 475 2320/9706
Visa required: No
Yellow fever certificate: Yes, if over 12 months old and arriving from (or having passed through within last 6 days) a country within the endemic zone
HIV test: Yes for workers/residence

Recommended health precautions
Immunisations: If you are stopping over in Singapore en route to Australia, etc., then tell your GP or clinic: it is unlikely you will need a huge defence against germs, as germs are outlawed in Singapore. But officially consider the usual Tet; Typh; Hep A; Pol. If staying long-term, as a care or health worker, Hep B should be considered. JE not needed for Singapore only

Malaria prophylaxis: There is no malaria, however, some dengue fever: take precautions against mosquito bites, particularly around Nov/Jan monsoons

There is no need to observe the full gamut of food and water hygiene: just take everyday precautions

---

THAILAND

+7 hours GMT
Capital: Bangkok
UK Tourist Office: 49 Albermarle Street, London W1X 3FE (0171-499 7679)
Embassy: 2930 Queen's Gate, London SW7 5JB (0171-589 0173). Consulates in Birmingham, Hull, Liverpool, Cardiff, Glasgow
British Embassy: Wireless Road, Bangkok 10330. Tel: (2) 253 0191; Fax: (2) 253 8619
Visa required: No
Yellow fever certificate: Yes, travelling from an infected area
HIV test: Usually no, but can be at authorities' discretion

Recommended health precautions
Immunisations: Again, it depends on itinerary. If you are only going to Bangkok, the biggest threat to your health will be the traffic. Elsewhere, choose from: Pol; Tet; Typh; Hep A. Give Rab careful consideration. Hep B if extended stay. If travelling rurally, consider JE (1000 cases per annum, mainly in north)

Malaria prophylaxis: No risk in Bangkok, other major cities or most coastal resorts, such as Phuket. Risk in forested or hilly areas, particularly border areas, with plenty of *P. falciparum*, much of it drug resistant. Seek specialist advice: there is high mefloquine resistance, so doxycycline (see Cambodia) often recommended in some areas. Check with your clinic or GP

Low risk of TD in most resorts, except that caused by gluttony: precautions should be instigated in rural areas. Worth sticking with bottled water everywhere, however, unless hotel has own treatment plant. Watch also for soil and water-borne parasites away from resorts

Rab is a risk, and there is the possibility of DF, particularly in rainy season, even in Bangkok: avoid mosquito bites

---

VIETNAM

+7 hours GMT
Capital: Hanoi
Embassy: 1214 Victoria Road, London W8 5RD (0171-937 1912)
British Embassy: 16 Pho Ly Thuong Kiet, Hanoi. Tel: (4) 252349; Fax: (4) 265 762
Visa required: Yes
Yellow fever certificate: Yes, all travellers over 12 months old coming from infected area
HIV test: No

Recommended health precautions
Immunisations: Tet; Typh; Pol; Hep A. Consider Rab; Hep B (15 per cent carrier rate) if extended stay. JE if travelling rurally (5000 cases per annum and rising)

Malaria prophylaxis: Not needed in urban areas. *P. vivax* dominant to the south, *P. falciparum* to the north. Drug resistance reported. Mefloquine (see Cambodia), with chloroquine/proguanil alternative, usually recommended. Use nets and repellents

Observe the usual battery of food and water hygiene precautions Protect against DF, Schis and food-, water- and soil-borne parasites

---

18.6 MIDDLE EAST

This region includes: Bahrain, Cyprus, Iran, Iran, Jordan, Kuwait, Lebanon, Oman, Qatar, Saudi Arabia, Syria, Turkey, United Arab Emirates (inc. Abu Dhabi and Dubai) and Yeman. Note that as of mid-1995 the dialling code to ring the UK from any of these countries should be 0044-, though the time of adoption of this code varies.

HEALTH RISKS THROUGHOUT THE REGION

Malaria: There is a malaria risk in parts of Iran, Iraq, Oman, Saudi Arabia, Syria, Turkey, United Arab Emirates and Yemen, all with much *P. falciparum* (up to 70 per cent) the rest *P. vivax*. The risk is not uniform throughout each country, with many parts visited by travellers free from the disease, and the risk to the average tourist is low. See individual countries for risk areas. Bahrain, Cyprus, Israel, Jordan, Kuwait, Lebanon and Qatar have no malaria risk.

Yellow fever: There is no yellow fever in the Middle East. Immunisation is not required if travelling from the UK, but some countries may want a certificate if travelling from a country on the WHO list of yellow fever countries, or countries they consider to be an infected area.

The infected countries, which does **not** mean the disease is active, are:

Angola, Belize, Benin, Bolivia, Botswana, Brazil, Burkina Faso, Burundi, Cameroon, Central African Republic, Chad, Colombia, Congo, Costa Rica, Cote d'Ivoire, Ecuador, Equatorial Guinea, Ethiopia, French Guyana, Gabon, Gambia, Ghana, Guatemala, Guinea, Guinea Bissau, Guyana, Honduras, Kenya, Liberia, Mali, Mauritania, Nicaragua, Niger, Nigeria, Panama, Peru, Rwanda, Sao Tome and Principe, Senegal, Sierra Leone, Somalia, Sudan, Suriname, Tanzania, Togo, Trinidad & Tobago, Uganda, Venezuela, Zaire and Zambia.

Not all of these may be recognised as countries requiring certification by your destination: check your itinerary carefully. Note, children under 9 months should not be immunised.

Other health risks: Dengue fever, disease spread by day-biting mosquitoes, common only in the Yemen; leishmaniasis (protozoa, spread by sandflies) and filariasis (worms, spread by mosquitoes). Various tick-borne diseases (e.g. Congo-Crimean haemorrhagic fever, relapsing fever) need to be protected against in many rural areas. Insects are best repelled by appropriate clothing (i.e. long sleeves, long trousers) and repellents containing DEET. Risks to travellers of insect-borne diseases are low

There are worm infections across the region, including soil-borne hookworm and strongyloides, which can be avoided by wearing shoes, and some risk of intestinal worms, such as roundworms, tapeworms and dracunculiasis (caused by the guinea worm). Schistosomiasis (bilharzia) is present in pockets throughout Saudi Arabia, Yemen, Iraq and Syria: avoid swimming or bathing in fresh water.

Typhoid and hepatitis A and the various dysenteries are all found throughout the region. There have been reports of cholera, and in some cases travellers may be asked for proof of immunisation if coming from, or occasionally, going to a cholera area. Although the WHO no longer recommends the immunisation, it may be worth some travellers having a single shot to obtain an officiallooking piece of paper. The best way to avoid cholera is good food and water hygiene (it is not a disease of tourism).

Rabies is present in most countries, except for Bahrain and Cyprus, which have had no cases in the last few years. Consider immunisation, but remember, post-exposure treatment also essential.

The number of HIV-positive individuals within the population is low, but many countries in this region require a test for people living and working in the country.

As always the most likely complaint the traveller will have to endure, particularly away from the cities, is the so-called travellers' diarrhoea. This may be caused by a variety of agents, from bacteria such as *Esherichia coli* and *Salmonella*, to protozoa such as *Entamoeba* and *Giardia*. Good food and drink hygiene is essential where water and food quality are suspect: wash hands, make sure all meat is cooked, drink bottled water, peel fruit, etc. Avoid unpasteurised dairy products, as there is a risk of brucellosis etc.

Immunisations for the region include tetanus, typhoid, hepatitis A, polio (endemic), plus rabies, meningitis (Saudi Arabia during Hajj pilgrimage only), hepatitis B (for health workers etc). Long-stay workers should ensure their diphtheria and tuberculosis are up to date.

Note that just because a disease is present in a country, it does not follow that a tourist or traveller will be exposed to it. Nor will they necessarily need all the advised immunisations, particularly if stopping over in one of the large cities of the region. Seek advice from your GP or travel clinic.

BAHRAIN

+3 hours GMT
Capital: Manama
Embassy: 98 Gloucester Road, London SW7 4AU (0171-370 5132)
British Embassy: PO Box 114, 21 Government Ave., Manama, Bahrain. Tel: 534 404; Fax: 531 273

Visa required: No
Yellow fever certificate: Yes, travellers over 1 year old arriving from an infected country
HIV test: No

Recommended health precautions
Immunisations: Pol; Tet; Typh; Hep A.

Consider Hep B

Malaria prophylaxis: Not required

Low risk of any form of TD, though it is best to stick with bottled water.

CYPRUS

+2 (3 in summer) hours GMT
Note that since the invasion (or liberation, depending on your point of view) of 1974, Cyprus is a divided island. This section refers to the southern, Greek, part. Although there is a tourist industry in the northern, Turkish, part, the Turkish Republic of Northern Cyprus remains, at the time of writing, unrecognised by everyone except Turkey
Capital: Nicosia
UK Tourist Office: 213 Regent Street, London W1R 8DA (0171-734 9822)
High Commission: 93 Park Street, London W1Y 4ET (0171-499 8272). Also in Manchester and Glasgow
British High Commission: PO Box 1978, Alexander Pallis Street, Nicosia. Tel: (2) 473131/7; Fax: (2) 367198
Visa required: No
Yellow fever certificate: No
HIV test: Yes, foreign workers in nightclubs, etc. may be required to take test. There are 6-monthly checks of people in high risk behaviour groups

Recommended health precautions
Immunisations: Many thousands of UK holiday makers travel to Cyprus without any jabs. However, checking Tet and Pol (no cases in recent years) may be a good idea. There is theoretical risk of Typh and Hep A, but the threat to the average traveller is very low

Malaria prophylaxis: None required

Food, water and dairy goods all generally safe. As in any hot climate, be wary of hotel buffets

---

IRAN

+3.5 hours GMT
Capital: Tehran
Embassy: 27 Prince's Gate, London SW7 1PX (0171-584 8101)
British Embassy: PO Box 113654474, 143 Ferdowsi Avenue, Tehran 11344. Tel: (21) 675011; Fax: (21) 678021
Visa required: Yes
Yellow fever certificate: Yes, all travellers over 1 year old arriving from an infected area (including anywhere in the endemic zone)
HIV test: Yes, if staying over 3 months

Recommended health precautions
Immunisations: Pol; Tet; Typh;Hep A. Consider Hep B; Rab if extended stay

Malaria prophylaxis: There is a risk of the disease in the provinces of Sistan-Baluchestan and Hormozgan, and the southern parts of Fars, Kohgiluyeh-

Boyar, Lorestan and Chahar Mahal-Bakhtiara and the north of Khuzestan. The threat is seasonal (Mar–Nov) in the north and NE, all year round elsewhere. Although some drug resistance reported, chloroquine and proguanil still preferred regime. Travellers to the SE may be offered mefloquine (not children under 15 kg, during the first trimester of pregnancy or if history of epilepsy or psychiatric disorders)

Mains water usually chlorinated, and safe in major centres, though bottled water is probably preferable. Pasteurised milk is available. Away from the best hotels observe food hygiene precautions, and treat water away from cities as suspect (according to CDC, giardiasis is common)

Fil (mosquitoes) and Leish (both varieties, spread by sandflies) present, plus tickborne relapsing fever in rural areas: protect against insect bites. Also Schis: do not swim/bathe in fresh water

---

IRAQ

+3 (4 in summer) hours GMT
Capital: Baghdad
Embassy: 21 Queen's Gate, London SW7 5JG (0171-584 7141)
British Embassy: Zukak 12, Mahala 218, Hay alKhelood, Baghdad. Tel: (1) 537 2121/5
Visa required: Yes
Yellow fever certificate: Yes, all travellers arriving from infected areas
HIV test: Yes, for visits over 5 days, at hospitals in Iraq. They test for syphilis too: take your own syringe and needles, etc. Check exemptions

Recommended health precautions
Immunisations: Pol; Tet; Typh; Hep A. Consider Hep B; Rab if extended stay

Malaria prophylaxis: Risk is May–Nov in northern rural areas. Chloroquine or proguanil is recommended

Treat all water as potentially contaminated, institute all food and drink hygiene precautions

There is Leish (Kala Azar: the visceral variety) and various tick- and louse-borne diseases in rural areas:avoid all biting insects. Schis present except in very far south: do not swim or bathe in freshwater. Protect against food and soilborne parasites

Check with Foreign Office before visiting Iraq

ISRAEL

+2 hours GMT
Capital: Jerusalem
UK Tourist Office: 18 Great Marlborough Street, London W1V 1AF (0171-434 3651)
Embassy: 2 Palace Green, Kensington, London W8 4QB (0171-957 9500)
British Embassy: 192 Rehov Hayarkon Street, Tel Aviv. Tel: (3) 5240171. Fax: (3) 291699. Consulates in Eilat and Jerusalem
Visa required: Yes
Yellow fever certificate: No
HIV test: Yes if seeking immigration, no if tourist staying up to 3 months

Recommended health precautions
Immunisations: Pol; Tet; Typh; Hep A. Consider Hep B; Rab if extended stay

Malaria prophylaxis: None required

Mains water normally chlorinated, though bottled water may be preferable. Food and drink safe in tourist resorts, hotels etc.; take more care in rural communities

There is a risk of various tick-borne diseases (e.g. MSF) away from towns and cities: avoid close contacts with animals, take care in rural vegetation. Some limited risk of Leish: avoid sandfly bites

---

JORDAN

+2 hours GMT
Capital: Amman
UK Tourist Office: 211 Regent Street, London W1R 7DD (0171-437 9465)
Embassy: 6 Upper Phillimore Gdns, London W8 7HB (0170-937 3685)
British Embassy: PO Box 87, Abdoun, Amman. Tel: (6) 823100; Fax: (6) 813 759
Visa required: Yes
Yellow fever certificate: Yes, all travellers arriving from endemic areas in Africa

HIV test: Yes, if applying for residence.

Recommended health precautions
Immunisations: Pol; Tet; Typh; Hep A. Consider Hep B; Rab if extended stay

Malaria prophylaxis: None required

Greatest risk is TD: treat all water as suspect (check whether hotel has purification plant); implement food and drink hygiene precautions, particularly in rural areas

Some Leish, Schis, flea- and tick-borne typhus

KUWAIT

+3 hours GMT
Capital: Kuwait City
Embassy: 45–46 Queen's Gate, London SW7 5HR (0171-589 4533)
British Embassy: PO Box 2, 13001 Safat, Arabian Gulf Street, Kuwait City. Tel: 243 2047; Fax: 240 7395
Visa required: Yes
Yellow fever certificate: No
HIV test: Yes, if applying for work permit, tested on arrival

Recommended health precautions
Immunisations: Pol; Tet; Typh; Hep A. Consider Hep B; Rab if extended stay
Malaria prophylaxis: None required

Mains water chlorinated and food generally safe in major towns and cities. Milk is usually pasteurised. Institute food/drink hygiene precautions in rural areas

Risks from insect-borne disease limited, though avoid sandfly and tick bites. There is little risk of Schis

---

LEBANON

+2 (3 in summer) hours GMT
Capital: Beirut
Embassy: 21 Kensington Palace Gardens, London W8 4QM (0171-229 7265/6)
British Embassy: Middle East Airlines Building, Tripoli Autostrade, Jal elDib, East Beirut. Tel: (1) 417 007. Consulate in Tripoli
Visa required: Yes
Yellow fever certificate: Yes, all travellers arriving from an infected area
HIV test: No

Recommended health precautions
Immunisations: Pol; Tet; Typh; Hep A. Consider Hep B; Rab if extended stay

Malaria prophylaxis: None required

Commonest ailment is likely to be TD. Mains water in major towns chlorinated, but bottled water may be preferable. Food, drink generally safe in larger towns, better hotels, etc., but implement all food and drink hygiene outside

There is a risk of Schis, some Leish, and the usual risk of tickborne diseases (e.g. MSF). Protect against soil-borne parasites: wear shoes

---

OMAN

+4 hours GMT
Capital: Muscat
Embassy: 167 Queen's Gate, South Kensington, London SW7 5HE (0171-225 0001)
British Embassy: PO Box 300, Muscat Oman 113. Tel: 738501; Fax: 736040

Visa required: Yes
Yellow fever certificate: Yes, all travellers arriving from an infected area
HIV test: Yes, if seeking work/residence. Tested on arrival, but not necessarily deported if positive

Recommended health precautions
Immunisations: Pol; Tet; Typh; Hep A. Consider Hep B; Rab if extended stay (amount of Rab increasing)

Malaria prophylaxis: Risk all year throughout the country. Mainly *P. falciparum*. Chloroquine or proguanil usually recommended, but drug resistance just starting, so mefloquine (see Iran) may eventually be suggested

Treat all water as potentially contaminated: instigate all food and drink hygiene precautions

Some risk of Leish, Schis: take usual precautions. Several tick-borne diseases and risk of soil- and food-borne parasites

---

QATAR

+3 hours GMT
Capital: Doha
Embassy: 27 Chesham Place, London SW1X 8HG (0171-235 0851)
British Embassy: PO Box 3, Doha. Tel: 421991; Fax: 438692
Visa required: No, if living or born in UK and UK passport holder
Yellow fever certificate: Yes, if more than 1 year old travelling from an infected area
HIV test: Yes, if student or worker. There may be other certificates (syphilis, TB, Hep B, leprosy) required: check with Embassy

Recommended health precautions
Immunisations: Pol; Tet; Typh; Hep A. Consider Hep B; Rab if extended stay

Malaria prophylaxis: None required

Water and food generally safe in major hotels and towns, less so outside: implement hygiene precautions if travelling rurally

---

SAUDI ARABIA

+3 hours GMT
Capital: Riyadh
Embassy: 32 Charles Street, London W1X 7PM (0171-917 3000)
Information Centre: 18 Cavendish Square, London W1 (0171-629 8803)
British Embassy: PO Box 94351, Riyadh 11693. Tel: (1) 488 0077; Fax: (1) 488 2373. Consulate also in Jeddah
Visa required: Yes
Yellow fever certificate: Yes, all travellers arriving from an infected country. Meningococcal meningitis also

required if attending for pilgrimage during Hajj
HIV test: Tests required for those applying for work visas

Recommended health precautions
Immunisations: Pol; Tet; Typh; Hep A. Consider Hep B; Rab if extended stay. Possibly Men (compulsory during Hajj, the annual pilgrimage to Mecca)

Malaria prophylaxis: There is a risk of the disease, though not in Jeddah, Mecca, Medina or Taif, or Riyadh, or the Eastern, Northern and Central provinces, nor over 2000 m. The west and south are the riskiest areas. For the moment chloroquine or proguanil are recommended, though changing patterns of drug resistance may alter that

The food and drink in all the major cities is generally very safe. Outside these more care should be taken

Some risk of DF, Leish and Schis: take usual avoiding action. Tickborne diseases, trachoma, Ech and other worm parasites exist in rural areas. Travax has informal reports of Men in Jeddah

---

SYRIA
(Syrian Arab Republic)

+2 hours (+3 in summer) GMT
Capital: Damascus
Embassy: 8 Belgrave Square, London SW1X 8PH (0171-245 9012)
British Embassy: PO Box 37, Quarter Malki, 11 rue Muhammed Kurd Ali, Immueble Kotob, Damascus. Tel: (11) 712 561/2/3; Fax: (11) 713 592. Consulate in Halab (Aleppo)
Visa required: Yes
Yellow fever certificate: Yes, all travellers over 1 year arriving from an infected area
HIV test: Yes, if student; if staying over 12 months applying for a work permit

Recommended health precautions
Immunisations: Pol; Tet; Typh; Hep A. Consider Hep B; Rab if extended stay

Malaria prophylaxis: Risk is May-Oct only, mainly in north-east of country. Chloroquine or proguanil recommended

Mains water normally chlorinated, but outside of hotels etc. instigate all food/drink hygiene. Reasonable risk of TD

Leish, Schis present in parts of the country

TURKEY

+2 (+3 in summer) hours GMT
Capital: Ankara
Embassy: 43 Belgrave Square, London SW1X 8PA (0171-235 5252)
Information Centre: 170/173 Piccadilly, W1V 9DD (0171-734 8681)

British Embassy: Fehit Ersan Caddesi 46/A, Cankaya, Ankara. Tel: (4) 427 4310; Fax: (4) 468 3214. Consulates in Antalaya, Bodrum, Iskenderun, Istanbul, Izmir, Marmaris and Mersin
Visa required: Yes, but obtained on arrival
Yellow fever certificate: No
HIV test: No

Recommended health precautions
Immunisations: Pol; Tet; Hep A; Typh (consult on whether your itinerary requires this). Consider Hep B; Rab if extended stay; rarely Men

Malaria prophylaxis: Risk from March-Nov in the east. No *P. falciparum* (yet). Those travelling extensively in the Anatalya or Iran/Iraq border areas, particularly Jun/Jul, should take chloroquine or proguanil

High risk of TD outside resorts (chlorinated water, but bottled may be preferable), and watch hotel buffets

Some risk of leishmaniasis, schistosomiasis (bilharzia) and various tick-borne diseases, inc.tick typhus: take usual precautions. Parasitic worms from both soil (wear shoes) and food found in rural areas

The refugee camps near Iraqi border have had various disease outbreaks, including Men

Note that in 1994 there were bombs in major resorts, deliberately targeting tourists, planted by the Kurdish Workers Party (PKK). Risk to individual travellers small, although there were injuries and a death; check current advice from Foreign Office

---

UNITED ARAB EMIRATES

+4 hours GMT
Capital: Abu Dhabi
Embassy: 30 Prince's Gate, London SW7 1PT (0171-581 1281)
British Embassy: PO Box 248, Abu Dhabi. Tel: (2) 326600 or 321364; Fax: (2) 341744
Visa required: No, for up to 30 days
Yellow fever certificate: No
HIV test: Yes, for work and residence

Recommended health precautions
Immunisations: Pol; Tet; Typh; Hep A. Consider Hep B; Rab if extended stay. (WHO reports rabies was absent, now present close to border with Oman)

Malaria prophylaxis: There is a slight year-round risk along the east coast and inland at oases. Cities, and much of the country, risk-free. Chloroquine or proguanil recommended

Water in most towns chlorinated and safe: boil/sterilise elsewhere. Institute food/drink hygiene precautions rurally, though dairy products should be treated with caution everywhere unless certain they are pasteurised

Cutaneous leishmaniasis and tick-typhus risk

YEMEN

+3 hours GMT
Capital: Sana'a
Embassy: 57 Cromwell Rd, London SW7 2ED (0171-629 9905)
British Embassy: PO Box 1287, 129 Haddah Rd, Sana'a. Tel: 215630; Fax: 263059
Visa required: Yes
Yellow fever certificate: Yes, all travellers over 1 year old arriving from an infected area
HIV test: No

Recommended health precautions
Immunisations: Pol; Tet;. Typh; Hep A. Consider Hep B; Rab if extended stay

Malaria prophylaxis: No risk around capital, but there is elsewhere, mainly Sep–Feb 90% *P. falciparum*, chloroquine and proguanil (Paludrine) recommended with mefloquine increasingly used

There is a risk of Leish, tick-borne typhus and fevers, Schis, Onch (tiny worms, spread by blackfly), dracunculiasis and a variety of other parasites are present in the country. Take appropriate precautions: avoid insect bites, wear shoes, institute all food/drink hygiene precautions

Note that in 1990 the two halves of Yemen merged; in 1994 they separated again, but at the time of writing, they were in the middle of kissing and making up, and tours had been resumed. Check current status with Foreign Office (0171-270 4129)

18.7 OCEANIA

This region includes Australia, New Zealand plus Christmas Island, Cook Islands, Federated States of Micronesia, Fiji, French Polynesia (including Tahiti), Guam, Kiribati, Marshall Islands, Nauru, New Caledonia, Niue, North Mariana Islands, Palau, Papua New Guinea, Pitcairn, American Samoa, Western Samoa, Solomon Islands, Tahiti (part of French Polynesia), Tokelau, Tonga, Tuvalu, Vanuatu, Wake Island, Wallis and Futuna.

By mid-1995 the code for dialling the UK from all these countries should be 0044-, but some countries are adapting the standard faster than others: check locally.

HEALTH RISKS THROUGHOUT THE REGION

Malaria: There is a risk of this disease in Papua New Guinea, the Solomon Islands and Vanuatu (not Futuna Island). The main type of *P. falciparum*, with much drug resistance, although *P. vivax* common. There is no risk elsewhere.

Yellow fever: There is no yellow fever in the region and immunisation is not required if travelling from the UK, but some countries may want a certificate if travelling from a country on the WHO list of yellow fever countries, or countries they consider to be an infected area.

The infected countries, which does **not** mean the disease is active, are:

Angola, Belize, Benin, Bolivia, Botswana, Brazil, Burkina Faso, Burundi, Cameroon, Central African Republic, Chad, Colombia, Congo, Costa Rica, Cote d'Ivoire, Ecuador, Equatorial Guinea, Ethiopia, French Guyana, Gabon, Gambia, Ghana, Guatemala, Guinea, Guinea Bissau, Guyana, Honduras, Kenya, Liberia, Mali, Mauritania, Nicaragua, Niger, Nigeria, Panama, Peru, Rwanda, Sao Tome and Principe, Senegal, Sierra Leone, Somalia, Sudan, Suriname, Tanzania, Togo, Trinidad & Tobago, Uganda, Venezuela, Zaire and Zambia. Not all of these may be recognised as countries requiring certification by your destination: check your itinerary carefully. Children under 9 months should **not** be immunised; some countries require all travellers who can have the immunisation to comply, others say all over 6 months, the majority all over one year.

Other health risks: Dengue fever, a viral disease (no immunisation) transmitted by day-biting mosquitoes, mainly in urban areas. The chances of the average traveller catching dengue are low. It occurs sporadically throughout the region, including Australia (N. Queensland and the Torres Straits Islands), Cook Islands, Fiji, Kiribati, New Caledonia, Niue, Palau, PNG, Samoa, Tahiti, Tokelau, Vanuatu, Wallis and Futuna. New Zealand and the rest are dengue-free.

There are other insect-borne diseases, including filariasis, worm infections spread by mosquitoes, and typhus spread by lice, but again the risk-factors are in your favour. Soil and food parasites (eg roundworm, hookworm, strongyloides, hydatid disease) are also present, but given the main reasons for travel to this area many of the hazards are to do with recreation: corals cuts, sharks, sea urchins, jellyfish, possibly citaguera (food poisoning from reef fish that have toxins in their flesh).

The number of HIV-positive individuals within the population is low. In the unlikely event of needing to, travellers should still avoid unscreened blood products: even without HIV, there is still a lot of hepatitis B around.

As always the most likely complaint the traveller will have to endure, particularly away from Australia, New Zealand and main tourist centres, is the so-called travellers' diarrhoea. This may be caused by a variety of agents, from bacteria such as *Esherichia coli* and *Salmonella*, to protozoa such as *Entamoeba* and *Giardia*.

Good food and drink hygiene is essential where water and food quality are suspect: wash hands, make sure all meat is cooked, drink bottled water, peel fruit, etc. Avoid unpasteurised dairy products, as there is a risk of brucellosis, etc.

Immunisations for the region include tetanus, typhoid, hepatitis A, polio, and hepatitis B (for health workers, etc). Long-stay workers should ensure their diphtheria and tuberculosis are up to date.

Note that just because a disease is present in a country, it does not follow that a tourist or traveller will be exposed to it. Nor will they necessarily need all the advised immunisations (e.g. typhoid is not used as often as it was), particularly if stopping over in Australia, New Zealand or one of the large resorts.

AUSTRALIA

+ 8 to + 10 hours GMT
Capital: Canberra
UK Tourist Office: Gemini House, 10–18 Putney Hill, London SW15 6AA (0181-7802227)
High Commission: Australia House, The Strand, London WC2B 4LA (0171-379 4334)
British High Commission: Commonwealth Ave, Yarralumla, 2600 Canberra. Tel: (6) 270 66666; Fax: (6) 273 3236. Consulates in Adelaide, Brisbane, Melbourne, Perth, Sydney and Darwin
Visa required: Yes
Yellow fever certificate: Yes, all travellers over 1 year old arriving within 6 days of a visit to an infected area (as defined by the WHO that week) OR if been infected within the last 10 years
HIV test: Yes, anyone over 15 years of age seeking residence, other long-term visitors who are considered 'at risk' of being HIV-positive

Recommended health precautions
Immunisations: None

Malaria prophylaxis: None required. There are a few mosquito nasties: dengue fever in northern Queensland and Torres Straits Islands (mainly summer, i.e. Nov–April) and Ross River Fever in Western Australia, South Australia and Victoria. Risk to most travellers low, but take precautions against mosquitoes

Food, water all safe. The most dangerous thing for adventurous travellers is the native fauna: watch for scorpions, snakes, jelly-fish, etc. Oh, and crocodiles, of course.

NEW ZEALAND

+12 hours GMT
Capital: Wellington.
UK Tourist Office: 80 Haymarket, London SW1Y 4TQ (0171-973 0360). High Commission at the same address. Tel: 0171-930 8422
British High Commission: PO Box 1812, 44 Hill Street, Wellington. Tel: (4) 472 6049; Fax: (4) 471 1974
Visa required: No
Yellow fever certificate: No
HIV test: No

Recommended health precautions
Immunisations: None

Malaria prophylaxis: None required

No above average risk of any diseases

CHRISTMAS ISLAND

+7 hours GMT
The island is part of Australia, so entry requirements etc. same as that country

Recommended health precautions
Immunisations: None

Malaria prophylaxis: None required

Note that there is a slightly higher risk of TD than Australia

---

COOK ISLANDS

+10 hours GMT
Capital: Avarua on Rarotonga
For tourism etc.: See New Zealand
Visa required: No, for less than 30 days
Yellow fever certificate: No
HIV test: No

Recommended health precautions
Immunisations: Pol; Tet; Typh; Hep A. Consider Hep B if extended stay. There is also JE, though only those spending much time in rural areas are at risk

Malaria prophylaxis: None required. There are mosquito-borne diseases, however (Fil, DF, Ross River fever, JE): avoid mosquito bites, use repellents

Food and water in resorts generally safe: take care away from tourist routes

---

FEDERATED STATES OF MICRONESIA

Part of Pacific Islands of Micronesia, the FSM are 600 plus islands; they used to be part of UK Trust Territory of The Pacific +9 or 10 hours GMT
Capital: Paliker

Visa required: No, not for less than 30 days
Yellow fever certificate: No
HIV test: Yes, if staying over 12 months

Recommended health precautions
Immunisations: Pol; Tet; Typh; Hep A. Consider Hep B if extended stay. There is a very small risk of JE, not enough to warrant routine immunisation

Malaria prophylaxis: None required

Mains water chlorinated, food generally safe in resorts and towns

---

FIJI

322 islands, many uninhabited
+12 hours GMT
Capital: Suva (on Viti Levu)
Embassy: 34 Hyde Park Gate, London SW7 5DN (0171-584 3661)
British Embassy: PO Box 1355, Victoria House, 47 Gladstone Road, Suva. Tel: 311 033; Fax: 301 406
Visa required: No
Yellow fever certificate: Yes, if over 1 year old arriving from an infected area
HIV test: No

Recommended health precautions
Immunisations: Pol; Tet; Typh; Hep A. Consider Hep B if extended stay

Malaria prophylaxis: None required, but watch for DF, Ross River and Fil, all spread by mosquitoes: avoid mosquito bites

Food and water in best hotels safe, mains water (heavily) chlorinated in larger towns; elsewhere treat water as suspect

---

FRENCH POLYNESIA

Includes Tahiti
9 to 10 hours GMT
Capital: Papeete on Tahiti
Embassy in UK: Contact French Embassy (0171-838 2055)
Visa required: No
Yellow fever certificate: Yes, if over 1 year old and arriving from an infected country
HIV test: No

Recommended health precautions
Immunisations: Pol; Tet; Typh; Hep A. Consider Hep B if extended stay

Malaria prophylaxis: No, but DF and Fil present: avoid mosquito bites

---

GUAM

+10 hours GMT
Capital: Agana
Embassy in UK: Contact US Embassy (0171-499 9000)
Visa required: No (requirements as USA)
Yellow fever certificate: No
HIV test: No

Recommended health precautions
Immunisations: Pol; Tet; Typh; Hep A. Consider Hep B if extended stay. There are some reports of JE, but immunisation not routine

Malaria prophylaxis: Not required, but DF and Fil present: avoid mosquito bites

Mains water chlorinated, food and drink generally safe, esp. in hotels

---

KIRIBATI
(formerly the Gilbert Islands)

+12 hours GMT
Capital: Tarawa
Consulate: Faith House, 7 Tufton Street, London SW1P 3QN (0171-222 6952)
British High Commission: PO Box 61, Bairiki, Tarawa. Tel: 21327; Fax: 21488
Visa required: No
Yellow fever certificate: Yes, all travellers over 1 year old arriving from an infected area
HIV test: No

Recommended health precautions
Immunisations: Pol; Tet; Typh; Hep A. Consider Hep B if extended stay

Malaria prophylaxis: None required, though DF and Fil reported: avoid mosquito bites

Water should be regarded as potentially contaminated: take all food and drink precautions

---

MARSHALL ISLANDS

+12 hours GMT
Capital: Majuro
Embassy: Contact US Embassy
Visa required: Yes
Yellow fever certificate: No
HIV test: No

Recommended health precautions
Immunisations: Pol; Tet; Typh; Hep A. Consider Hep B if extended stay

Malaria prophylaxis: None required

Food and water generally safe

NAURU

+12 hours GMT

Capital: Yaren District

Government Office: 3 Chesham Street, London SW1X 8ND (0171-235 6911)

British Embassy: Contact PO Box 1355, Victoria House, 47 Gladstone Road, Suva, Fiji. Tel: (202) 337 8320. Fax: (202) 337 1996

Visa required: Yes

Yellow fever certificate: Yes, travellers over 1 year old arriving from an infected area

HIV test: No

Recommended health precautions

Immunisations: Pol; Tet; Typh; Hep A. Consider Hep B if extended stay. JE reported, but routine immunisation not advised

Malaria prophylaxis: None required, but Fil, DF and JE occur sporadically: repel all mosquitoes

Mains water chlorinated, but bottled may be preferable. Local food generally safe

---

NEW CALEDONIA

+11 hours GMT

Capital: Noumea

Embassy in UK: Contact French Embassy (0171-838 2055)

Visa required: No

Yellow fever certificate: Yes, all travellers over 1 year old arriving from an infected area

HIV test: No

Recommended health precautions

Immunisations: Pol; Tet; Typh; Hep A. Consider Hep B if extended stay

Malaria prophylaxis: None required, but some Fil and DF: avoid mosquito bites

Mains water chlorinated, but take precautions outside towns by drinking bottled or sterilised water; local food generally safe

---

NIUE

-11 hours GMT

Capital: Alofi

Embassy: Contact New Zealand tourism

Visa required: No, not for under 30 days

Yellow fever certificate: Yes, all travellers over 1 year old arriving from an infected area

HIV test: No

Recommended health precautions

Immunisations: Pol; Tet; Typh; Hep A. Consider Hep B if extended stay

Malaria prophylaxis: None required, but be aware that mosquitoes may carry DF or Fil: avoid bites

Risk of TD low

NORTHERN MARIANA ISLANDS

Part of the pacific Islands of Micronesia: Saipan, Tinian and Rota
+10 hours GMT
Capital: Saipan
Embassy in UK: Contact US Embassy (0171-499 9000)
Visa required: No, not for less than 30 days
Yellow fever certificate: No
HIV test: No

Recommended health precautions
Immunisations: Pol; Tet; Typh; Hep A. Consider Hep B if extended stay. Some JE, but immunisation not routinely recommended

Malaria prophylaxis: None required, but JE, DF and Fil present: avoid mosquito bites

Water should be regarded as contaminated except in best hotels: stick to bottled water, take food hygiene precautions away from resorts

---

PALAU

+9 hours GMT
Capital: Koror
Embassy in UK: Contact US Embassy (0171-499 9000)
Visa required: No, not for less than 30 days
Yellow fever certificate: No
HIV test: No

Recommended health precautions
Immunisations: Pol; Tet; Typh; Hep A. Consider Hep B if extended stay

Malaria prophylaxis: None required, but some cases of DF, JE and Fil: avoid mosquito bites

Take care with food and water outside best hotels

PAPUA NEW GUINEA

+10 hours GMT
Capital: Port Moresby
High Commission: 14 Waterloo Place, London SW1Y 4AR (0171-930 0922)
British High Commission: PO Box 4778, Kiroki Street, Waigani, Boroko, PNG. Tel: 251 677; Fax: 253 547
Visa required: Yes
Yellow fever certificate: Yes, all travellers over 1 year old entering from infected area
HIV test: Yes, if seeking residence or if longstay worker

Recommended health precautions
Immunisations: Pol; Tet; Typh; Hep A. Consider Hep B if extended stay. JE present, though immunisation is not routine unless long stay in rural areas

Malaria prophylaxis: Year-round risk, everywhere below 1800 m. Chloroquine resistance and Fansidar (which is used for treatment) resistance common. The recommended regime is usually mefloquine (not for children under 15 kg, during first trimester of pregnancy or if history of epilepsy or psychiatric problems), or sometimes maloprim and chloroquine. Note that maloprim has problems of its own: deaths have occurred when recommended dose exceeded. Take specialist advice. Note that other mosquito-borne diseases are found (dengue, filariasis, Japanese encephalitis): use nets and repellents and avoid bites

There is a high risk of TD away from resorts and hotels: all hygiene precautions should be instigated

Soil- and food-borne parasites are common: wear shoes to prevent former, make sure all meat cooked, avoid raw fish, etc. for latter. Leeches are found in parts of the region, expect to be attacked if trekking up country

---

PITCAIRN ISLAND

+8.5 hours GMT

Visa required: No

Yellow fever certificate: Yes, all travellers over 1 year old coming from an infected area

HIV test: No

Recommended health precautions

Immunisations: Pol; Tet; Typh; Hep A. Consider Hep B if extended stay

Malaria prophylaxis: None required, but some dengue fever: avoid mosquito bites

Food and drink generally safe

AMERICAN SAMOA

-11 hours GMT

Capital: Pago Pago

Embassy in UK: Contact US Embassy (0171-499 9000)

Visa required: No

Yellow fever certificate: Yes, travellers over 1 year old arriving from an infected area

HIV test: No

Recommended health precautions

Immunisations: Pol; Tet; Typh; Hep A. Consider Hep B if extended stay. JE present, but immunisation not routinely recommended

Malaria prophylaxis: None required, but DF, JE (low risk) and Fil present: avoid mosquito bites

Food and water in hotels and resorts generally safe

WESTERN SAMOA

-11 hours GMT
Capital: Apia (Upolu)
UK Tourist Representative: Destination Marketing, 2 Cinnamon Row, Plantation Wharf, York Place, London SW11 3TW (0171-978 5262)
Honorary British representative: C/o Apia Kruse Va'ai and Barlow, PO Box 2029, Apia. Tel: 21895; Fax: 21407
Visa required: No
Yellow fever certificate: Yes, all travellers over 1 year old arriving from an infected area
HIV test: No

Recommended health precautions
Immunisations: Pol; Tet; Typh; Hep A. Consider Hep B

Malaria prophylaxis: None required, but DF and Fil: avoid mosquito bites

Mains water chlorinated, though bottled might be preferable; local food safe

---

SOLOMON ISLANDS

+11 hours GMT
Capital: Honiara
Consulate: 19 Springfield Road, London SW19 7AL (0181-946 5552)
British High Commission: PO Box 676, Soltel House, Mendana Avenue, Honiara. Tel: 21705; Fax: 21549
Visa required: No
Yellow fever certificate: Yes, all travellers arriving from an infected area
HIV test: No

Recommended health precautions
Immunisations: Pol; Tet; Typh; Hep A. Consider Hep B if extended stay. JE is present in rural areas (sporadic outbreaks only), but immunisation not routine

Malaria prophylaxis: There is a malaria risk. Recommendations as for Papua New Guinea: usually mefloquine with maloprim/chloroquine alternative, but take specialist advice. Fil and JE also present: use nets and repellents. Fairly high risk of TD: treat all public water supplies as hostile, and institute the usual hygiene precautions

Protect against mites and soil parasites (e.g. hookworm) in rural areas: wear long trousers/shoes if hiking

---

TAHITI

See French Polynesia

TOKELAU

Details as New Zealand.

Recommended health precautions
Immunisations: Pol; Tet; Typh; Hep A. Consider Hep B if extended stay. Some JE present, but immunisation not routine

Malaria prophylaxis: None required, but the other mosquito-borne threats (DF, JE, Fil) are present: avoid bites

Food and water safe in resorts and hotels, take hygiene precautions elsewhere

---

TONGA

172 islands, Tongatapu being the largest
+13 hours GMT
Capital: Nuku'alofa (Tongatapu Island)
High Commission: 36 Molyneux Street, London W1H 6AB (0171-724 5828)
British High Commission: PO Box 56, Vuna Road, Nuku'alofa. Tel: 21020/1; Fax: 24109
Visa required: No, not under 30 days
Yellow fever certificate: Yes, all travellers over 1 year old entering from an infected area
HIV test: No

Recommended health precautions
Immunisations: Pol; Tet; Typh; Hep A. Consider Hep B if extended stay. Sporadic JE, but immunisation not routinely recommended

Malaria prophylaxis: None required, but DF, JE and Fil present: avoid mosquito bites

Food and drink safe in capital and resorts, take hygiene precautions elsewhere

---

TUVALU

+12 hours GMT
Capital: Funafuti
British Embassy: Contact Suva, Fiji
Visa required: No (proof of onward travel needed)
Yellow fever certificate: Yes, all travellers over 1 year old arriving from an infected area
HIV test: No

Recommended health precautions
Immunisations: Pol; Tet; Typh; Hep A. Consider Hep B if extended stay. Some JE, but immunisation not routinely recommended

Malaria prophylaxis: None required, but DF, Fil and occasional JE present: avoid mosquito bites

---

VANUATU

Formerly the New Hebrides

+12 hours (+11 in summer) GMT
Capital: Port Vila (Efate Island)
UK Tourist representation: Destination Marketing, 2 Cinnamon Row, Plantation Wharf, York Place, London SW11 3TW (0171-978 5262)
British High Commission: PO Box 567, KPMG House, rue Pasteur, Port Vila. Tel: 23100; Fax: 23651
Visa required: No
Yellow fever certificate: No
HIV test: No

Recommended health precautions
Immunisations: Pol; Tet; Typh; Hep A. Consider Hep B if extended stay

Malaria prophylaxis: Required everywhere except Futuna Island. Much drug resistance, recommendations much as for Papua New Guinea: mainly mefloquine (maloprim/chloroquine alternative), but seek up-to-date specialist advice. JE, Fil and DF occasionally reported: avoid mosquito bites

Mains water chlorinated on Vila, and is safe (though bottled water may taste better), and food and drink is reliable in resorts and hotels. Institute hygiene precautions elsewhere

Hikers should protect against ticks and mites which can carry disease

---

WAKE

Basically an air strip owned by the US Air Force

WALLIS AND FUTUNA

+12 hours GMT
Embassy in UK: Contact French Embassy (0171-838 2055)
Visa required: No
Yellow fever certificate: No
HIV test: No

Recommended health precautions
Immunisations: Pol; Tet; Typh; Hep A. Consider Hep B and perhaps JE if extended stay

Malaria prophylaxis: None required, but JE, filariasis, DF and River Ross fever are present: protect against bites

Food and water generally safe

18.8 WESTERN EUROPE

This region includes Andorra, Austria, Azores, Belgium, Denmark, Faroe Islands, Finland, France, Germany, Gibraltar, Greece, Greenland, Iceland, Ireland, Italy, Liechtenstein, Luxembourg, Madeira, Malta, Monaco, Netherlands, Norway, Portugal, San Marino, Spain, Sweden and Switzerland.

Note that as of mid-1995 the code for dialling for the UK from any of these countries should be 0044, but some countries are adapting the standard faster than others: check locally.

HEALTH RISKS THROUGHOUT THE REGION

Malaria: There is no risk of native malaria.

Yellow fever: There is no yellow fever in the region, but a minority of countries may want a certificate if travelling from a country on the WHO list of yellow fever countries, or countries they consider to be an infected area. The infected countries, which does **not** mean the disease is active, are:

Angola, Belize, Benin, Bolivia, Botswana, Brazil, Burkina Faso, Burundi, Cameroon, Central African Republic, Chad, Colombia, Congo, Costa Rica, Cote d'Ivoire, Ecuador, Equatorial Guinea, Ethiopia, French Guyana, Gabon, Gambia, Ghana, Guatemala, Guinea, Guinea Bissau, Guyana, Honduras, Kenya, Liberia, Mali, Mauritania, Nicaragua, Niger, Nigeria, Panama, Peru, Rwanda, Sao Tome and Principe, Senegal, Sierra Leone, Somalia, Sudan, Suriname, Tanzania, Togo, Trinidad & Tobago, Uganda, Venezuela, Zaire and Zambia. Not all of these may be recognised as countries requiring certification by your destination: check your itinerary carefully. Children under 9 months should not be immunised; some countries require all travellers who can have the immunisation to comply, others say all over 6 months, the majority all over 1 year.

Other health risks: There are a variety of tick-borne diseases, including the bacterial Lyme disease (woods in mainland western Europe: Austria, Scandinavia, Germany, etc.), tick-borne encephalitis (Austria, Germany, Switzerland and parts of Scandinavia) and Mediterranean Spotted Fever (Mediterranean coast). Leptospirosis, a viral disease transmitted through animal's urine, is a hazard to recreational water users (canoeists, etc.), but still relatively rare. Rabies is present on mainland Europe. Generally, however, there are few nasty endemics likely to affect the traveller.

As always the most likely complaint the traveller will have to endure, particularly in the warmer southern regions, is the so-called travellers' diarrhoea. This may be caused by a variety of agents, from bacteria such as *Esherichia coli* and *Salmonella*, to protozoa such as *Entamoeba* and *Giardia*. Good food and drink hygiene is essential where water and food quality are suspect; be particularly wary of hotel buffets. Avoid unpasteurised dairy products, as there is a risk of brucellosis, etc.

Immunisations for the region are minimal, though being up to date with tetanus is always a good idea.

ANDORRA

-1 hours (+2 summer) GMT
Capital: Andorra la Vella
Andorran Delegation: 63 Westover Road, London SW18 2RF (0181-874 4806)
British Consulate: Contact Barcelona (3419 9044)
Visa required: No
Yellow fever certificate: No
HIV test: No

Recommended health precautions
None

AUSTRIA

+1 (+2 in summer) hours GMT
Capital: Vienna
UK Tourist Office: 30 St George Street, London W1R 0AL (0171-629 0461)
Embassy: 18 Belgrave Mews West, London SW1X 8HU (0171-235 3731)
British Embassy: Jauresgasse 12, A1030 Vienna. Tel: (1) 713 1575; Fax: (1) 712 7316. Consular section: Tel (1) 871 461/17/18; Fax (1) 757 824
Visa required: No
Yellow fever certificate: No
HIV test: No

Recommended health precautions
Both TBE (viral) and Lyme disease (bacterial) are a risk in forested areas in summer. There is an immunisation for TBE but it is only recommended for those working (or walking) for prolonged periods in at-risk areas. Otherwise avoid tick bites

---

AZORES

See Portugal

BELGIUM

+1 hour (+2 in summer) GMT
Capital: Brussels
UK Tourist Office: 29 Princes Street, London W1R 7RG (0171-629 0230)
Embassy: 103 Eaton Square, London SW1W 9AB (0171-235 5422)
British Embassy: 85 rue d'Arlon, B1040 Brussels. Tel: 2 287 6211; Fax: 2 287 6355. Consulates in Antwerp and Liege
Visa required: No
Yellow fever certificate: No
HIV test: Yes, for non-EC nationals studying/working

Recommended health precautions
Some risk of Lyme disease in the Ardennes area in summer: protect against tick bites

---

DENMARK

+1 (+2 summer) hour GMT
Capital: Copenhagen
UK Tourist Office: 55 Sloane Street, London SW1X 9SY (0171-259 5959).
Embassy: Same address. Tel: 0171-333 0200
British Embassy: Kastelsvej 36–40, DK2100, Copenhagen 0. Tel: 31 26 46 00; Fax: 31 38 10 12. Consulates in: Abenra, Alborg, Arhus, Esbjerg, Ferdericia, Herning, Odense, Ronne and the Faroe Islands
Visa required: No
Yellow fever certificate: No
HIV test: No

Recommended health precautions
Some risk of Lyme disease in forested areas during summer: protect against bites. There have been cases of TBE, but it is rare

---

FAROE ISLANDS

See Denmark

FINLAND

+2 (+3 in summer) hours GMT
Capital: Helsinki
UK Tourist Board: 6668 Haymarket, London SW1Y 4RF (0171-839 4048)
Embassy: 38 Chesham Place, London SW1X 8HW (0171-235 9531)
British Embassy: Itainen puistotie 17, 00140 Helsinki. Tel: (0) 661 293; Fax: (0) 661 342. Consulates in Jyvaskyla, Kotka, Kuopio, Mariehamn, Oulu, Pori, Tampere, Turku and Vaasa
Visa required: No
Yellow fever certificate: No

HIV test: Yes, for some foreign students

Recommended health precautions
Both TBE (viral) and Lyme disease (bacterial) are present in forested areas in summer, though both are fairly rare. There is an immunisation for TBE but it is only recommended for those working for prolonged periods in at-risk areas. Otherwise avoid tick bites. Avoid also mosquito bites, there is a small risk of viral encephalitis

---

FRANCE

+1 (+2 summer) hours GMT
Capital: Paris
UK Tourist Board: 178 Piccadilly, London W1V 0AL (0171-499 6911)
Embassy: 58 Knightsbridge, London SW1X 7JT (0171-201 1000)
British Embassy: 35 rue du Faubourg St Honore, 75383 Paris. Tel 1 42 66 91 42; Fax: 1 42 66 95 90
British Consulate: 9 avenue hoche, 75008 Paris. Tel: (1) 42 66 38 10; Fax: (1) 40 76 02 87. Consulates in Biarritz, Bordeaux, Lille, Calais, Boulogne, Cherbourg, Dunkirk, Lyon, Marseille, Perpignan, Ajaccio (Corsica), Le Havre, Nantes, Nice, St Malo-Dinard and Toulouse
Visa required: No
Yellow fever certificate: No
HIV test: No

Recommended health precautions
Some Lyme disease, some risk of MSF in summer (also tick-borne) and even Leish is present (avoid sandfly bites), but the risk to the average traveller is low

---

GERMANY

+1 (+2 summer) hour GMT
Capital: Berlin
UK Tourist Office: 65 Curzon Street, London W1Y 7PE (0171-495 3990)
Embassy: 23 Belgrave Square, London SW1X 8PZ (0171-824 1300). Consulates in Manchester and Edinburgh
British Embassy: Friedrich-Ebert-Allee 77, 53113 Bonn. Tel: 228 234 061. Fax: 228 234 070. Consulates in Dusseldorf, Frankfurt, Hamburg, Bremen, Nuremberg, Frieberg, Hannover, Munich, Stuttgart, Kiel and Berlin
Visa required: No
Yellow fever certificate: No
HIV test: Yes, for residence permits in certain parts of the country (not EC nationals)

Recommended health precautions
Note that water in the former Eastern part may be more polluted (usually with industrial waste) than in the old West Germany. Both TBE (viral) and Lyme

disease (bacterial) are present in forested areas in summer. There is an immunisation for TBE but it is only recommended for those working for prolonged periods in at-risk areas. Otherwise avoid tick bites

GIBRALTAR

+1 hours GMT
Information Bureau: Arundel Great Court, 179 The Strand, London WC2R 1EH (0171-836 0777). The island is a British Crown colony
Visa required: No
Yellow fever certificate: No
HIV test: No

Recommended health precautions
None

GREECE

+2 (+1 end Sept–end Oct)
Capital: Athens
UK Tourist Office: 4 Conduit Street, London W1R 0DJ (0171-734 5997)
Embassy: 1a Holland Park, London W11 3TP (0171-221 6467)
British Embassy: Odos Ploutarchou 1, 106 75 Athens. Tel: (1) 723 6211; Fax: (1) 724 1872. Consulates in Crete, Corfu, Kavala, Patrai, Rhodes, Salonika, Samos and Valos
Visa required: No
Yellow fever certificate: Yes, all travellers over 6 months old arriving from an infected area
HIV test: Some students, check with Embassy

Recommended health precautions
No recommended immunisations

Care should be taken with tap water if TD to be avoided. Some Leish (esp. Crete: avoid sandfly bites), TBE and other diseases reported, but risks to most travellers very low

GREENLAND

See Denmark

ICELAND

GMT
Capital: Reykjavik.
UK Tourist Office: 172 Tottenham Court Road, London W1P 9LG (0171-388 5346)
Embassy: 1 Eaton Terrace, London SW1W 8EY (0171-730 5131)
British Embassy: PO Box 460, Lau-

fasvegur 49, 121 Reykjavik. Tel: (1) 15883; Fax (1) 27940
Visa required: No
Yellow fever certificate: No
HIV test: No

Recommended health precautions
None

REPUBLIC OF IRELAND

GMT
Capital: Dublin
UK Tourist Board: 150–151 New Bond Street, London W1Y 0AQ (0171-493 3201)
Embassy: 17 Grosvenor Place, London SW1X 7HR (0171-235 2171)
British Embassy: 31–33 Merrion Road, Dublin 4. Tel: (1) 269 5211; Fax: (1) 283
Visa required: No
Yellow fever certificate: No
HIV test: No

Recommended health precautions
There are no recommended immunisations. There are occasional incidents of Lyme disease, but risk to visitors very low

---

ITALY

+1 (+2 summer) hour GMT
Capital: Rome
UK Tourist Office: 1 Princes Street, London W1R 8AY (0171-408 1254)
Embassy: 14 Three Kings Yard, Davies Street, London W1Y 3EH (0171-629 8200)
British Embassy: Via XX Settembre 80A, 00187 Rome. Tel: (6) 482 5551; Fax: (6) 482 5551. Consulates in Bari, Brindisi, Florence, Milan, Turin, Trieste, Genoa, Venice and Naples
Visa required: No
Yellow fever certificate: No
HIV test: No

Recommended health precautions
There are no recommended immunisations. Some TBE and Lyme disease present: avoid bites. Similarly, there are sporadic ocurrences of Leish: treat sandflies as potentially hostile

---

LIECHTENSTEIN

+1 (+2 in summer) hour GMT
Capital: Vaduz Embassy in UK: Contact Swiss Embassy (0171-723 0701) and Swiss Tourism (0171-734 1921)
Visa required: No
Yellow fever certificate: No
HIV test: No

Recommended health precautions
None

LUXEMBOURG

+1 (+2 in summer) hour GMT
Capital: Luxembourgville
UK Tourist Office: 122 Regent Street, London W1R 5FE (0171-434 2800)
Embassy: 27 Wilton Crescent, London SW1X 8SD (0171-235 6961)
British Embassy: BP 874, 14 boulevard Roosevelt, L2108 Luxembourgville. Tel: 229 864; Fax: 229 867
Visa required: No
Yellow fever certificate: No
HIV test: No

Recommended health precautions
None

MADEIRA

See Portugal

MALTA

+1 (+2 in summer) hour GMT
Capital: Valletta
UK Tourist Office: Suite 300, Mappin House, 4 Winsley Street, London W1N 7AR (0171-323 0506)
High Commission: 16 Kensington Square, London W8 5HH (0171-938 1712)
British High Commission: PO Box 506, 7 St Anne Street, Floriana, Valletta VLT 15. Tel: 233 134; Fax: 622 001
Visa required: No
Yellow fever certificate: Yes, all travellers over 9 months old arriving from an infected area
HIV test: No

Recommended health precautions
Pol and Tet are often recommended, with Hep A and Typh sometimes thrown in for good measure, though for most travellers, certainly those staying at the popular resorts, this seems excessively cautious. Discuss your itinerary with your GP or travel clinic. Note that the incidence of Hep B in the population is quite high, so longstay workers should consider immunisation. There have been reports of Leish: avoid sandfly bites

---

MONACO

+1 (+2 in summer) hours GMT
Capital: Monacoville
UK Tourist Office: 3–18 Chelsea Garden Market, Chelsea Harbour, London SW10 0XE (0171-352 9962)
Embassy: 4 Cromwell Place, London SW7 2JE (0171-225 2679)
British Consulate: 24 avenue du Prado, 13006, Marseille, France. Tel: 91 53 43 32; Fax: 91 37 47 06

Visa required: No
Yellow fever certificate: No
HIV test: No

Recommended health precautions
None

NETHERLANDS

+1 (+2 in summer) hours GMT
Capital: Amsterdam (seat of Government, The Hague)
UK Tourist office: PO Box 523, London SW1E 6NT (0891-200 277)
Embassy: 38 Hyde Park Gate, London SW7 45DP (0171-584 5040)
British Embassy: Lange Voorhout 10, 2514 ED, The Hague. Tel: (70) 364 5800; Fax: (70) 360 3839
Visa required: No
Yellow fever certificate: No
HIV test: No

Recommended health precautions
There are no recommended immunisations. Some Lyme disease reported in wooded areas in summer: avoid tick bites

NORWAY

+1 (+2 in summer) hours GMT
Capital: Oslo
UK Tourist Board: 5–11 Lower Regent Street, London SW1Y 4LR (0171-839 6255)
Embassy: 25 Belgrave Square, London SW1X 8QD (0171-235 7151)
British Embassy: Thomas Heftyesgate 8, 0244 Oslo 2. Tel: (22) 552 400; Fax: (22) 551041. Consulates in Alesund, Bergen, Harstad, Haugesund, Kristiansund, Stavanger, Tromso and Trondheim
Visa required: No
Yellow fever certificate: No
HIV test: No

Recommended health precautions
No recommended immunisations. Occasional Lyme disease: avoid tick bites

PORTUGAL

0 (+1 in summer) hour GMT
Capital: Lisbon
UK Tourist Board: 2nd Floor, 22–25a Sackville Street, London W1X 1DE (0171-494 1441)
Embassy: 11 Belgrave Square, London SW1X 8PP (0171235 5331)
British Embassy: Rua de S Domingos a Lapa 35–37, 37 1200 Lisbon. Tel: (1) 396 1191; Fax: (1) 397 6768. Consulates in Funchal (Madeira), Oporto, Ponta Delgada (Azores) and Portimao
Visa required: No

Yellow fever certificate: Yes, for Madeira and Azores ONLY, travellers over 12 months are required to produce a certificate
HIV test: No

Recommended health precautions
There are no recommended immunisations. Leish and various tick-borne diseases are present, but risk to most travellers is very low. Avoid tap water outside major cities and towns

---

SAN MARINO

See Italy

SPAIN

+1 (+2 in summer) hours GMT; Canaries are GMT
Capital: Madrid
UK Tourist Office: 57–58 St James's Street, London SW1A 1LD (0171-499 0901)
Embassy: 39 Chesham Place, London SW1X 8SB (0171-235 5555)
British Embassy: Calle de Fernando el Santo 16, 28000 Madrid. Tel: (1) 319 0200; Fax: (1) 319 0423. Consulates in Algeciras, Alicante, Barcelona, Bilbao, Lanzarote, Las Palmas, Santa Cruz (Canaries), Malaga, Menorca, Palma, Ibiza, Santander, Seville, Tarragona and Vigo
Visa required: No
Yellow fever certificate: No
HIV test: No

Recommended health precautions
There are no recommended immunisations, though Typh and Hep A sometimes suggested for long-stay workers in rural areas. There is some Lyme disease in wooded areas, some MSF (dog ticks) and reports of Leish (avoid sandfly bites). The risks to most travellers is small

---

SWEDEN

+1 (+2 in summer) hours GMT
Capital: Stockholm
UK Tourist Office: 73 Welbeck Street, London W1M 8AN (0891-200 280)
Embassy: 11 Montague Place, London W1H 2AL (0171-724 2101)
British Embassy: PO Box 27819, Skarpogatan 6–8, 115 93 Stockholm. Tel: (8) 667 0140; Fax: (8) 662 9989. Consulates in Gothenburg, Malmo, Lulea and Sundsvall
Visa required: No
Yellow fever certificate: No
HIV test: No

Recommended health precautions

There are no recommended immunisations. Some tickborne diseases in rural areas (Lyme disease, TBE): avoid tick bites.

SWITZERLAND

+1 (+2 in summer) hours GMT
Capital: Bern
UK Tourist Office: Swiss Centre, Swiss Court, London W1V 8EE (0171-734 1921)
Embassy: 16–18 Montague Place, London W1H 2BQ (0171-723 0701)
British Embassy: Thunstrasse 50, CH3005 Bern 15. Tel: (31) 352 5021; Fax: (31) 352 0583. Consulates in Geneva, Montreux, Zurich and Lugano
Visa required: No
Yellow fever certificate: No
HIV test: No

Recommended health precautions
There are no recommended immunisations. There is Lyme disease in forested areas and TBE (though the risk to most travellers is low): avoid tick bites. TBE immunisation is sometimes recommended for forest workers

---

18.9 EASTERN EUROPE

This region includes Albania, Bosnia/Herzegovina, Bulgaria, Croatia, Czech Republic, Hungary, Macedonia, Poland, Romania, Slovak Republic, Slovenia and Yugoslavia (Serbia/Montenegro). The countries of the former USSR, including Russia, are dealt with separately.

Note that as of mid-1995 the code for dialling the UK from any of these countries should be 0044-, but some countries are adapting the standard faster than others: check locally.

Health risks throughout the region
Malaria: There is no risk of malaria.

Yellow fever: There is no yellow fever in the region, but a minority of countries may want a certificate if travelling from a county on the WHO list of yellow fever countries, or countries they consider to be an infected area.

The infected countries, which does **not** mean the disease is active, are:

Angola, Belize, Benin, Bolivia, Botswana, Brazil, Burkina Faso, Burundi, Cameroon, Central African Republic, Chad, Colombia, Congo, Costa Rica, Cote d'Ivoire,

Ecuador, Equatorial Guinea, Ethiopia, French Guyana, Gabon, Gambia, Ghana, Guatemala, Guinea, Guinea Bissau, Guyana, Honduras, Kenya, Liberia, Mali, Mauritania, Nicaragua, Niger, Nigeria, Panama, Peru, Rwanda, Sao Tome and Principe, Senegal, Sierra Leone, Somalia, Sudan, Suriname, Tanzania, Togo, Trinidad & Tobago, Uganda, Venezuela, Zaire and Zambia.. Not all of these may be recognised as countries requiring certification by your destination: check your itinerary carefully. Children under 9 months should not be immunised; some countries require all travellers who can have the immunisation to comply, others say all over 6 months, the majority all over 1 year.

Other health risks: There is a variety of tick-borne diseases, including the bacterial Lyme disease (many rural areas of eastern Europe), the viral tickborne encephalitis (Hungary, Poland, Czech Republic, Slovak Republic, countries of former Yugoslavia) and the Crimean-Congo haemorrhagic fever (Albania, Bulgaria). There is also haemorrhagic fever with renal syndrome, a disease spread by rat droppings, in the south and east of the region. The risk to travellers is quite small, however.

Rabies is present, as is echinococcosis (hydatid disease, cysts from dog faeces), leptospirosis (virus, from rodent urine in water), leishmaniasis (from sandfly bites) and, in poorer rural areas, various intestinal parasites, both soil- and food-borne.

As always the most likely complaint the traveller will have to endure, particularly in the warmer southern regions, is the so-called travellers' diarrhoea. This may be caused by a variety of agents, from bacteria such as *Esherichia coli* and *Salmonella*, to protozoa such as *Entamoeba* and *Giardia*. Good food and drink hygiene is essential where water and food quality are suspect. Avoid unpasteurised dairy products, as there is a risk of brucellosis,tickborne encephalitis (which can be passed on in milk), etc.

Immunisations for the region include polio, typhoid, hepatitis A, tetanus. Health workers and others coming into prolonged contact with locals should consider diphtheria, hepatitis B and tuberculosis. Note that individual travellers very unlikely to come across all the diseases and parasites mentioned. Check your itinerary with travel clinic or GP.

ALBANIA

+1 hour (+2 in summer) GMT

Capital: Tirana

Embassy: 6 Wilton Court, 59 Eccleston Square, London SW1V 1PH (0171-834 2508). Tourist information from Regent Holidays: 01272-211 711

British Embassy: Office of the Charge

d'Affaires, Rruga Skenderbeg 14, Tirana. Tel: (42) 34250
Visa required: No, entry fee
Yellow fever certificate: Yes, if over 1 year old and arriving from an infected country
HIV test: No

Recommended health precautions
Immunisations: Tet; Pol; Typh; Hep A. Sometimes Rab; Hep B; diphtheria. There are various tick-borne diseases: take precautions against bites. TBE immunisation may be suggested for at-risk workers

Water in Tirana is chlorinated, but treat supplies elsewhere as suspect and institute food and drink hygiene precautions

---

BOSNIA/HERZEGOVINA

+1 hour GMT (+2 in summer)
Capital: Sarajevo
Embassy: contact the Foreign Office (0171-270 4125/9) for up-to-date information

Recommended health precautions
Immunisations: Pol; Tet. Sometimes Hep A; Typh

There are Leish, tick-borne diseases (Lyme disease, TBE: immunisation available if at risk) and sandfly fever in the region: avoid bites

---

BULGARIA

+2 hours GMT
Capital: Sofia
UK Tourist Office: 18 Princes Street, London W1R 7RE (0171-499 6988)
Embassy: 186–188 Queen's Gate, London SW7 5HL (0171-584 9400)
British Embassy: Boulevard Vasil Levski 6567, Sofia 1000. Tel: (2) 879 575; Fax: (2) 462 065
Visa required: Yes, unless booked through recognised agent, can be obtained at border
Yellow fever certificate: No
HIV test: Yes, if staying longer than 1 month. UK test accepted

Recommended health precautions
Immunisations: Tet; Pol. Sometimes Typh (15 cases in 1993, risk low); Hep A, depending on itinerary. Rab and TBE may also be offered. Long-stay workers may wish to consider Hep B

Note that there are reports of malaria to the south of the country, though prophylaxis not officially suggested: avoid mosquito bites

Mains water normally chlorinated, but stick to bottled water outside main hotels/restaurants

There are the full complement of tick-borne diseases present: take precautions against bites

---

CROATIA

+1 hour GMT (+2 summer)

Capital: Zagreb

Embassy: 18–21 Jermyn Street, London SW1Y 6HP (0171-434 2946)

British Embassy: PO Box 454 4100, Ilica 12/11, Zagreb. Tel: (41) 424 888; Fax: (41) 420 100

Visa required: No

Yellow fever certificate: No

HIV test: No

Recommended health precautions

Immunisations: Tet; Pol. Sometimes Hep A; Typh; Rab

High risk of TD outside of large towns: all food and drink hygiene must be instituted. There are Leish, tick-borne diseases (Lyme disease, TBE: immunisation may be suggested if at risk) and sandfly fever in the region: avoid bites

For the latest travel advice, given the political situation, call the Foreign Office (0171-270-4129)

CZECH REPUBLIC

+1 hour GMT (+2 summer)

Capital: Prague

Embassy: 26–30 Kensington Palace Gardens, London W8 4QY (0171-243 1115). Tourist Advice from Cedok, 49 Southwark St, SE1 1RU (0171-378 6009)

British Embassy: Thunovska 14, 125 50 Prague 1. Tel: (2) 533 340; Fax: (2) 539 927

Visa required: No

Yellow fever certificate: No

HIV test: No for tourists, but foreign students may need one (at the time of writing this did not apply to UK nationals: check current requirements with Embassy)

Recommended health precautions

Immunisations: Pol; Tet

Mains water usually chlorinated, but take care in remote rural areas

TBE is present in wooded areas, and those at-risk may be immunised. Lyme disease also present

---

HUNGARY

+1 hour GMT (+2 in summer)

Capital: Budapest

Embassy: 35 Eaton Place, London SW1X 8BY (0171-235 4048). For travel advice contact Danube Travel, 6 Conduit St, London W1R 9TG (0171-493 0263)

British Embassy: Harmincad Ucta 6, Budapest V. Tel: (1) 266 2888; Fax: (1) 266 0907

Visa required: No

Yellow fever certificate: No

HIV test: Yes, for sub-Saharan African students only

Recommended health precautions
Immunisations: Tet; Pol; rarely Hep A. There is TBE in the forested areas, and an immunisation is available for at-risk groups. Hep B sometimes suggested for long-stay workers

Lyme disease present in forested areas: avoid tick bites.

MACEDONIA

Also known as the Former Yugoslav Republic of Macedonia
+1 hour GMT (+2 summer)
Capital: Skopje
Embassy: C/o Macedonia Steel, Kingsway House, 103 Kingsway, London WC2B 6QX (0171-404 6558)
British Representative: Ul Veljko Vlahokic 26, 9100 Skopje. Tel: (91) 116 772; Fax: (91) 117 005
Visa required: No
Yellow fever certificate: No
HIV test: No

Recommended health precautions
Immunisations: Tet; Pol. Sometimes Hep A; Typh; Rab

Mains water in large towns chlorinated and fairly reliable; elsewhere institute food and drink hygiene precautions

This part of the former Yugoslavia is not a prime area for TBE, though it does exist

---

POLAND

+1 hour GMT (+2 summer)
Capital: Warsaw
Embassy: 73 New Cavendish Street, London W1M 7RB (0171-580 0476). For travel information contact Polorbis, 82 Mortimer Street, W1N 7DE (0171-637 4971)
British Embassy: Aleja Roz 1, 00556, Warsaw. Tel: (2) 628 1001/5; Fax: (22) 217 161
Visa required: No, unless working
Yellow fever certificate: No
HIV test: Yes, if extended-stay student

Recommended health precautions
Immunisations: Pol; Tet. Sometimes Hep A; Hep B if extended stay. Possibly TBE if working in forested areas

Mains water chlorinated, but it is advisable to stick to bottled water, especially outside large cities

Lyme disease is also present: avoid tick bites

ROMANIA

+2 hours GMT (+3 in summer)

Capital: Bucharest

UK Tourist Office: 83a Marylebone High Street, London W1M 3DE (0171-224 3692)

Embassy: Arundel House, 4 Palace Green, London W8 4QD (0171-937 9666/8)

British Embassy: Strada Jules Michelet 24, 70154 Bucharest. Tel: (1) 312 0303; Fax: (1) 312 0229

Visa required: Yes

Yellow fever certificate: No

HIV test: No

Recommended health precautions

Immunisations: Tet; Pol. Sometimes Hep A; Hep B (4% carrier rate); Typh; TB; Dip. Chol previously reported, but immunisation not advised. TBE immunisation may be suggested to those at risk

Tap water supplies sporadic and, though chlorinated, bottled water is preferable

There is a risk of HIV if medical or dental procedures undertaken: consider taking your own supply of sterile syringes, needles, etc.

Lyme disease also present: avoid tick bites

SLOVAK REPUBLIC

+1 hour GMT (+2 in summer)

Capital: Bratislava

Embassy: 25 Kensington Palace Gardens, London W8 4QY (0171-243 0803). For travel information contact Cedok (0171-378 6009)

British Embassy: Groslingova 35, 811 09 Bratislava. Tel: (7) 364 420; Fax: (7) 364 396

Visa required: No

Yellow fever certificate: No

HIV test: No for tourists, but students/workers may be required to have test. Check with Embassy for current status

Recommended health precautions

Immunisations: None, except possibly for TBE if in atrisk occupation. There have been recent cases of travellers infected with TBE from unboiled goat's milk

Mains water chlorinated and usually safe in larger towns. Take care in rural areas

---

SLOVENIA

+1 hour GMT (+2 summer)

Capital: Ljubljana

UK Tourist Office: 57 Grosvenor Street, London W1X 9DA (0171-495 4688)

Embassy: Suite 1, Cavendish Court, 11–15 Wigmore Street, London W1H 9LA (0171-495 7775)

British Embassy: 4th Floor, TRG Republike 3, 61000 Ljubljana. Tel: (61) 157 191; Fax: (61) 150 174

Visa required: No

Yellow fever certificate: No

HIV test: No

Recommended health precautions

Immunisations: Tet; Pol. Sometimes Hep A; Typh; Rab; TBE (common in wooded areas: avoid tick bites)

YUGOSLAVIA: SERBIA/ MONTENEGRO

At the time of writing the situation in Yugoslavia was still unresolved, with UN sanctions in force, The Foreign Office advises against travel

+1 hour GMT (+2 summer)

Capital: Belgrade

Embassy: 57 Lexham Gardens, London W8 5JJ (0171-370 6105)

British Embassy: Ulica Generala Zdanova 46, 11000 Belgrade. Tel: (11) 645 055; Fax: (11) 659 651

Visa required: Yes

Yellow fever certificate: No

HIV test: No

Recommended health precautions

Immunisations: Tet; Pol. Sometimes Hep A; Typh; Rab; TBE

18.10 RUSSIA AND THE COUNTRIES OF THE FORMER SOVIET UNION

This now fragmented political group consists of: Armenia, Azerbaijan, Belarus, Estonia, Georgia, Kazakhstan, Krygyzstan, Latvia, Lithuania, Moldova, Russia (Russian Federation), Tajikistan, Turkmenistan, Ukraine and Uzbekistan.

Note that as of mid-1995 the code for dialling the UK from any of these countries should be 0044-, but some countries are adapting the standard faster than others: check locally.

HEALTH RISKS THROUGHOUT THE REGION

Malaria: Most of the region is malaria free, with some reports of the disease on the Afghanistan, Iran and Turkey borders, and also in Tajikistan, Uzbekistan and Kazakhstan.

Yellow fever: There is no yellow fever in the region, but a minority of countries may want a certificate if travelling from a county on the WHO list of yellow fever countries, or countries they consider to be an infected area.

Other health risks: Health care and immunisation programmes have been highly disrupted by the political changes in this region, so the disease profile is changing rapidly, with diseases such as diphtheria (a very large jump in cases from 1992 to 1993) and poliomyelitis becoming a problem. Check current status with your GP or travel clinic.

There are a variety of tick-borne diseases, including Lyme disease, tick-borne encephalitis and Crimean-Congo haemorrhagic fever, plus some other local specialities. Travellers to forested rural areas should take precautions against tick bites. Leptospirosis, a viral disease transmitted through animal's urine, is a hazard to recreational water users (canoeists, etc.), but still relatively rare. Rabies is present, with an increase in the number of cases reported. There are isolated foci of plague, particularly in the Asia countries. Immunisation is suggested for those at-risk, but the vast majority of visitors do **not** come under this category. Leishmaniasis occurs in sporadic foci. There have been outbreaks of cholera, though again the average traveller is at little risk.

As always the most likely complaint the traveller will have to endure is the so-called travellers' diarrhoea. This may be caused by a variety of agents, from bacteria such as *Esherichia coli* and *Salmonella*, to protozoa such as *Entamoeba* and *Giardia*. Good food and drink hygiene is essential where water and food quality are suspect: be particularly careful with hotel buffets. Avoid unpasteurised dairy products, as there is a risk of brucellosis, tick-borne encephalitis, etc. Rural areas pose a threat from both soil and food-borne parasites. Wear shoes and ensure all meat is thoroughly cooked.

Immunisations for the region include polio, tetanus, diphtheria, typhoid, hepatitis A, hepatitis B (carrier rates up to 20 per cent of population in some areas), possibly tuberculosis, rabies, plague (travellers rarely at risk) and tick-borne encephalitis if working in an at-risk occupation. *Plague* is sometimes recommended for some of those countries with foci but the immunisation is hard to come by, expensive and can cause a severe reaction. Tetracycline can be taken instead.

Note, the immunisations you need depend on your itinerary: trips to Moscow and St Petersburg will have a very different profile to hiking in Uzbekistan. Consult your travel clinic or GP. Visa requirements also subject to change: check with a specialist such as Intourist (0171-538 8600) or Worldwide Visas (0171-240 5454).

ARMENIA

-3 hours GMT

Capital: Yerevan

Embassy: 25A Cheniston Gardens, London W8 6TG (0171-938 5435)

British Embassy: N/a. At the time of writing political instability has made Armenia an unsafe place for tourists. Contact the Foreign office (0171-270 4129) for advice

Visa required: Yes

Yellow fever certificate: No

HIV test: No

Recommended health precautions

Immunisations: Tet; Pol. Possibly Hep A; Typh; Rab. Those working closely with local populace should consider also Hep B and Dip and TB boosters. Those travelling extensively in forested areas should consider TBE

Malaria prophylaxis: There is no reported malaria

Treat all water as potentially contaminated, and institute the usual food and drink hygiene precautions

---

AZERBAIJAN

+4 hours GMT

Capital: Baku

Embassy: To be opened

British Embassy: C/o Hotel Intourist, Room 215, Baku. Tel: 926 306

Visa required: Yes (until the Embassy opens can be obtained from Russian Embassy)

Yellow fever certificate: No

HIV test: No

Recommended health precautions

Immunisations: Pol (59 cases in 1993); Tet. Possibly Hep A; Typh; Rab. Those working closely with local populace should consider also Hep B and Dip booster and check on TB. Plague in the south of the country carry tetracycline. Those travelling extensively in forested areas should also consider TBE

Malaria prophylaxis: There is malaria, in the benign *P. vivax* form. Chloroquine or proguanil recommended

Water is suspect throughout the country: take appropriate precautions

There have been cases of Leish: avoid sandfly bites. Risk of food- and soil-borne parasites in rural areas (eat only well cooked food and wear shoes)

BELARUS

+2 hours GMT

Capital: Minsk

Consulate: 1 St Stephen's Crescent, Bayswater, London W2 5QT (0171-221 3946)

British Embassy: Zakharova 26, Minsk. Tel: (0172) 330 752

Visa required: Yes

Yellow fever certificate: No
HIV test: No

Recommended health precautions
Immunisations: Pol; Tet. Possibly Hep A; Typh; Rab. Those working closely with local populace should consider also Hep B and Dip and TB boosters. Those travelling extensively in forested areas should consider TBE

Water in large towns usually chlorinated, but bottled water may be preferable. Make sure all food cooked: risk of trichinosis, etc.

Note that the region is extensively forested and other tick-borne disease (e.g. Lyme disease) may be present: avoid bites. There have been some cases of Leish: avoid sandfly bites

---

ESTONIA

+2 hours (+3 in summer) GMT
Capital: Tallinn
Embassy: 16 Hyde Park Gate, London SW7 5DG (0171-589 3428)
British Embassy: Kentmanni 20, EE-0001, Tallinn. Tel: (2) 455 328; Fax: (2) 298 107
Visa required: No
Yellow fever certificate: No
HIV test: No

Recommended health precautions
Immunisations: Pol; Tet. Possibly Hep A; Typh; Rab. Those working closely with local populace should consider also Hep B and Dip booster and a TB check. Those travelling extensively in forested areas should consider TBE (60 cases a year). Plague sometimes reported.

Water supplies vary in quality: stick to bottled water. Risk of TD outside better hotels

Other tick-borne diseases (e.g. Lyme disease) present: avoid bites

---

GEORGIA

+4 hours GMT
Capital: Tbilisi
Embassy: contact Russian Embassy or Intourist, 219 Marsh Wall, London E14 9F (0171-538 8600)
British Embassy: Not at the time of writing. Note that Georgia is politically unstable, and there has been fighting. Contact the Foreign office (0171-270 4129) for travel advice
Visa required: Yes
Yellow fever certificate: No
HIV test: No

Recommended health precautions
Immunisations: Pol; Tet. Possibly Hep A; Typh; Rab. Those working closely with local populace should consider also Hep B and Dip booster and a TB check. Plague in south of country.

Those travelling extensively in forested areas should consider TBE

High risk of travellers' diarrhoea outside major cities. Treat all water supplies as suspect, stick to bottled water and take care with food

Leish also present in south of country

KAZAKHSTAN

+5 hours (+6 in summer) GMT
Capital: Almaty
Embassy: No, contact Intourist (see Georgia)
British Embassy: 173 Furmanov Street, Almaty. Tel: (3272) 506 191; Fax: (3272) 506 260
Visa required: Yes
Yellow fever certificate: No
HIV test: No

Recommended health precautions
Immunisations: Pol; Tet. Possibly Hep A; Typh; Rab. Those working closely with local populace should consider also Hep B and Dip and TB boosters. Plague foci. Those travelling extensively in forested areas should consider TBE. Some Chol reported in 1993, little risk to travellers
High risk of TD: observe all water/food hygiene precautions

Tick-borne (Lyme disease, Crimean-Congo haemorrhagic fever) and various mosquito-borne diseases present, also Leish: avoid insect bites

---

KRYGYZSTAN

+5 hours GMT
Capital: Bishkek
Embassy: Contact Intourist (see Georgia)
Visa required: Yes
Yellow fever certificate: No
HIV test: No

Recommended health precautions
Immunisations: Pol; Tet. Possibly Hep A; Typh; Rab. Those working closely with local populace should consider also Hep B and Dip booster and a TB check. Plague (rarely) suggested sometimes. Those travelling extensively in forested areas should consider TBE

Water supplies generally safe, but bottled water may be preferable (according to CDC high metal content in public supplies). Ensure food thoroughly cooked: risk of TD and parasitic infections

---

LATVIA

+2 (+3 in summer) hours GMT
Capital: Riga
Embassy: 72 Queensborough Terrace, London W2 3SP (0171-727 1698)
British Embassy: 3rd Floor, Elizabetes Iela 2, 226010 Riga. Tel: (2) 320 737; Fax: (2) 322 973
Visa required: No
Yellow fever certificate: No
HIV test: No

Recommended health precautions
Immunisations: Pol; Tet. Possibly Hep A; Typh; Rab. Those working closely with local populace should consider also Hep B and Dip and TB boosters. Plague foci in south. Those travelling extensively in forested areas should consider TBE

All food and, especially, water should be considered suspect

LITHUANIA

+2 hours (+3 in summer) GMT
Capital: Vilnius
Embassy: 17 Essex Villas, London W8 7BP (0171-938 2481)
British Embassy: PO Box 863, Antakalnio 2, 2600, Vilnius. Tel: (2) 222 070; Fax: (2) 357 579
Visa required: No
Yellow fever certificate: No
HIV test: No

Recommended health precautions:
Immunisations: Pol;. Tet. Possibly Hep A; Typh; Rab. Those working closely with local populace should consider also Hep B and Dip and TB boosters. Plague (v. rarely) sometimes. Those travelling extensively in forested areas should consider TBE

Water supplies generally reliable in cities, less so outside. Institute food and drink hygiene precautions, esp. if travelling rurally

---

MOLDOVA

+2 hours GMT
Capital: Chisinau
Embassy: Contact Intourist (see Georgia)
British Embassy: Contact Moscow
Visa required: Yes
Yellow fever certificate: No
HIV test: No

Recommended health precautions
Immunisations: Pol; Tet. Possibly Hep A; Typh; Rab. Those working closely with local populace should consider also Hep B and Dip booster and a TB check. Occasional plague cases in south. Those travelling extensively in forested areas should consider TBE

Mains water chlorinated, but bottled preferable

Other tick-borne diseases (e.g. Lyme disease, boutenneuse fever), sandfly fever and Leish reported: protect against insect bites

---

RUSSIA

(Russian Federation)

+3 (Moscow) hours GMT, though ranges to +13
Capital: Moscow
Embassy: 13 Kensington Palace Gardens, London W8 4QX (0171-229 3628)
British Embassy: Sofiyskaya Naberezhnaya 14, Moscow 72. Tel: (095) 230 6300; Fax: (095) 233 3563. The British Consulate in St Petersburg is at Ploshad Proletarskoy, Dictatury 5, 1913124. Tel: (0812) 119 6036); Fax: (0812) 110 6037
Visa required: Yes
Yellow fever certificate: No
HIV test: Yes, for foreigners staying over 3 months. Check with Embassy

Recommended health precautions
Note that across such a large country, the requirements may vary considerably (e.g. Typh not required for much of the western territories)

Immunisations: Pol; Tet. Possibly Hep A; Typh; Rab (number of cases increased in 1993). Those working closely with local populace should consider also Hep B (up to 20% carrier rate) and Dip (there were 3897 cases in 1992, which leapt to 15,211 in 1993, though most tourists not at risk) and TB boosters. Those travelling extensively in forested areas should consider TBE

Water supplies vary widely: stick to bottled water if possible. There was an outbreak of Chol in Daghestan in 1994; immunisation not advised, but again usual hygiene precautions essential

Risk of Lyme disease, etc.: avoid all tick bites

TAJIKISTAN

+5 hours GMT
Capital: Dushanbe
Embassy: Contact Intourist (see Georgia)
British Embassy: Contact Moscow
Visa required: Yes
Yellow fever certificate: No
HIV test: No

Recommended health precautions
Immunisations: Pol; Tet. Possibly Hep A; Typh; Rab. Those working closely with local populace should consider also Hep B and Dip booster and a TB check. Some plague foci. Those travelling extensively in forested areas should consider TBE

Malaria prophylaxis: There is malaria

on the southern border region: chloroquine or proguanil (Paludrine) recommended; avoid mosquito bites

Chol also reported, so food/drink hygiene precautions very important. Stick to bottled water

There are reports of Leish in the south: avoid sandfly bites

TURKMENISTAN

+5 hours GMT
Capital: Ashgabat
Embassy: Contact Intourist (see Georgia)
British Embassy: Contact Moscow
Visa required: Yes
Yellow fever certificate: No
HIV test: No

Recommended health precautions
Immunisations: Pol; Tet. Possibly Hep A; Typh; Rab. Those working closely with local populace should consider also Hep B and Dip booster and a TB check. Some plague foci. Those travelling extensively in forested areas should consider TBE

Malaria prophylaxis: There have been reports of malaria in the east of the country. Chloroquine or proguanil recommended, as are insect repellents and nets

All water should be considered contaminated: instigate usual hygiene precautions for food and drink

A variety of tick-borne diseases present: avoid tick bites

UKRAINE

+2 hours (+3 summer) GMT
Capital: Kiev
Embassy: 73 Kensington Park Road, London W11 2PL (0171-727 6312)
British Embassy: ul. Desyatinna 9, 252025 Kiev, Ukraine. Tel: (044) 228 0504; Fax: (044) 228 3972
Visa required: Yes
Yellow fever certificate: No
HIV test: Yes, if staying more than 3 months

Recommended health precautions
Immunisations: Pol; Tet. Possibly Hep A; Typh; Rab. Those working closely with local populace should consider also Hep B and Dip booster and a TB check. Plague (v. rarely) suggested. Those travelling extensively in forested areas should consider TBE

Risk of TD and food and soil-borne parasites: good food and water hygiene recommended

Lyme disease (ticks) and Leish/sandfly fever reported: avoid bites

---

UZBEKISTAN

+5 hours GMT
Capital: Tashkent
Embassy: Contact Intourist (see Georgia) or HY Travel (0171-935 4775)
British Embassy: Contact Moscow
Visa required: Yes
Yellow fever certificate: No
HIV test: Yes, may be a condition of granting visa (not usually if arranged through Uzbekintour or agent). Check carefully

Recommended health precautions
Immunisations: Pol; Tet; Hep A; Typh. Possibly Rab. Those working closely with local populace should consider also Hep B and Dip booster and a TB check. Those travelling extensively in forested areas should consider TBE (and protect against bites: other tick-borne diseases present)

Malaria prophylaxis: There have been a few cases of malaria on the Afghan border: chloroquine or proguanil (paludrine) plus nets and repellents recommended in that area

There have been Chol outbreaks around Tashkent: good food and drink hygiene essential, stick to sterilised or bottled water

Leish also reported: protect against sandfly bites. Some risk of food-borne parasites, ensure all meat thoroughly cooked

POSTSCRIPT

Reading through the preceding pages, it is amazing how a country that one already knows, and knows to be quite survivable, suddenly transmutes into a repository of vile worms, bacteria and viruses on the page. I hope the list hasn't put anybody off going off and experiencing them – the countries, not the diseases – for themselves. It hasn't me: next stop, India, followed, I hope, by Mexico. Just be careful out there. And keep taking the tablets.

Rob Ryan, London 1994

Further reading

I am not about to give a comprehensive bibliography, after all this book was not aimed at those who regularly flick through the *Weekly Epidemiological Review* or *Travel Medicine International*. However, the following books are recommended for those who want to dig a little deeper than snide remarks about mosquitoes:

The Tropical Traveller by John Hatt. Penguin. Opinionated, readable and informative. An excellent pre-travel guide, full of I-wish-I-had-thought-of-that tips. My regular driver to the airport objects strongly to the part that says 'avoid minicab firms, as they are often a magnet for villains, and frequent places for the exchange of criminal information'. I feel he was too soft: he missed out the X-reg Datsuns and rotten driving.

Where There is No Doctor by David Werner. Teaching Aids at Low Cost, St Albans. Everything you need to know about basic health care in the developing world.

Health Advice for Travellers. Dept of Health (free on 0800 555 777). Includes the E-111 form and some basic advice, plus what you have to pay for in EC and non-EC countries.

The Traveller's Handbook (ed. Sarah Gorman). WEXAS. Not just travel health but every aspect of leaving the country, from photography to off-road driving plus very useful appendices of world currencies, voltage, visa requirements etc.

Useful addresses and contact numbers

AIDS/HIV products and information
Blood Care Foundation
01274 531723
01723 742427

Call of the Wild
017687 71014

Homeway
01962 881526

InterHealth
0171 729 4230

MASTA
0171 631 4408
01274 531723

National AIDS Helpline
0800 555 777

SAFA
0151 708 0397

SafariQuip
01433 620320

Travel Medicine Centre
01272 354447

Back pain
The Back Shop
24 New Cavendish Street
London W1M 7LH
0171 935 9120

Culture shock/working abroad
Kuperard
0171 372 4722

Women's Corona Society
35 Belgrave Square
London SW1X 8QB

Clothing
Genuine Panama Hat Co
0171 720 3300

Nomad
0181 889 7014

Norfolk Headwear
0171 498 2099

SafariQuip
01433 620320

Diabetes advice
British Diabetic Association
10 Queen Anne Street
London W1M 9LD
0171 323 1531

Douglas Cox-Tyrie
0181 534 9595

LeisureCare
01793-514199

Medic Alert
0800 581420

Disability advice
The Disabled Drivers' Association
14 Belmont Park Road
Maidenhead
Berks SL6 1HT
01628 26767

Disabled Living Foundation
380–4 Harrow Road
London W9 2HU
0171 289 6111

Holiday Care Service
2 Old Bank Chambers
Horley
Surrey RH6 9HW
01293 774535

RADAR
250 City Road
London EC1V 8AS
0171 250 3222

Spinal Injuries Association
76 St James's Lane
London N10 3DF
0181 444 2121

First aid courses and kits
Advanced Medicine for Remote Foreign Travel
c/o Barry Roberts
25 Beaconsfield Street
Leamington Spa
Warwickshire CV31 1DT
01926 882763

InterHealth
0171 729 4230

Medic Alert
0800 581420

SAFA
0151 708 0397

St Andrew's Ambulance
041 332 4031

St John Ambulance
1 Grosvenor Crescent
London SW1X 7EF
0171 235 5231

Travel Medicine Centre
0172 354447

WellCare
01225 446220

General
African Medical & Research Foundation
2nd Floor
8 Bourdon Street
London W1X 9HX
0171 409 3230

American Express
Global Assist Emergency Service
0044 181 469 3742

British Red Cross
0171 235 5454

Foreign Office
0171 270 4129

International Association for Medical Assistance to Travellers
417 Center Street
Lewiston
NY 14092
USA
0101 716 754 4883

and

40 Regal Road
Guelph
Ontario
Canada
0101 519 836 0102

Medical Service for Travellers Abroad (MASTA)
0171 631 4408
0891 224100 *for up-to-the-minute travel medicine information*

Travax
NHS on-line Database
0141-946 7120 (x 1277)

Traveller Database
For nearest pharmacy/GP ring
0742-854 443

Insect repellants
Ghurka
01666 822518

MASTA (Mosi-Guard)
0171 631 4408

Nomad
0181-889 7014

SafariQuip (Mosi-Mil)
01433 620320

Tony Pisacana (X-Gnat)
01236 722374

Insurance companies
Age Concern
01883 346964

American Express/
Centurion
0800 700707

BCWA
01272 293742

Club Direct
01730 817533

Columbus
0171 375 0011

Commercial Union
0171 283 8611

Crispin Speers
0171 480 5083

Douglas Cox-Tyrie
0181 534 9595

Europ Assistance
01444 442211

Frizzell
01202 292333

General Accident
01738 212021

Leisure Care Insurance
01793 514199

Travel Direct
01903 893333

TSB
Contact local branch

WEXAS
0171 589 0500

Jet-lag
Danielle Ryman
c/o The Park Lane Hotel
0171 499 6321

Mosquito nets
Appropriate Applications
01442 879750

Clothtec
01726 813602

InterHealth
0171 729 4230

Long Road
0101 510 540 4763

MASTA
0171 631 4408

Mission Supplies
0181 337 0161

Nomad
0181 889 7014

Oasis
01366 500466

SafariQuip
01433 620320

Travel Medicine Inc.
0101 413 584 0381

Off-road driving tuition
Barony College
Parkgate
Dumfries
01387 85251
Use Land Rovers in 20,000 acres

Brands Hatch Off-Road Centre
Longfield
Kent
01474 872331
Use Suzukis in 100 acres

Canterbury Off-Road Centre
Hoath
Kent
01227 728268
Use Discoverys and Land Rover Defenders in 7 acres

Don Coyote
Lamancha Village
Near Edinburgh
0131 443 2881
Use Land Rovers in 230 acres

4x4 Drive Off-Road Centre
Castle House
Rock Park
Wirral
0151 645 8124
Use Land Rovers and others in 90 acres

Fresh Tracks
Ware
Herts
01920 438758
Access to public sites in London, Manchester and Bristol using Land Rovers, Range Rovers and Suzukis

Gotwick Off-Road Centre
Holtye Road
East Grinstead
01304 315504
Use various 4x4s in 10 acres, but also specialises in expedition preparation

Ian Wright Off-Road School
7 Church Row
West Peckham
Maidstone
Kent
01622 817509
Various sites in Kent using Patrols, Discoverys and Troopers

Lakeland Safari
9 Castle Way
Boughton-in-Furness
Cumbria
01229 89333
Use Land Rovers in 75 acres

Landcraft
The Steppes
Pen-y-Ball Hill
Holywell
Clwyd
01352 711855
Use various 4x4s on several sites from 200 acres up

Mid Norfolk Off-Road Centre
Wood Farm
Runhill
Norwich
01362 859233
Use Diahatsus and Land Rovers in 25 acres

Motor Safari
Treetops
Mold
Clwyd
01352 770769
Use variety of 4x4s on 50 sites

North Herts Off-Road Driving School
Marden
Herts
01568 84372
01568 84372
Use Land Rovers and Suzukis in 295 acres

North Yorks Off-Road Centre
Bay Ness Farm
Robin Hood's Bay
Whitby
N Yorks
01947 880371
Use Land Rovers in 15 acres

Off-Road Motivations
Salisbury Road
Andover
Hants
01264 710113
Use Discoverys and Suzukis in 15 acres

Ronnie Dale Off-Road Adventure Driving School
Abbey St Bathans
Duns
Berwickshire
013614 244
Use various 4x4s in 2000 acres

Spectrum 4x4 Driving Centre
PO Box 9
Holyland
Barnsley
S Yorks
01226 748822
Use Range Rovers and Land Rovers on three sites of 65 acres

Tuf Going
Coldharbour Lane
Rainham
Essex
01268 764830
Use Land Rovers in 12 acres

Tuff Terrains
Abbeycwmhir
Llandrindod Wells
Powys
01597 851551
Use Suzukis and Land Rovers in 138 acres

Venture 4x4s Off-Road Centre
Eastern Grove
Wisbech
Cambs
01945 772270
Use Range Rovers and Land Rovers in 10 acres

Warwickshire College
Moreton Morell
Warwick
01926 651367
Use Land Rovers in 20 acres

Weardale Off-Road Centre
Coves House Farm
Wolsingham
Co Durham
01388 527375
Use Land Rovers and Range Rovers in 400 acres

Wild Rovers
38 Chatsworth Road
Hazel Grove
Stockport
0161 449 0725
Use Land Rovers in 30 acres

Yorkshire 4x4 Exploration
West Pasture
Crakehall
N Yorks
01677 424824
Use Land Rovers in 1600 acres

Safety devices and information

Semmco (intruder alerts/ smoke alarms)
01483 295803

UIAA Mountain Medicine Centre (mountain safety)
St Bartholomew's Hospital
London EC1A 7BE
0171 359 6412

Sleeping bags

Exodus
01252 316016

Nomad
0181 889 7014

SafariQuip
01433 620320

Travel clinics and hospitals

British Airways Travel Clinic
0171 831 5533 *for your nearest clinic*

Centre for Tropical Medicine
John Radcliffe Hospital
Headington
Oxford OX3 DU
01865 741166

Communicable Disease (Scotland) Unit
Ruchill Hospital
Glasgow G20 9NB
0141 946 7120

Department of Communicable and Tropical Disease
East Birmingham Hospital
Birmingham B9 5ST
0121 766 6611

Hospital for Tropical Diseases
4 St Pancras Way
London NW1 0PE
0171 387 4411
0171 637 9899 *for travel clinic*

Liverpool School of Tropical Medicine
Pembroke Place
Liverpool L3 5QA
0151 708 9393
Travel clinic every afternoon 1–4pm

London School of Hygiene and Tropical Medicine
Keppel Street
London WC1E 7HT
0171 636 8636
0891 600350 *malaria information line*

Medical Advisory Services for Travellers Abroad (MASTA)
Telephone information service with postal back-up
0891 224100
Calls cost 49p/min peak, 39p/min cheap; average call costs £2.50–£3

Nomad
3 Turnpike Lane
London N8 0PX
0181 889 7014
Travel equipment shop plus pharmacy and free advice on immunisations (by appointment)

PPP Medical Centre
New Cavendish Street
London W1M 7FQ
0171 436 0224

Thomas Cook
45 Berkeley Street
London W1A 1EB
0171 499 4000

Trailfinders
194 Kensington High Street
London W8 7RG
0171 938 3444

Water purification equipment

Explore Direct
01252 316016

Nomad
0181 889 7014

SafariQuip
01433 620320

Visa information

Thames Consular Services
0181 995 2492

Thomas Cook
0171 499 4000

Visaservice
0171 833 2709

Worldwide Visas
0171 240 5454

Index

STOP PRESS

Ch. 3 Immunisations

'Traveller' is a software programme for pharmacists/GPs, giving the latest travel health information. Updated every month, countries can be called up to show immunisations, malaria distribution, health advice, etc. It also handles complicated itineries/different types of travel (hotel, safari, etc). Data sheets can be run out for clients to take to immunisation centres. For your nearest Traveller user call 01742 755057.

Ch.5 Malaria

Up to end of March 1994, 352 cases of malaria were imported into the UK. There were two deaths (in both cases drug regimes had been stopped on returning to the UK, so remember - always complete the course). Self-treatment of malaria is very complex for the lay person - you could easily exacerbate the problems. For example, quinine is not advisable as treatment if mefloquine is used as a prophylaxis. But if Fansidar resistance is common, it may have to be - in which case the dose should be modified and given intravenously if possible.

Ch.6 Coping with the journey

Some doctors have expressed disquiet about melatonin, especially as it's being marketed in the US as a food supplement rather than the hormone it actually is. Originally withdrawn, it has now satisfied toxicology tests and is again available. I know six people who've used it - three said it was effective. Some doctors suggest using a sunbed upon arrival to suppress the melatonin and help re-set the body clock, rather than take drugs - but as we all know, sunbeds have their own set of problems...

Ch.10 Diarrhoea and how to avoid it

Prof. Farthing's study on commandos in Belize suggests that one 500mg dose of ciprofiaxacin (Ciproxin), given soon after symptoms start, is useful in treating serious diarrhoea, although fluid replacement (esp. in children) is vital. The problem in using antibiotics for such treatment has long been the worry about compliance with the course (only one dose in this case) and the promotion of resistance among the organisms. Ciproflaxacin, Farthing points out, has a relatively short half-life in the body (3.5 - 4.5 hours) and so serious side effects and long-term resistance problems are less likely (*The Lancet*, Dec 3, 1994).

Ch. 12 Being bitten

1994 saw an outbreak of dengue fever in Puerto Rico (25,000+ affected). Island health authorities say that tourists are at little risk but insect repellents are advisable.

Not all the exotic diseases live outside the UK. In December 1994, a rambler died of Q fever after a tick bite in the West Country. Q fever ('Q' is 'query') is caused by rickettsiae, the same bacteria-like organisms which cause typhus. Ticks are becoming more of a problem in many heath areas as bracken is no longer burnt off each Spring.

Ch. 18 Country-by-country

Albania: 10/94 cholera reported in SW Albania. Angola: 11/94 outbreak of meningoccal meningitis - immunisation advised. Columbia: 11/94 large outbreak of gastrointestinal illness among tourists on San Andreas island - take all precautions. Hong Kong: 8/94 some cholera cases reported - average tourist not at risk. Georgia: 8/94 diphtheria outbreak spreading from Russia and Ukraine into Georgia. Immunisation recommended for at-risk groups. Guinea-Bissau: 11/94 outbreak of cholera close to the border with The Gambia. Kenya: 7/94 some authorities estimating 25% failure rates of mefloquine in some areas of the country. Not being bitten still very important. Libya: 11/94 reports of Libya demanding cholera certificates from travellers entering overland from Tunisia and Algeria. Mozambique: 10/94 outbreak of bubonic plague near Malawi and Zambia borders. Sierre Leone: 10/94 cholera outbreak. Somalia: 8/94 major cholera outbreak. Thailand: 12/94 increase in dengue fever among returning travellers. Precautions against mosquito bites very important. Ukraine: 10/94 outbreak of diphtheria waning but immunisation still advised. Vanuatu: 12/94 malaria increasing. Precautions essential. Vietnam: 12/94 malignant malarial forms now nationwide, with chloroquine resistance very high in south. Zaire: 10/94 continued outbreaks of bubonic plague - carry antibiotics.

(*Dates indicate when warnings appeared on Travax.*)

December 1994: Yellow fever active in Angola, Bolivia, Brazil, Cameroon, Equador, The Gambia, Ghana, Guinea, Mali, Nigeria, Peru, Sudan, Zaire.

Visas

Note: all visa requirements relate to British Passport holders only.

Sri Lanka: visas not required by tourists.

Thailand: At the moment visa needed for over 15 days, but at time of writing was about to change.

Israel: visa stamp issued on arrival.